MONSTER HUNTERS

On the Trail with Ghost Hunters, Bigfooters,
Ufologists, and Other Paranormal Investigators

TEA KRULOS

CHICAGO
REVIEW
PRESS

Copyright © 2015 by Tea Krulos
All rights reserved
Published by Chicago Review Press Incorporated
814 North Franklin Street
Chicago, Illinois 60610
ISBN 978-1-61374-981-4

Library of Congress Cataloging-in-Publication Data
Krulos, Tea, author.
    Monster hunters : on the trail with ghost hunters, bigfooters, ufologists,
and other paranormal investigators / Tea Krulos.
       pages cm
    Summary: "Journalist Tea Krulos joins paranormal investigators in the
field as they explore haunted houses, trek through creepy forests in search
of Bigfoot, scan the skies for UFOs, and more. Along the way, he meets a
diverse cast of characters—true believers, skeptics, and hoaxers—from the
credible to the quirky"— Provided by publisher.
    Includes bibliographical references and index.
    ISBN 978-1-61374-981-4 (paperback)
    1. Parapsychology—Miscellanea. 2. Supernatural—Miscellanea. I. Title.

BF1031.K78 2015
001.94—dc23

                        2015002299

Cover design: Andrew Brozyna, AJB Design Inc.
Cover images: (top) Fexel/Shutterstock; (bottom) Tea Krulos
Interior design: Jonathan Hahn
Illustrations: Courtesy of David Beyer Jr.

Printed in the United States of America
5 4 3 2 1

To my parents, Marty and Joy,
for encouraging me to read monster stories

CONTENTS

INTRODUCTION:
INVISIBLE MONSTERS

MILLIONS OF AMERICANS go about their lives in what is considered a "normal" way. Their interests are not the supernatural but ESPN, Wall Street, *Better Homes and Gardens*. They wonder, *What's on TV tonight?* and *What's for dinner?* Sometimes they enjoy a ghost story, or catch a rerun of a popular reality show like *Ghost Hunters* or *Finding Bigfoot*. Maybe they have had an eerie experience, but they just shrug it off. Maybe they think it's all foolish folklore, kid stuff. And then back to the routine. Job promotion. Parking ticket. Pay bills. Field trip permission form.

And for downtime? Weekend fishing trip. Art museum. Video games. Curl up with a good book. Meet up with friends for a drink. Millions and millions of people, normal lives, normal hobbies.

This book is not about those people.

▲ ▲ ▲

The universe is full of mystery, I thought to myself after getting off the bus and wandering into an unfamiliar neighborhood in Milwaukee named Granville. I've lived in Milwaukee most of my life, but I had never set foot there before.

I walked into a quiet subdivision and dug my notepad out of my pocket to check the address. I looked up and saw the house down

1

the street: a nice townhouse with the garage door open and a classic, freshly washed hot rod parked inside. I rang the doorbell.

A woman with a wavy mane of red hair answered the door and looked at me curiously.

"Tea?" she said, smiling. "Come in."

She motioned for me to follow her down a hall. We walked by a living room table with a spread of potato chips, pretzels, and two-liter bottles of soda. I walked in and found a group of nine people seated on couches and chairs, staring at me politely. They all had matching shirts that identified them as the Paranormal Investigators of Milwaukee (PIM).

"Hi," I said.

Then I walked around the room shaking hands as people introduced themselves. I had spent some time studying the "Members" section of the PIM website, and my brain worked to match the two-dimensional profiles with the living people in front of me.

The redheaded woman at the door was Jann Goldberg, boisterous paranormal investigator and paralegal. Then there was Noah Leigh, meticulously organized team leader and founder, a research scientist with three degrees. I met Michael "Gravy" Graeve, with a soul patch and arms sleeved in tattoos, who worked at a printing company; Missy Bostrom, a polite, petite hair stylist; and John Krahn, a gruff ex-cop—you know he likes you when he starts viciously making fun of you. Three other team members introduced themselves: Chris Paul, in the auto parts and salvage biz, his gray hair pulled back in a ponytail; Tony Belland, intense-looking guy with a shaved head and beard, an HVAC repairman and construction worker; and Randy Soukup, a kindly pharmacist. A ninth member was present but would be parting ways with the team before I saw him again.

I felt a touch of nervousness. It was obviously a tight-knit group. One of the first things that happened as I made introductions was that one of the members made an inside joke and everyone laughed while I looked around, puzzled. PIM was a little different than my usual peer group, too. PIM is composed of white suburbanites, most between thirty and forty-five years old and middle to upper-middle class—and all of them are married with children. Ghost hunting is apparently something that appeals to those in the suburbs who need a more exciting and mysterious hobby than forming a bowling league.

After introductions, I sat down. All eyes were on me. And then I realized this wasn't just a casual PIM meeting I was sitting in on. I had been called in front of the board for a job interview.

"Could you tell us more about yourself and the book you want to write?" Leigh asked.

"Well, I uhh . . ."

▲▲▲

My own interest in the paranormal began when I was young. My library card was a prized possession that I used to check out every book I could find on UFOs, ghosts, and Bigfoot. I particularly remember Time Life Books' *Mysteries of the Unknown*, a popular thirty-three-volume series that covered everything from "Alien Encounters" to "Visions and Prophecies." I would load these books up in my gangly arms and haul them to the checkout desk. I also occasionally caught the classic mystery documentary shows *In Search Of . . .* and *Unsolved Mysteries*. I loved these stories, and part of me believed them.

As I got older, a new love—journalism—turned me into more of a skeptic, a person who needed fact-checking and hard evidence to be satisfied. I still thought the topic was fun stuff, but my view on it had changed. Bigfoot was nothing more than foolish folklore, wasn't it?

I imagined Jason Robards's Ben Bradlee in *All the President's Men* frowning at me for even daring to consider approaching the topic as news.

▲▲▲

My interest in the paranormal was piqued again with the same thing that captivated a lot of people's attention, a reality show that premiered in 2004 titled *Ghost Hunters*. Although ghost hunting dates back to the Spiritualist movement of the 1840s and has had a devoted following ever since, *Ghost Hunters* popularized paranormal investigation for a new generation. After the show premiered, amateur ghost hunting groups spread quickly and widely. There are now hundreds of these groups all over the country, in cities big and small.

Noah Leigh, PIM's founder, was inspired by *Ghost Hunters* as well. Leigh had a prior interest in ghost stories, reading them as a kid growing up in the small rural town of Berlin, Wisconsin.

"When I was younger, I liked Halloween," Leigh later told me in an interview. "Not the gory stuff, but the spooky stuff that really intrigued me and scared me a bit. I remember there was one book on ghosts in our middle school library that I would check out."

In high school, Leigh was intrigued with a piece of local ghost lore, a legend that a plot in a Berlin graveyard was supernatural. "A certain sarcophagus with a lid featuring a hand holding a dagger in the local cemetery was the resting place of a man and two ex-wives he had murdered. When it rained, supposedly the dagger would bleed, is the story," Leigh said. After a cross-country training session near the hills of the graveyard one day, Leigh decided to look for the grave. He found it.

"It had rained the night before and there was water in the depression. You could see a red tint." But Leigh suspected that it was something more commonplace than blood, and ultimately "I found the rusty color was indeed iron oxide." Leigh moved to another small town—Ripon, Wisconsin—to go to Ripon College, where in 2004 he got a bachelor's degree in biology with a minor in history. While there, he also studied papers on local ghost stories.

After graduating, Leigh moved to the big city of Milwaukee, where he continued his education at the Medical College of Wisconsin.

His schedule changed drastically.

"I only had class once a week, for eight hours on Thursdays. Other than homework, the rest of the time I didn't have anything to do. I was used to having class four to five days a week and homework at night and on weekends. So, as a bachelor guy in Milwaukee, I filled my days with video games quite a bit. But that got old after about a year. By August 2005 I was bored. During that summer, there were previews for this *Ghost Hunters* show that I happened to catch. I thought, *Huh, that's interesting.*"

The gears started turning.

"I thought, *These guys are plumbers and going around doing this. Come on. I have a master's degree in biology, I should be able to do this easily.* So I started looking into it and found someone who was on the ground level of starting a group in Milwaukee."

This group was the Greater Milwaukee Paranormal Research Group (GMPRG), and Leigh joined in 2005. Eager to fill his time with this new hobby, Leigh immersed himself in learning everything he could about paranormal investigation. He contributed so much, he was given the title of cofounder. But after a year and a half, he had a falling-out with other members of the team and was ousted from the organization. Using what he had already learned, Leigh faced the rejection by becoming highly motivated to start his own group.

"After I got kicked out of the group, I was pretty ticked off," Leigh admitted. "Nothing motivates me more than showing people they're wrong. And so what I wanted to do is build a group that was better than the group I was kicked out of, to show them that they had made a mistake."

After a lot of work, Leigh put together Paranormal Investigators of Milwaukee in 2007. The group slowly began to expand membership and build a base of clients, and it gained publicity through a series of events, media appearances, and social networking.

Leigh taught a Paranormal Investigation 101 class, in which I later enrolled, and hosted workshops and presentations at public libraries and other venues. The team sometimes has tagalong investigations open to the public, so the curious masses can try their hand at finding a ghost. The team grew, and now membership fluctuates between eight and ten members at any given time.

Leigh gave the group a simple descriptive tagline: "No charge. Scientific. Professional."

▲▲▲

PIM concentrates on looking for evidence of ghosts, but *paranormal* is an umbrella term that covers several areas that participants call "fields" but skeptics deride as "pseudoscience."

Besides ghost hunting, there is cryptozoology, which is the study of unknown animals such as the hairy hominid Bigfoot, the elusive Loch Ness Monster, and perennial bloodsuckers known as the Chupacabras. Ufology is the study of unidentified flying objects, aliens, and related topics. The term *demonology* is sometimes used to describe the study of demonic entities, possession, and exorcism. Other related fields include parapsychology, which is the study of psychic ability, and cerealogy, the study not of breakfast cereals but of crop circles.

These are the people that I wanted to learn about, that I wanted this book to explore: people who have dedicated a significant part of their lives to looking for evidence or hunting for unknown entities—ghosts, aliens, Bigfoot, demons . . . entities very real to some yet dismissed by others.

▲ ▲ ▲

After scouring the Internet and looking at a couple of groups in the southeastern corner of Wisconsin, I decided that PIM would be the best group to contact.

PIM seemed professional and dedicated to active investigation. Some paranormal groups have every intention of being active but are able to schedule a hunt only once in a blue moon. Many groups form but after the initial excitement fizzle out. Leigh would later tell me that a lot of groups don't even make it to their one-year anniversary. Others do a sloppy, half-hearted job of learning to do an effective investigation.

"For them, it's a fun Friday night, but for us it's more," Leigh explained.

PIM has maintained a busy schedule. In 2013 it conducted about forty investigations, a large amount by any group's standards. These cases are all thoroughly documented in case reports on PIM's website, accompanied by any relevant audio or video clips.

I e-mailed Leigh and explained that I really wanted to be part of the team. I wanted to join them in investigations, not just stand there gawking. I wanted to learn how to investigate and help with their cases. After a talk on the phone, Leigh invited me to meet at Jann's house to talk to PIM at the monthly team meeting. Walking in, I could tell they wanted to size me up, and I didn't blame them. It may be spooky to track ghosts, but inviting a writer to snoop around in your affairs is an equally hair-raising concept. I met the team and explained my intentions as best I could.

"You know what I'm concerned about," Michael Graeve said at the meeting, "is what your expectations might be. This isn't like you see on the reality show, where there's lots of evidence and spook factor. Investigations can be really long and uneventful."

The team discussed my request after I left the meeting, and Leigh sent me an e-mail the next day that said, "Welcome aboard!"

▲ ▲ ▲

After receiving that e-mail, I enrolled in Leigh's Paranormal Investigation 101 class and signed up for a Cryptozoology 101 class online. I started following a media company that specialized in information on UFOs and began to amass a couple of huge stacks of books on various paranormal topics that covered most of my desk.

I was preparing for the hunt, but was there anything to find?

« 1 »

THE MONSTER HUNTER
AND HIS MUSEUM

A VON STREET, in the Arts District of Portland, Maine, is a small, narrow avenue that seems more like an alleyway. As I turned onto it and stepped onto the sidewalk—more of a curb—everything seemed all too much of an urban reality. A large graffiti-style mural covered the side of a building, and spray-painted orange arrows pointed out the uneven street. Squiggly graffiti tags surrounded a No Parking sign. The traffic of Congress Street hummed along, a car honking. Approaching 11 Avon Street, I stopped to wonder if this were the right place. But then I spotted the flag flapping in the breeze. It said International Cryptozoology Museum.

I walked through a bland steel door, down the hall, and, hearing strains of classical music playing on a radio, turned, and there I was, inside the museum.

More often than not, if he's not on the road, the museum's founder, Loren Coleman, is at the door to greet visitors. His neatly trimmed white beard and hair, bright blue eyes, and jet-black eyebrows give him an Obi-Wan Kenobi Jedi master appearance. Dressed in a safari style shirt and khakis, he seems wise and scholarly, but he has a certain boyishness to him. That mixture suits him, because Coleman has a unique profession: he is a cryptozoologist.

Cryptozoology, from the Latin, means "study of hidden animals" and purports to study evidence of creatures like Bigfoot and Lake Monsters.* These unknown animals are called *cryptids*.

I learned about this field through an online program—actual college courses are few and far between. My lessons included "The Foundations of Cryptozoology," "Existing Species that Were Once Cryptids," and "Bigfoot Evidence."

"We are the world's only cryptozoology museum," Coleman explained to me soon after I walked through the door. "We've become the reservoir for a lot of people's collections, as well as my own fifty-three years of collecting."

The museum now has about ten thousand cryptozoology-related items, Coleman said. These are rarities that you won't find anywhere else in the world. There is a hair sample from a Yowie, Australians' variant of Bigfoot, a huge hairy creature that wanders the outback.

Another display is dedicated to the Jersey Devil, a horse-faced,

---

* Coleman uses the following style guide: unknown animals capitalized, discovered animals lowercase, native names italicized. So, for example, before the okapi was discovered it was the Okapi, and natives spoke legend of an *okapi*.

bat-winged creature said to terrorize the Garden State. A statue of a Cadbrosaurus, a mysterious Sea Serpent that supposedly swims the Pacific coast of North America, glides through a display in a corner of the museum.

Always a labor of love, the museum opened in 2003 and for its first five years was based out of Coleman's home. Eventually he found a small public space, sharing it with the Green Hand, a mystical bookstore just up the street on Avon and Congress.

"In 2011 we moved to this space, became a nonprofit, and really expanded," Coleman told me. The building is more than a hundred years old, and the museum space was originally used as a showroom for a furrier. It is now a two-room boutique museum, a mix of Victorian sensibility and monster folklore.

Handing me a photocopied hand-drawn map of the museum layout, Coleman began to show me around. The first room was called the Evidence Room, he explained, and he led me to the first display: "Classic Animals of Discovery."

"There's really two forms of cryptids," Coleman explained. "The cryptids that are actually new species—brand-new discoveries—and cryptids that are extinct animals that may still be around."

For example, the International Cryptozoology Museum's mascot—featured as part of its logo—is the coelacanth, which Coleman called a "darling of cryptozoology." There was a model of one hanging near the front door of the museum.

"This is the full-size replica of the first living coelacanth ever discovered in 1938 off of Africa," Coleman explained, pointing at the model. "They're bright blue like that, five and a half feet long. It had not been seen in sixty-five million years."

This prehistoric fish embodies the philosophy of cryptozoology: if we didn't know that the coelacanth still swam in our oceans, despite declaratively being categorized as "extinct," what other unknown fauna is alive out there?

Underneath the coelacanth Coleman had a display case featuring models of many examples of animals that were formerly known as cryptids. The mountain gorilla, for example, was sort of a nineteenth-century version of Bigfoot. Reports of the animals date back to 1861, but explorers believed the stories were village myth until Captain Robert von Beringe and his crew shot two of them in 1902.

The examples go on and on. The weird-looking megamouth shark, first discovered in 1976. Even the platypus was originally written off as a hoax. Scientists believed a duck's beak had been sewn to a beaver's body by a jokester taxidermist.

"What happens is people come in and they begin to understand that we're interested in animals, we're interested in mysteries, and new species being discovered, which happens all the time. In cryptozoology, the celebrity cryptids are Bigfoot, Yeti, Lake Monsters, Sea Serpents, and Chupacabras," Coleman said as we walked through the museum.

"Those get the press, but it's all these little ones—like the new animal discovered in South America a couple weeks ago related to the raccoons [the olinguito], or a new turtle was discovered in Pearl River, Mississippi [the Pearl River map turtle]. I'm happy when people see we're skeptical of most of the bizarre cases and really grounded zoologically and anthropologically about normal animals being discovered."

Discovery of new animals is an ongoing process, even in this modern day and age. A new species of tapir, the kabomani tapir, was discovered in South America in 2013. The animal was known to locals and evidence had been gathered in the past, but it wasn't scientifically confirmed until December 2013. "The [kabomani tapir's] discovery was definitely cryptozoological, as this species first came to Western Science's attention based on ethnoknown information," Coleman declared in his year-end "Top Cryptozoology Stories of 2013," on his blog *CryptoZooNews* (www.cryptozoonews.com).

Also in 2013 a team captured the first video of the giant squid, tempted out of hiding with a bioluminescent lure. Although bodies of the animal had been found, this was the first live footage of the animal that is thought to be the basis of the mythological sailor lore of the Kraken. And so, while some of the inhabitants of the International Cryptozoology Museum might seem bizarre and far-fetched, some of them potentially could be real, and it is this excitement of discovery that the museum tries to tap into.

"All of us—myself, [assistant director] Jeff Meuse, [tour guide and "Crypto Queen"] Sarah McCann—try to be passionate with people here at the museum, in a short term," Coleman said. He quoted Bernard Heuvelmans, Belgian-French scientist, founding father of cryptozoology and author of seminal cryptozoology book *On the Track of Unknown Animals*: "He said cryptozoology is about two things: patience and passion."

THE PANGBOCHE HAND

Pangboche Hand replica.
COURTESY OF JEFF MEUSE / INTERNATIONAL CRYPTOZOOLOGY MUSEUM

SOME OF THE MANY ITEMS with an interesting story behind them in the International Cryptozoology Museum are the artifacts related to the Pangboche Hand, which come from a monastery in Nepal.

These artifacts were gathered during the 1959 Slick–Johnson Snowman Expedition, which searched for evidence of the Yeti in the Himalaya Mountains. It was bankrolled by Texas millionaire and adventurer Tom Slick and his friend in the oil business F. Kirk Johnson Sr. A large expedition had been undertaken the previous year that featured a trek into the mountains by a team including Irish big game hunters Peter and Bryan Byrne and more than a dozen Sherpas. The expeditions and others sponsored by Slick are documented in Loren Coleman's book *Tom Slick: True Life Encounters in Cryptozoology.*

After hearing a legend of a mummified Yeti hand in the Pangboche monastery from a monk visiting the expedition camp, Peter Byrne stopped by for a visit and took pictures of the artifact. The Pangboche lamas forbade him from taking the hand or part of it, saying that it must not leave the temple.

Determined to get evidence, Peter Byrne returned to the Pangboche monastery as part of the 1959 expedition. According to an account he gave *Unsolved Mysteries* in 1992, Byrne gave the lama who had introduced him to the artifact a bottle of scotch. When the lama passed out, Byrne set to work and removed parts of two of the fingers from the Pangboche Hand. He replaced them with bones from a human skeleton, carefully wiring them into place.

"I shall not go into the details of how we got the thumb and phalanx of the Pangboche hand, but we have them. The main thing is that we have them, and that the lamas at the monastery do not know we have them," Byrne wrote Tom Slick on February 3, 1959.

Now he just needed to sneak them out of Tibet. Byrne turned to an unlikely ally, a friend of expedition bankroller

Johnson: actor Jimmy Stewart. Byrne crossed the border into India, where he met Stewart and his wife, Gloria, in Calcutta. The famous couple smuggled the fingers out of the country in Gloria's underwear bag and took them to England. From India, the samples made their way back to Slick and Johnson, who had them scientifically analyzed. The results were inconclusive.

In 1960 Sir Edmund Hillary voyaged to Nepal to conduct his own hunt for the Yeti, sponsored by *World Book Encyclopedia*. Hillary visited the Pangboche monastery and examined the hand, and he and his experts concluded that "this is essentially a human hand, strung together with wire, with the possible inclusion of several animal bones." As Coleman pointed out in his book, Hillary and the world at large were unaware that Byrne had indeed replaced part of the hand with human bones and wired it together.

The ICM has an artist's representation of the hand on display, along with a skin sample from the hand as well as hair and, yes, even a fecal sample, all of which were also collected on the expedition. "These were donated to me by the scientist who was Slick's collection point for extra samples not tested, as he was dying," Coleman said. A letter from Jimmy Stewart to Coleman, which confirms the actor's involvement in the events, is also part of the exhibit.

Coleman saw the incident as a controversial but historic chapter of cryptozoology. "I strongly disagree with the tactics of mutilating this sacred relic and with the apparent theft of the hand's parts from Nepal. But I also understand this event in the context of the 1950s and the strong notion that by proving the existence of the Yeti, the Slick–Johnson Snowman Expedition personnel hoped to establish the Yeti's place in zoology," Coleman wrote in his book on Tom Slick.

Young Cryptozoologist

Coleman grew up in Decatur, Illinois. He was the oldest of four, the son of a firefighter and a housewife. "I was a shy young nerd. It's fascinating that I became a university professor for twenty years and have been on TV, because I started out a quiet boy, and there still is a little bit of that quiet boy in me."

Coleman's mother was supportive of him and encouraged him to get books with his spending money. Although his father sometimes helped out by giving him permission to go on jaunts with game wardens, Coleman said, "He was challenged by my intellect. We would get into tussles over who was smarter. I saw my father and I did everything he didn't do. I was the only one in the family to get an education, I didn't drink, I didn't smoke, and I didn't abuse women, so there's a lot. In psychology it's called reaction formation. I decided to be different from him, but I appreciated baseball* like he did."

Loren Coleman's introduction to cryptozoology came about when he was twelve and saw a movie that would forever change his life. As he writes in his 2003 book, *Bigfoot! The True Story of Apes in America*:

> I now look back on one March evening in 1960 as a critical juncture that changed my life. I was watching the broadcast on the local Decatur TV station of a science fiction movie, a Japanese picture entitled *Half Human: The Story of the Abominable Snowman* (Ishiro Honda, 1957), about the search for the Abominable Snowman in the mountains of Asia. It was fascinating, for even though I knew it was fiction, there appeared to be an underlying truth to this tale of an expedition in pursuit of an unknown species of hairy, upright creature. One does not pick their entries into mysteries, I suppose; for me this just happened to be the one.
>
> I went to school the next week and asked my teachers about this elusive, mysterious creature called the Abominable Snow-

---

* "I grew up a Cardinals fan. Everyone in my family liked the Cubs, and I had to be different," he laughed. After moving to New England in 1975, he switched allegiance to the Red Sox.

man. They were discouraging and lacked interest. They told me I was wasting my time on a "myth." But their words did little to put out the fire in my belly. I was one very curious young man. I began looking for everything I could read on the Abominable Snowman.

A framed movie poster of *Half Human* now hangs on the museum's wall. The film was originally released in Japan under the title *Jūjin Yuki Otoko* in 1955. It was created by the Toho film production company, the same company that made the original *Godzilla*. An American version, which features footage from the original spliced with scenes with actors such as John Carradine, was released in 1958. The film's movie trailer claims the film also stars "the mountain creature of Asia, whose name has become a symbol of terror and mystery . . . the Abominable Snowman!" The poster boasts that the monster is 1400 POUNDS OF FROZEN FURY, although the actual movie creature looks to be more like a couple hundred pounds of actor, rubber, and fake hair.

After seeing the film, Coleman began his path to a lengthy career in researching cryptozoology. Nowadays, people interested in cryptozoology just need the Internet to get started. With some simple searching, you'll be able to find dozens upon dozens of forums, blogs, Internet radio shows, and videos by budding cryptozoologists on the subject. But when Coleman started, he was one of an elite few who was taking the subject seriously, and in the early 1960s making connections on the topic took some effort.

"Younger groups that come in, I point this out," Coleman said at a "Classic Cryptozoologist Study" exhibit, pointing out an old rotary telephone. "I ask if they know what this is, and sometimes they don't! The other thing I say is that before e-mail, we actually wrote letters." Letter writing was the method Coleman used to begin his research into and expertise on the subject at a young age.

"I had four hundred correspondents I wrote to when I was fourteen. I would take a book like *Abominable Snowmen: Legend Comes to Life* [1961] by Ivan Sanderson, I would go through page by page and find who the experts or newspaper writers were, and I started writing everybody. I wasn't thinking, *Oh, this is an exalted expert or someone I want to put on a pedestal.* These were people I wanted to exchange information with or I wanted articles from that they'd written in the past."

Coleman's contacts included several who are now considered important researchers of what was then commonly called the "Fortean studies." Named after writer and unexplained phenomenon researcher Charles Fort (d. 1932), the Forteans became disciples of his philosophy of being neither a "true believer" nor a "skeptic" but somewhere in between.

A novelist and journalist, Fort examined reports of poltergeists, rains of animals, spontaneous combustion, strange artifacts, and UFOs. Fort's name lives on with publications like the *Fortean Times*, published in London, and groups like the International Fortean Organization.

Among Coleman's Fortean researcher correspondents were the aforementioned Scottish zoologist and author Ivan S. Sanderson, the "father of cryptozoology" Bernard Heuvelmans, early ufologist John Keel, Bigfoot researcher John Green, and Peter Byrne, Irish big game hunter turned Yeti tracker.

"So I would write everybody, and before I knew it I had all these correspondents. Back then there wasn't even Xerox. What I would do is, I worked as a paperboy and knew where the newsstands were. Say there was an article about an Illinois Bigfoot sighting—I would get ten copies of that paper, cut them out individually, put the citation, page number, and what paper, and I would mail it to Ivan Sanderson and my friends all across the country. And they were mailing items to me. I have five hundred boxes of archives in my basement at home that I need to organize someday," Coleman said.

Coleman's circle of correspondents became an early newswire of the weird, and information was gladly shared and forwarded.

John Keel's book *Strange Creatures from Time and Space* (1970) includes a chapter on Bigfoot largely based on reports Coleman had sent him.

"That's just what we did," Coleman continued. "I appreciated his thank-you, but I didn't expect more than that. The only way of getting information was giving information, I thought."

Coleman was soon doing fieldwork as well. He was traveling around the country in his spare time, interviewing witnesses who had seen Lake Monsters, camping out in Bigfoot hot spots, investigating any strange cases that came his way.

Even life choices like college were influenced by his cryptozoological interests. "I picked my college and its location—Southern Illinois University in Carbondale—because folklorist John W. Allen had written of authentic sightings of these animals by a minister and farmers from the area's bottomlands. I studied anthropology, minored in zoology, to have some scientific background to pursue these Bigfoot," Coleman wrote in *Bigfoot!*

▲▲▲

As Coleman's letters began to stack up, he was encouraged to write.

"I had a friend [Fortean and ufologist] Lou Farish, he was a researcher in Arkansas. He said, 'You write such good letters, write an article.'

"I wrote an article, and someone said, 'You write such good articles, put thirty of them together and write a book.' I never knew I was going to be a writer. I didn't want to be a writer. I just wanted to share my passion and the cases. It kind of snuck up on me."

Thirty-some books later, Coleman has written, coauthored, and edited books on cryptozoology from every angle. From field guides on cryptids like Lake Monsters (*Field Guide to Lake Monsters, Sea Serpents, and Other Mystery Denizens of the Deep*, 2003) to individual cryptid cases (*Mothman and Other Curious Encounters*, 2002), state guides (*Monsters of Massachusetts*, 2013), books on other cryptozoologists (*Tom Slick: True Life Encounters in Cryptozoology*, 2002), and an all-encompassing reference (*Cryptozoology A to Z: The Encyclopedia of Loch Monsters, Sasquatch, Chupacabras, and Other Authentic Mysteries of Nature*, 1999).

That last book, coauthored with Fortean researcher Jerome Clark, was not more than an arm's length away from me as a reference guide while working on this book. In addition to his hundreds of blog posts—he wrote for a popular cryptozoology blog called

Cryptomundo before starting his own *CryptoZooNews*—and short articles for various publications, Coleman is frequently called on to be an expert for a variety of media, including radio shows like *Coast to Coast AM* and TV shows like *Unsolved Mysteries*, to cite just a couple of examples.

There are many other noteworthy cryptozoologists, like Dr. Karl Shuker, a zoological consultant and editor of the *Journal of Cryptozoology*, and Dr. Jeff Meldrum, an anthropologist and leading Bigfoot researcher. But Coleman remains cryptozoology's most familiar face.

"Now someone said, 'You're the world's leading living cryptozoologist,' and I say, 'I'm just glad I'm living,'" Coleman quipped, laughing.

Cryptozoology Evolves

"In the '60s, Sanderson said to me, 'You're one of only five people or so in the country that is into this.' It was a small fraternity," Coleman recalled. "And it *was* a fraternity: there weren't that many women. We were guys across the country, usually well grounded, balanced, and interested in a wide variety of subjects. We knew that life didn't start or stop with Bigfoot or Yeti. I was interested in the Civil War, politics, girls. I didn't live in my parents' basement, all those things that get portrayed."

As the fraternity experienced a population explosion, expanding from a handful into the hundreds, though, human nature began to rear its ugly head. People became secretive, jealous, and dismissive.

"It was interesting to me in the '80s and '90s when I started noticing Bigfoot researchers weren't saying where the sightings were and became territorial and 'my sightings are my sightings.' Before that, we had all been sharing so much."

Coleman easily made the transition online around 1995. "I don't really think Facebook is real," Coleman said, smiling. "I have over three thousand friends on Facebook and two thousand followers on Twitter. So are there five thousand people that are my friends? No. But it does give you a sense of the four or five in 1960 and then the four hundred in 1963 to 1964. The number started growing and now literally there are thousands! After being on TV last week, I opened my e-mails the next day. There were people who want to volunteer here at the museum, even though they live far away. One said, 'Hi, I'm thirteen, can you send me everything you know on cryptozoology?'" Coleman chuckled.

Although getting e-mails from budding thirteen-year-old cryptozoologists makes Coleman proud, the Internet culture has also made it easier for those secretive, dismissive, jealous, ugly feelings to spread around, too. And with Coleman's stature in the media as an expert, he began to experience sour grapes from others in the field, people who perhaps envisioned themselves giving some snapping sound bites for *MonsterQuest* or *Weird Travels*.

"It gets into this territorialism that you didn't have back in the '60s. It is really brutal now—people are nasty to each other. Here's something an artist sent me," he said, pointing to an illustration that hangs by his desk of a cute Bigfoot strolling along with a thought balloon over his head that reads, "Haters Gonna Hate."

"There is part that is really like that, the trolling and the haters in the Bigfoot field now, because it's become part of the social media."

A Unique Wedding Gift

Next to the "Classic Animals of Discovery" display is a life-size bronze statue of the thylacine, commonly known as the Tasmanian tiger, yawning hugely. The Tasmanian tiger's population rapidly decreased due to human development until the last specimen, named Benjamin, died in the Hobart Zoo in 1936.

But did the species somehow survive? Coleman explains that Australians continue to report sightings, with more than four hundred reports since the animal's alleged extinction.

This dynamic statue was a wedding gift for the museum, bought by an online crowdsourcing effort to cover the cost. About a month after my visit to the museum, Coleman married his fiancée on Halloween day. It was his third marriage. The wedding's reception was

a costume party at the museum and featured a Día de los Muertos–
themed cake.

"I haven't been married in twenty years, so I've had time to assess
what that should be," Coleman said. He met his current wife, Jenny,
after she contacted him online with some questions about cryptozoology. Love blossomed.

Coleman is also the father to three sons: Desmond from his first
marriage, and Malcolm and Caleb from his second. "Being a father,
what was always important to me was that my sons follow their
dreams, not that they have a certain career or do it my way," he said.

Although his sons aren't actively pursuing cryptozoology, it is
inadvertently a family thing. "I've never taken a vacation that wasn't
cryptozoology related, so we'll go to places and I'll investigate. I
took [Malcolm and Caleb] to Loch Ness—Drumnadrochit—in 1999.
Malcolm wrote this essay about how we went to Scotland and looked
for the Loch Ness Monster. His teacher actually called me up and
said, 'We need to have a conference—we think your son has some
attention problems.' I said, 'No, we really did do that. I may be the
one with the problem, he's OK!'" Coleman laughed.

Although a large body of his work has been on cryptozoology,
Coleman has also authored a few titles that have nothing to do with
living dinosaurs or mystery hominids but instead highlight his career
as a social worker. After his studies at Southern Illinois University at
Carbondale, he got a graduate degree in psychiatric social work from
the School of Social Work at Simmons College in Boston in 1978. He
also studied social anthropology at Brandeis University and sociology
at the University of New Hampshire's Family Research Laboratory.

Topics he has examined in his writing include causes of suicide
and suicide prevention. He wrote the acclaimed 1987 book *Suicide
Clusters* and appeared on *Larry King Live* to discuss it. He also worked
on copy for a series of training manuals for suicide prevention at the
University of Southern Maine that same year, and trained and con-
sulted around North America on suicide clusters and school violence.

Other titles he has written, coauthored, or edited include *Unat-
tended Children* (1987), *Working with Older Adoptees* (1988), *Adoption and*

the Sexually Abused Child (1990), and *The Copycat Effect: How the Media and Popular Culture Trigger the Mayhem in Tomorrow's Headlines* (2004). Coleman taught a course on the social impact of documentary films from 1990 to 2003. My visit to the museum fell on a memorable day for both of us—September 25 is my birthday, and a date Coleman will always remember. In 1993, wearing a T-shirt with a Yeti on it and rock climbing with his sons in rural Maine, Coleman slipped and fell about forty feet, bursting one of his vertebrae. He had two weeks of operations in the hospital. Despite the setbacks involved, Coleman views the accident as a blessing in disguise.

"Breaking one's back can change how you view the world," he said. "For me, I decided to leave my 50-hours-plus-a-week university jobs. If I was going to devote as much time to cryptozoology and my sons as I wanted to, it was now or never. And so I did it, full time," Loren wrote in a blog post. His productivity in writing definitive books on cryptozoology increased exponentially.

▲ ▲ ▲

Back in the ICM, I was joined by more curious patrons wandering through the museum. There was a college student who told Coleman he was from South Carolina.

"I've never been to Portland before, and when I saw this, it became my number one need-to-go-to place," he declared. A young couple on vacation from Long Island looked around curiously. A woman came through, talking to herself, and then cornered Coleman, who politely listened as she rambled on about different theories of aliens and different interdimensional vibrations for a solid ten minutes.

Coleman said that although the museum draws an occasional strange character, about half the museum's visitors are tourists, who find the museum in a guidebook or online. The other half are people familiar with cryptozoology or his work in particular. "Or it could be a family, and one is really a cryptozoologist at heart. That's how it was with a family of four who was here this morning before you arrived."

These visitors have a lot of questions. The most popular one for Coleman is "Have you ever seen a Bigfoot?" he told me. "No,

I've never seen a Bigfoot. I've found tracks and heard high-pitched calls that I was told matched local Southern Illinois unknown apes, but I definitely entered the field out of curiosity, not because I am a participant-observer."

But Coleman says he did spot a cryptid, back in 1969: a mystery Black Panther, not native to his home state, crossing a highway near Anna, Illinois.

"I was going to work as a therapist at a state mental health hospital with coworkers. I was not driving. They refused to turn the car around to look for signs and prints. I see in that one experience what often happens in short-term observations with uninterested eyewitnesses who do not wish to pursue the matter scientifically but instead use mundane ridicule to continue with their day-to-day activities. No hard feelings against them. I was just disappointed."

▲▲▲

In 2011 the museum became an official State of Maine nonprofit corporation, and in 2012 Coleman began filing for federal 501(c)(3) status. Coleman is hopeful the status will enable him to reach out for larger funding, since it will allow him to get tax-deductible donations from corporations and foundations as well as individuals.

Funding has been a challenge for Coleman. In January 2014, for example, hit by a nasty wave of snowstorms that saw snow day closures and low museum attendance, Coleman had to turn to media contacts and social networks to ask for donations to make rent.

Besides donations, the museum sells merchandise in-house and online. While Coleman talked to me, ICM assistant director Jeff Meuse was in the background, photographing merchandise to post in the museum's online store. Products included T-shirts, books by Coleman and other cryptozoologists, coelacanth key chains, replicas of Bigfoot footprint casts, even a Chupacabras* finger puppet.

▲▲▲

* This cryptid may be referred to in the singular as either "Chupacabra" or "Chupacabras." I've used the latter except when quoting from print sources that have alternate spellings.

Looking around the museum, one has to pause and wonder, *Is this stuff real? Or are the displays filled with invisible monsters?*

Although I would label Coleman a "believer," he said that he is skeptical and scientific in what he examines. He admitted that about 80 percent of reports he gets of cryptids are merely misidentifications. For example, he said a would-be cryptozoologist sent him a photo of what the correspondent said was an unidentified animal. Upon examination, he discovered it was a kinkajou. Coleman smiled. "A fairly common animal, but sometimes people want to believe. Besides the large percentage of misidentification, there is a small percentage which are straight-up fakes or hoaxes." Leading me to a display case of artifacts related to the Chupacabras, he pointed out a perfectly cast plaster "Chupacabras footprint."

"In 1995 when there was a big explosion of Chupacabras reports, there were T-shirts online, all kinds of stuff. Then this website came about where someone in Miami said, 'I've got the footprint of the Chupacabras.' I said, 'OK, I got to have one' and sent my twenty-five dollars in, and I get the package, get it open," Coleman said, miming himself excitedly ripping a package open, like a Christmas present, "and . . . it's the best dog print I've ever seen!" he laughed.

Such a large wall of fail might be seen as daunting and frustrating, but it is that small 10 to 15 percent of true mystery that keeps Coleman and the field of cryptozoology going.

Preserving a Legacy

"I worry about the legacy, obviously, or I wouldn't have created the museum. People don't live forever; I'm not going to," Coleman said. "I wanted to figure out—can I create something that will live on beyond me?

"You need to have a small board in Maine: six people. Two of the people on the board are my sons, not because they're interested in cryptozoology," Coleman said. His sons' involvement is purely to be sure that the legacy doesn't end with his death.

"They're not interested in selling this on eBay or breaking the museum up. They want it to live on in my name." This is important to Coleman, because there have been horror stories of families not quite sure what to do with their relatives' collections of oddities. Coleman encountered one such cautionary tale when the family of deceased cryptozoologist Scott Norman called Coleman and asked if he would pen his obituary. Norman had gone on six expeditions to Africa to look for the allegedly living dinosaur Mokèlé-mbèmbé ("one who stops the flow of rivers" in the Lingala language), described as a sauropod.

I learned about the Mokèlé-mbèmbé in lesson 12 of my Cryptozoology 101 class. It has been reported in Congo, Gabon, and Cameroon, often in the Likouala Swamp, which covers fifty-five thousand square miles and is largely unexplored. The creature is reported to be anywhere from fifteen to seventy-five feet long, gray or reddish brown, and to feast on the malombo plant. A few brave cryptozoologists have led expeditions over the past few decades to find evidence of the creature, but other than an unclear photo and some possible footprints, the dinosaur remains anecdotal. Norman read works by cryptozoologists Roy Mackal and Herman Reguster on the Mokèlé-mbèmbé and set up his own website on the cryptid in 1996. Sporting his favorite hat, an Indiana Jones–style fedora, he joined a team of investigators in 2001 in his first expedition to search for the creature in the Republic of Cameroon.

"He came to the museum in 2008, and the following February he died," Coleman explained to me. "A young guy, forty-three. I got some details and wrote an obituary. A lot of his friends told me it was great. His mother called me a couple days later, said 'Wonderful obituary that touched my heart. And by the way, you don't need to worry about any of his possessions—I threw them away in the Dumpster, so no one would have to worry about them,'" Coleman said, smiling grimly at the memory.

"It hit me then in a very real way, that people celebrate death in two fashions. They celebrate the person's life, they remember them, and they grieve. And then some loved ones want to get as far away as possible, and they don't want anything around to remind them of that person, and they think they are doing everyone a favor. And of course his whole legacy of going on all those expeditions looking for living dinosaurs was lost—his files . . . he had an enormous collection, in a huge glass tower, of dinosaur figurines and native art from Africa. Gone, all gone!"

Norman's mom told Coleman, who was desperate to save anything, that some of the dinosaur figurines had been donated to a local church. Coleman tracked down a couple of the dinosaurs, which now stand posing behind protected glass in the museum.

"It's not so much that I want people to donate their stuff here, but I want to serve as a model. Donate to your alma mater, have someone inherit it in a university or museum, but think of your cryptozoology collection as worthy of keeping, not destroying or throwing away.

"So I think that's part of my mission, to say that that stuff is worthy of keeping, there's a history here, each piece has an individual story," Coleman concluded.

2

TIME STAMP

"HELLO, MY NAME IS NOAH. These are all my friends," Noah Leigh declared, his voice echoing in the empty concert hall. "We are not here to hurt you or to try to make you leave; we're just trying to communicate with you. So if there is anyone that would like to communicate with us, would you please come forward and tell us your name?"

Silence.

I was sitting in row S, seat 1, inside the beautiful old Riverside Theater in downtown Milwaukee. Not that I could admire its beauty or anything else—the theater was pitch black, and I was sitting silently listening to three members of the Paranormal Investigators of Milwaukee at work.

"Did you used to work here?" Leigh asked. After he asked the question, there was about ten seconds of silence.

Dead silence.

"Were you a performer onstage at one point?"

Nothing.

That last question was the booming voice of Michael "Gravy" Graeve, sitting on the stage of the Riverside.

"Do you prefer comedy . . . or tragedy?" Leigh asked.

This was what paranormal investigators call an Electronic Voice Phenomenon (EVP) session. The ghost hunters were inviting spirits to interact with them, hoping to catch their ethereal voices on the electronic recorders they had on their person and set up around the room.

"What was that?" asked PIM member Jann Goldberg. She was sitting several rows behind me.

"It's just a chair from next door," Leigh said. The restaurant next door to the Riverside was closing up, and the staff was pushing tables around.

"Do you have a favorite performer?" Gravy asked. "Someone you'd like to see again?"

Silence.

The Riverside hosts concerts—outside the marquee was advertising Steely Dan, Melissa Etheridge, and Diana Ross. After hours, a stranger spectacle takes place. There had been reports of ghostly footsteps walking across the stage. An apparition had been spotted hanging out in one of the back rows. Ghostly children ran and laughed up in the fourth-floor hall. A shadow entity was spotted in the third-floor men's room, and a mischievous ghost turned a light on and off up in the light booth. Employees said this was the ghost of a light operator who died of a heart attack in the booth.

"Can you leave here if you want to?" Jann asked.

In the silence, I suddenly felt a chill, a patch of cold air moving across my back and neck. I shuddered. But that must just have been a draft in the old building . . . right?

Riverside Theater, June 6, 2013

"OK, I'm recording," I said. My first ghost hunt with PIM had started shortly before our EVP session of the Riverside's main hall.

"Seven eighteen and thirty-four seconds," Leigh time-stamped after I turned my recorder on, his voice echoing across the Riverside stage. Time stamps are given to mark the beginning and end of investigations and to document any significant events—moving to a different room, hearing an unexplained noise, any other strange occurrences. Leigh was wearing a PIM baseball cap with a row of LED lights clipped to the visor to illuminate one of his cases of equipment spread out across the stage.

To get started, Leigh told me, I needed to get two basic pieces of equipment—an ultraviolet flashlight and a Zoom H1 digital audio recorder. These are a bit more expensive than your average audio recorders, but as the old axiom goes, you get what you pay for. The H1 is also popular among musicians for its high sound quality, and with a mega memory chip it can hold forty hours of audio. PIM sets these recorders up in different rooms of a building the team is investigating. In addition, each member has a recorder attached to his or her person; these are called "control recorders." They allow the room audio to be cross-checked to see if a sound is potentially an EVP or just a team member across the room sneezing.

Audio recorders were just one piece of equipment used by PIM. Leigh and Gravy both wore military-style flak vests, which held their H1 recorders (mine was held to my sweatshirt with electrical tape) and other devices. Spread out on the Riverside's stage in front of them were eight or so industrial suitcases filled with thermal imaging cameras, infrared lights, electromagnetic field (EMF) detectors, and other gizmos that remain a mystery to me.

All of this gear costs money, of course, and ghost hunting can be an expensive hobby. Just buying an adequate supply of batteries can be quite a tab.

"Noah has more gear personally than most groups have combined. Which is why he is telling his children that they need to get scholarships," Jann laughed, noticing that I was staring with puzzlement at the long line of equipment. My first PIM assignment was to follow Jann as she wandered around the Riverside to record "baseline readings" of "environmental data" while I scratched them down in my notepad. Jann was looking to record the temperature and electromagnetic field (EMF) level in each room as a reference point. Her multifunctional device is called a Mel Meter. I later learned it was developed by inventor Gary Galka, who lost his teenage daughter Melanie in a car crash and has since created a line of inventions to help paranormal investigators in the field.

"EMF is 1.2 and temperature is 65.5," Jann said, reading the glowing orange screen of the Mel Meter as she stood at a spot on the right side of the stage. I wrote that down. A serious fluctuation of these numbers could be a sign of paranormal activity, I was told, a ghost trying to manifest. After the baseline readings were complete, the outer ring of doors to the theater were closed and the lights turned off. The EVP session began.

PIM has a set of rules for EVP sessions. First, there is absolutely no whispering. This is at times a challenge for newcomers, because a natural reaction to darkness is to whisper. But whispering sounds too close to an actual EVP and muddies the audio, so investigators must speak in a distinct voice.

Also, if you do make a noise, it must be "tagged" or identified. If your stomach growls, you should say, "That was my stomach," or if you're a little shy on declaring your bodily functions, simply say, "That was me." And then, during an EVP session, wait ten seconds between questions to give a chance to capture a clean EVP.

▲▲▲

"Eight thirty-five. Let's move to the upper floors now," Leigh said after about fifteen to twenty minutes of EVP in the silent concert hall. We moved up to the third floor, where one of the Riverside managers claimed to have spotted a shadowy entity in the men's room.

"He was washing his hands and he saw something out of the corner of his eye to the right," Leigh said, directing the beam of his flashlight, "in this area here. He said it shot out the door and went to the left out onto the balcony area. He chased after it, and when he got to the balcony he couldn't find it. This was the middle of the day."

We spread out and sat along the hallway floor. I took a seat on a small table in the foyer of the men's room. It was completely pitch black.

"We don't do it for the spook factor," Leigh later explained to me about the "lights-out" style of investigating. "The vast amount of claims we hear about happen at night with the lights out." He added that PIM's video equipment also relies on infrared (IR) lights and that most evidence they collect is audio. "So with lights on you're using your eyes a lot, when in fact you should be focusing on your ears."

Each of the EVP sessions starts with a couple minutes of "control silence." This is used to tune the ears in to any noises that might already be in the background—traffic, a heating or air-conditioning system, water pipes, and so on. After listening and not hearing anything, Gravy led off the EVP session.

"Hello, my name is Gravy, these are my friends. We're not here to hurt you or make you leave, we just have a couple questions. Can you start off by telling us your name?"

Silence.

"How old are you?"

Silence.

"Are you from Milwaukee originally?" Gravy asked.

"If you are, you probably like beer. What is your favorite beer?"

It was completely silent when I heard a *fffffffffft!* sound. My heart jumped and I leapt to my feet, turning on my flashlight. I was thinking this might be a ghostly cobra, but when I looked into the

bathroom, I spotted the spook—an automatic air freshener that emitted a blast of scent on a timed basis.

After a couple more EVP questions, Leigh asked, "Did you hear
that?"

He and Gravy took off down the hall. The rest of us followed
to find Leigh and Gravy looking around the main concert hall from
the balcony. They heard a disembodied voice but soon found the
source—high above, in the Riverside's ceiling, we saw flashlight
beams and heard distant voices.

Leigh called the Riverside manager to confirm.

"It's Noah. Quick question: Are there maintenance people above
the house? Because we're hearing voices and there's a light on above
the house ceiling." The manager checked it out and called back.

"There were guys up there," Leigh told us. "They didn't get the
memo, but they're cleared out now."

Continuing the investigation up to the fourth floor, we found a
small group of "trigger objects" PIM had placed in the hallway where
ghosts of small children running and playing had allegedly been spotted. There was a baseball, a toy car, and a stuffed cat. The idea behind
trigger objects is that they will entice activity from a ghost. If PIM is
investigating a former speakeasy, for example, team members might
put out playing cards or cigars or small bottles of alcohol.

"I'm told there are some children that like to hide in this closet
next to me," Gravy said. "If you want to come out and play, we have
some toys for you to play with."

Only silence.

With no activity, the group headed for their last stop, the light
booth, where the aforementioned booth operator was rumored to
have died from a heart attack. Staff now reported that the control
booth light mysteriously blinked on by itself. The concrete walls of
the control booth had signatures from famous guests written in chalk.
My flashlight fell on Alice Cooper's signature, and Gravy moved over
to a wall that had PIM WAS HERE scrawled on it and changed the tally
mark from four to five.

▲ ▲ ▲

PIM first investigated the Riverside on September 9, 2011, which they documented in case report #110909. They caught an EVP of an indistinguishable whisper in the Riverside's basement. In report #111203 they documented their December 3, 2011, investigation, in which they caught another soft and subtle EVP whisper. They returned February 18, 2012, for case #120218. That time they used a boom box playing music, as a familiar tune can also be considered a trigger object. That case yielded a pretty solid-sounding EVP. As I listened to the audio on PIM's case file on their website, I heard a female whisper say something indistinguishable and then what sounded like (to me, anyway) "Get. Out." It was spooky.

In the light booth, PIM's fifth Riverside investigation was drawing to a close.

"Working up here, you must have seen a lot of great shows. Can you tell me what your favorite show was?" Gravy asked.

Silence.

Jann was sitting in the narrow stairwell that leads to the lighting room. "If it's too crowded up there, you can come down here and let me know you're here by tapping me on the shoulder," she said.

Nothing.

"Or pushing her down the stairs," Gravy quipped.

"Or punching Gravy in the face!" Jann shot back.

Still nothing.

Leigh got things back on track. "We've been told someone passed away from a heart attack. Is that true?"

Silence.

After a couple more questions, Noah offered the same concluding statement he does whenever leaving a room: "If you've been communicating with us, thank you very much. We have to leave now."

Back on the Riverside stage, the process of packing up began, a process that you don't see in the reality show edits. Lots of equipment has to be broken down, cords rolled up, devices powered down. PIM has been doing it long enough that the process moves along quickly. Leigh and Gravy knelt before their cases, packing the compartments with audio recorders and EMF detectors.

"Almost done," Gravy said. "For once I think I had more gear than you did."

"That's definitely not true," Leigh said, matter-of-fact.

"Well, I had lights out . . ."

"I had lights!"

"Yeah, your little lights that take two seconds to put away! Mine had cords I had to wrap up!" Gravy declared. Jann looked at me and rolled her eyes.

"Noah and Gravy bicker like they've been married for about thirty years," she laughed.

"Does anyone mind walking me to my car so I don't murder or rape anyone along the way?" she asked, displaying her trademark crude humor.

I told her I would, and we parted ways from the rest of the group. As we walked through downtown, I asked her how she got involved with PIM, and I later sat down to do a one-on-one interview with her at a coffee shop.

The Sailor Sister

Jann studied anthropology and forensic death investigation but eventually settled for a job as a paralegal for a bank.

"It's all right. I like my job as much as anyone likes their job. It's tolerable—I don't hate it," she told me. A horror and sci-fi fan, Jann is married and has a young son. Although she cleans up nicely when she has to act in a professional capacity, Jann is loud and loose with her raunchy sense of humor. For a while on Facebook, for example, she was posting the same picture of actor Bradley Cooper frolicking on a beach every Friday and adding lusty comments speculating on his genitals. Another time she publicly posted that her love for a honey-flavored peanut butter was so great that she would lick it off a baboon's intimate regions to taste it.

"My sister used to work with me, and they used to call us the sailor sisters because of our filthy mouths and shit, but I mean, that's just how we were raised. My mom says, 'God, I hate it when people don't know how to fucking swear,'" she told me, laughing.

Jann began to take an interest in the paranormal after she and her sister Maggie started watching the reality show *Ghost Adventures*, starring investigators Zak Bagans, Nick Groff, and Aaron Goodwin. After the success of *Ghost Hunters*, reality show producers have bet heavily on paranormal-themed shows, and *Ghost Adventures* was a payoff. In 2014 the show entered its ninth season.

The sisters at first enjoyed the show for comedic value.

"We used to call the show *Three Bros and a Ghost*," Jann recalled. "The first episodes, where they didn't know what they were doing and were freaking out all the time, are hilarious."

Interested, Jann kept an eye out for local groups and attended one of PIM's library meetings. She later filled out the application to join the team, found on PIM's website.

"Leigh sent the standard 'We're not looking for anyone right now blah blah blah blah blah.' But he said, 'If you have any questions, I'd be happy to answer them.' So I said, 'Yeah, I got some fucking questions,'" Jann laughed. "I wrote him this great big long thing: Do you see any correlation between these things and the environment? What do you think of this, what do you think of that?

"He said, 'Well, obviously you have some decent questions. Here's the thing: we don't need investigators at the moment, but would you mind coming in for an interview, and then you could start tracking space weather for us?'"

"Space weather?" I asked her.

"Yeah, there's certain types of evidence that correlate with weather environmental events," she explained. Jann began monitoring space weather activity for the team through the National Weather Service Space Weather Prediction Center website.

Soon Jann became active on investigations with the group and helped with PR work for the team as well.

I enjoyed talking to Jann, because she was extremely candid about the pros and cons of being on a paranormal investigation team. You didn't have to try to break the ice with Jann; she immediately crashed through it. For example, when I asked her what her husband thought of her unusual hobby, she replied, "It causes friction at home. I get it, but from my standpoint—what the hell would we be doing? You'd be washing your car like you do every weekend, and I'd be dicking around on the computer. So at least I'm doing something."

"So he is annoyed by it?" I asked.

"Oh yeah, they're all annoyed by it! If the others say their spouses aren't," Jann replied, finishing with a mock whisper, "they're lying. Once in a while [Jann's spouse, Jeremy] will say, 'I think it's kinda cool you do that,' but I think he just wants to get played with, so I dunno. It's one of those things husbands do—take an interest in what their wives are doing in hopes of getting their wiener touched."

One cause of these stresses, Jann says, is the time commitment that PIM demands, particularly on the weekends.

"It's like a fifteen-hour-a-week job you pay for instead of get money," Jann told me, letting out a short laugh. "This isn't a paying job. You travel together, sleep on hotel floors together, you're eating in crappy restaurants, investigating bat-infested, rat-infested shitholes. In the middle of the night you're looped up, buzzed on caffeine, talking about your marriage and your kids and all this shit. Honestly, with the exception of my parents and husband, I'm tighter with these guys than anyone else in my family. It's just . . . really a different thing."

"I Don't Want Her to Go Up the Ladder Like That"

Willow Creek Farm, outside of Shannon, Illinois, is a popular destination for paranormal investigators around the Midwest. PIM members have frequented this haunted farm as guests several times since their first investigation there in 2009. They feel that some of their most compelling evidence and experiences have occurred here, ranging from odd sensations to recorded EVPs.

As noted in the "Reported Activity" section of case report #130525:

There are reports of several resident spirits on this property including: Archibald Graham who may have been a doctor, reverend or both, and a young male named Robbie who are said to reside in the Northwest Bedroom; Sarah who resides upstairs mainly in the Master Bedroom; Lily and Mary who are believed to stay mainly in the Northeast Bedroom; and an older woman, possibly a nanny, who is said to stay in the Nursery.

The reported activity is varied and is spread throughout the house and outbuildings. Reports include seeing balls of light, objects being moved, being touched, the sound of a barking dog heard in the house, unexplained tapping noises, and many more reports.

On March 7, 2009 (case #090306), time-stamped at 3:05 PM, Leigh and a former PIM member were about to pull down the stairs from the ceiling that led to the farmhouse's attic. Unknown to them at the moment, their audio equipment was capturing a bizarre whisper. It was a Class A EVP (the best level), and its message was oddly relevant to what they are doing.

▲▲▲

"If you listen again, it's before the third and fourth pop," Leigh said. He was standing in front of an audience at a lecture hall in the Milwaukee Public Museum. It was close to Halloween—the busiest time of year for PIM and about four months after the Riverside Theater investigation. Inside the museum were Halloween activities for families, including trick-or-treating and art projects. PIM had been invited to give a half-hour presentation of what paranormal investigation is about.

For this part of his PowerPoint, Leigh was playing some Class A EVPs the team had captured in the past. He played the clip from Willow Creek again, and the audience was silent, straining their ears to make out the unearthly whisper.

"It sounds like . . . 'I don't want her there, something something'?" an audience member suggested.

"What we think it is saying is, 'I don't want her to crawl up the ladder like that.'" He played the clip again, and then that is exactly what everyone heard.

"I don't want her to crawl up the ladder like that."

"Wow," a woman sitting in the row behind me said. She sounded a little creeped out.

Noah's presentation led through the founding of PIM and some of its methods. A bullet point flashed on the screen behind him.

"I use my scientific background as much as I can when it comes to investigation," Noah read.

The Scientist

"Having a hard science background is pretty rare," Leigh told me in his interview, when I asked him how many other paranormal investigators had scientific careers. "I can probably count them on one hand. There's some computer scientists I know, but that's about it."

Leigh has a BA in biology and an MS in epidemiology and cell biology. At the time of the interview, he worked as a lab manager and cell biologist at a Milwaukee-area research facility.

"We study vascular development, using zebra fish as a model. We study how veins and arteries develop in the fish and hopefully can apply that to humans."

▲▲▲

Leigh's falling-out with the Greater Milwaukee Paranormal Research Group was over ego.

"[The other cofounder] was worried I was trying to take over the group or something. Because if I say I'll do something, I'll do it. Like I'll say, 'Hey, I think we need business cards.' Then instead of waiting around for someone to make them, I'll just make them. They might not look the best, but at least it's a start. I figure if I can get the ball rolling, something will happen," Leigh told me. "They ended up kicking me out of the group—this was November of 2006, I think. I had put a lot of time into the group, so I was upset for that reason."

Leigh turned to a veteran ghost investigator, Jaeson Jrakman, to give him advice on starting a new group. Jrakman had been investigating ghosts since 1997.

"He wrote this—it's a pretty good reference guide," Leigh later told me at his home, handing me a well-worn copy of a 2003 book by Jrakman—*The Art of Ghost Hunting*—off his bookshelf.

"I don't think he's investigating anymore," Leigh told me as I flipped through the book. "Last I heard, he was doing cryptozoology-type stuff."

Leigh and Jrakman talked about criteria for group members that didn't have anything to do with paranormal investigation skills—no felons, must have own vehicle. Leigh also factored in experiences from his previous group. "They had taught me what not to do," he said.

Annoyed by his old group's frequent cigarette breaks, for example, he forbade smoking on investigations. "If anything, it's motivation for people to quit the habit," he said. PIM's application also stated that couples aren't allowed to be on the team, which again was based on negative experience.

Jrakman also gave him technical advice on how to do an investigation. "He gave me my start on techniques, and I built on that," Leigh said. PIM's first official investigation was case #070512 on May 12, 2007, at Elsing's 2nd Hand Shop in Stoughton, Wisconsin. "It was me and Jrakman and that was it. He helped out until I got more people on my team," Leigh said.

▲▲▲

Back at the Milwaukee Public Museum presentation, Noah led the audience through a crash course of paranormal investigations. He ran through the four types of suggested hauntings—residual (a ghost that flickers in for a moment), intelligent (a responsive spirit), poltergeist (historically an entity that moves things around but is probably faked, Leigh said), and inhuman (angels, demons).

John Krahn and Gravy were also on hand, sitting in the front row, to help answer questions after the presentation. They had a table set up with a display of all the equipment PIM commonly uses. Spread out and carefully labeled were an EM pump (a device that emits electromagnetic waves to "help ghosts do their thing," as Jann put it), a flashlight, the Kestrel weather station, a Geiger counter, a three-axis EMF meter, and a geophone.

But the part that was most impressive to the audience was the sampling of EVPs that PIM has captured.

He played another Class A EVP from Willow Creek. It sounded like it was saying, "You're crazy." Another EVP from an unnamed business in a suburb of Milwaukee called Greenfield had an ominous threat for PIM: "Get out of here."

Brumder Mansion, November 9, 2013

It was missing spooky cobwebs and poor lighting, but other than that, the 1910 gothic brick Brumder Mansion was the perfect setting for a ghost story. There was an antique piano in the parlor, and looking up the main stairwell to the second floor revealed a chandelier and walls filled with old portraits. I could almost feel the eyes following me as I walked up the stairs.

By now I had gained some additional experience in paranormal investigation. I took a Paranormal Investigation 102 class taught by Leigh, where I learned a lot about techniques and equipment. I learned why a three-axis EMF detector is considered better than a single-axis EMF detector. The final part of the class was getting out to do a field trip to a location with haunting claims, in this case Lincoln Intermediate School in West Allis, where ghostly voices were heard in the basement and black shadows were seen moving in the detention room. The entire class sat in various rooms of the school, doing EVP sessions and reading equipment. Nothing significant happened.

▲ ▲ ▲

Constructed as a home to the Brumder family, the historic mansion became a boarding house, a parsonage, and an activity center for the Lutheran Church, according to *Milwaukee Ghosts* by Sherry Strub. In

1978 it was renovated and converted to a bed and breakfast. Brumder's neighborhood, around Thirtieth Street and Wisconsin Avenue, used to be a wealthy section of town, but the neighborhood has since deteriorated.

PIM was there to do a public event. Once a year, team members spend a couple nights at Brumder, letting people pay a modest fee ($40 per session, all four for $135) to join them for a night of paranormal investigating. The Brumder offers a special room rate to those brave enough to spend the night after a long evening of ghost hunting.

More and more businesses are starting to see their ghost stories as a selling point instead of a drawback. If they have the ghosts hanging around anyway, why not make a buck off it? It's the American way.

For PIM, this session was a fundraiser—like a bake sale or carwash. The group split the money with the Brumder and allocated its half to the team fund, used for transportation, website costs, and other business expenditures.

PIM ran two short investigation shifts over the course of Friday and Saturday nights, for four shifts total. Around ten to twenty people showed up and were split into two smaller groups, one led by Leigh and one led by Gravy. The groups rotated around the building, talking about the building's ghost lore. And of course, like all buildings with a history, it has accumulated quite a bit of it. There are ghosts in the basement, which has a small theater in it; in the various suites; and in the parlor. The building's most notorious ghost, named Aunt Pussy, is said to be a former resident of the boarding house and lived in what is now the Gold Suite. No one is quite sure where her head-turning name stems from, but it is assumed it was for her love of felines and not other connotations.

As I strolled up the stairs to the second floor, taking in the portraits on the wall, I ran into John Krahn, who was busy shuttling equipment to different rooms.

"Hey, Tea, don't screw things up tonight!" he said gruffly, displaying his trademark affection-through-insult personality quirk.

The first session was scheduled for 7–10 PM, and people began

The Brumder Mansion. COURTESY OF WENDY OTT

showing up and assembling in the parlor. For the first part of the evening I joined a group of ten people following the team of Gravy, Jann, and Tony Belland. We started in the basement. Tony sat onstage; Gravy stood stage right.

After the control silence, someone in our group said, "Is it just me or is the air really heavy in here?"

"Yeah, I agree," someone else said. I took a deep breath but didn't notice anything.

"Tony, you want to start us off?" Gravy asked.

"Hi. We're back," Tony said. "Some of us were here last night. We just want to get to know you. So if there's anyone here, can you knock on something for us?"

After some questions from PIM, the first of their participants opened up.

"Is my great-grandfather Frank down here?" a woman in her fifties asked. She explained that her great-grandfather used to socialize at the Brumder.

"Oh, man, it just got really cold over here," a young woman sitting near me said.

"Yeah," said her boyfriend, sounding scared. He was dressed kind of like Eminem, with short bleached hair, a baseball hat, a gold chain necklace, a white T-shirt, and baggy white denim pants.

"Now is your chance to meet me. Come sit next to me. I've been waiting a long time to meet you," the woman said.

"Is there like . . . a draft coming out this fireplace?" the scared guy asked.

"Not the fireplace, but probably off the windows behind you," Tony said.

▲ ▲ ▲

At 8 PM we switched places, moving from the basement to the suites on the third floor. After an uneventful session, we moved to the second floor. Some of the group went to Aunt Pussy's room, the Gold Suite, while the rest of us moved into the Red Suite, said to be inhabited by a ghost named George. Equipment was spread out on a coffee table.

"This is a geophone—it detects vibrations," Tony told the participants. "What we have here is a touch light. If you touch it, it turns on. A deck of cards, whiskey, a doll—these are trigger objects—a Geiger counter, and a data logger here." A couple sat on the bed, and another woman was encouraged to sit in the closet. Jann and I sat in plush chairs by the coffee table. I decided to give it a go.

"I got a deck of cards in front of me," I said. "Want to play? You deal."

Silence, and no card dealing.

"Do you mind everyone hanging out in your room like this, George?" Jann asked.

More silence.

The group switched locations again, returning to the basement.

▲ ▲ ▲

Down in the basement, an EVP session was going pretty normally. The young man with the bleached hair who felt the cold air earlier was with us again, sitting by himself in the small theater's prop and costume room on a metal folding chair. I'll call him Marshall. Tony was saying: "It seems kind of stupid, us asking you to knock, but it's the only way we can communicate with you. We can't hear you, we can't see you, so knocking is like a Morse code for us."

Silence, no knocks.

"Give me three really loud knocks, and we'll be done with this whole thing. We'll leave you alone."

"Oh fuck! I'm out of here!" Marshall shouted from the dressing room, then a thrashing sound was heard as he jumped to his feet and crashed into the hallway wall outside the room.

"It's OK, you're OK, you're OK, you're OK!" Jann, closest to him, soothed.

"Oh!" Marshall, said, breathing heavily.

"That scared the hell out of me!" a woman next to me said, holding her hand to her heart.

"I'm outta here! OK!" Marshall said.

"What happened!" Gravy asked.

"It just shook my whole body!" Marshall said. "The chair just started going *zeeeew*, and my whole body was shocked! Like shook! Like I ran into a wall and hit my funny bone or something."

"He flew out of there like his ass was on fire," Jann said.

"I did not expect that, it was way too dramatic for me!" Marshall said. I had walked over to see what was going on.

"You all right, man?" I asked. He was standing with his hands on his knees, breathing heavily.

"*Foo. Foo.* Yeah. Just trying . . . to get my footing, what's real and what's not. It felt like the chair was shaking, vibrating my whole body. Like all over my body!"

I walked back to the costume room, where a prop sword fell onto the floor, further scaring everyone. Gravy and Tony were examining the chair, trying to find an explanation. After catching his breath, Marshall returned to the scene.

"So did you feel that sensation of your body shaking first or the chair and then the sensation?" Gravy asked.

"It was really fast, but I think the chair got stiff and then shook and then . . . but it happened in milliseconds because I had no time to go, 'Oh, what was that?'"

"All right, let's reset," Gravy said, but then his walkie-talkie crackled. "Oh, I guess we're moving."

"Gravy, don't tell them what happened," Tony said. "No one tell them what happened."

Back up on the second floor, Tony slyly pulled Leigh aside to let him know about the chair so he could put someone from his group in the same position to see if he got a similar reaction.

"That guy really lost it; we heard him up on the third floor," Leigh told me later, when I asked what his group experienced in the basement. "We had a woman who said she had a weird feeling in that room, but she didn't freak out at all."

▲▲▲

After the session, the groups gathered in the parlor, and Leigh addressed them from the stairwell.

"So did you guys have some experiences while you were here tonight?"

A few people said "Yes" or nodded their heads.

Leigh told them any evidence would be placed on PIM's website and wished them a good night.

PIM members took a short break to slam energy drinks, which many of them rely on to combat late-night fatigue. There's usually a good supply of Rockstars, Monsters, and 5-Hour Energy bottles. The group has also come up with its own caffeinated concoction called "PIM juice," which is made from 50 percent Coca-Cola, 50 percent Mountain Dew.*

Soon the second groups for the evening showed up. For the second session I followed around Leigh, Missy Bostrom, and John Krahn in their group. After the excitement in the basement, not much

---

* It is an acquired taste, but effective. In fact, I'm drinking PIM juice as I write this.

happened. We rotated through the rooms and did EVP sessions. After the second group departed, PIM began packing up equipment. It was now around 1 AM, and I called for a taxi.

The cab dispatch said, "Brumder Mansion? I hear that place is haunted!"

"Yes," I replied. "I hear that, too."

« 3 »

THE SLAYING OF THE CHUPACABRAS

"IT WAS JUST SO MUCH MORE . . . it was so beefy," Sharon Hill told me via Skype from her home in Philadelphia. She wasn't talking about the latest beef jerky endorsed by a cartoon Sasquatch but her introduction into skeptical literature in the early 1990s. "It actually had evidence to it, whereas all these volumes of ghost stories and UFO stories were just recycled from book to book. The same stories were just reported over and over, and I got bored with that, so when I found the skeptical literature I thought it was great. It was exciting, and I liked thinking about it this way," Hill said. She was wearing a headset with a microphone and took a sip from a wine glass. A parody of Leonardo da Vinci's *The Last Supper* featuring the classic Universal Studios monsters hung in the background.

Hill's interest led to her becoming part of a group of people who proudly call themselves skeptics, a network of people who examine claims of the paranormal with a shrewd, scrutinizing look. They are going to tell you that the ghost you think is in your house is a creaky floorboard, your alien abduction was a case of sleep paralysis, and your Lake Monster is just a funny-looking log. They are seen as the much-needed voice of reason and sanity by some but as killjoys pulling the wings off pixies by others.

Hill, who works as a geologist, has had a long interest in monsters. "The first books I read were about dinosaurs and monsters. Always been into animals, nature. I collected bugs and liked Dr. Seuss books with all the funny creatures in them. Always read about Bigfoot. When I was in third grade, I read all the 001 books on the shelf [the Dewey Decimal assignment for books on 'knowledge,' where you'll find the paranormal section of the library], the paranormal things, Lake Monster, UFO stuff. I was a bookworm as long as I can remember. Godzilla, Dracula, ghosts. I liked the ghost stories but not the idea of being scared."

Hill's introduction to skeptical literature came after she graduated from college in 1992. "I was unemployed for a summer, and I just caught up on all my reading. I was reading stuff like Stephen Jay Gould, who was key in the skeptical sphere at that time. He would be talking about things like creationism. I think being a geologist and talking about how creationism reflects geology is the key to what got me into the skeptical approach to things."

Interested, Hill began to join e-mail lists and visited online bulletin boards. "I ended up on a skeptic mailing list, where I met a lot of the people I still interact with today. That was 1993 or 1994."

Hill explained to me the mind-set of this networking group of skeptics. "*Skeptic* is an approach, a process. You decide you want to use evidence to draw your conclusions. Some people are OK just taking other people's word for it, without any evidence except that one piece of testimony, whereas a skeptic looks at it from a more objective perspective by saying, 'Yeah, people make mistakes and they exaggerate and their senses deceive them and they misremember, and I'm going to look for more objective evidence.'"

Hill attended her first skeptic conference with a friend in 2000. It was a much different scene than it is today. "You could have counted the number of people thirty or younger on one hand. It was a very old, academic crowd. Typical white-haired, white-bearded professors. There were some women, but the original skeptic community was old, white, male. And now, today—and this has a lot to do with the Bush years and the Internet—it has pulled in a whole pile of younger people who were kind of disgusted with the idea that religion should play such a big part in your life or that you should believe in all these faith-based things. They were disillusioned with magical thinking."

Criticizing a "Scientifical" Approach

In 2010 Hill wrote a thesis paper titled "Being Scientifical: Popularity, Purpose and Promotion of Amateur Research and Investigation Groups in the U.S." It focuses on paranormal researchers and their methods, specifically ghost hunting groups.

"They are the epitome of scientifical," Hill said, using her term for methods that appear to be scientific but really aren't. "I don't know what it was like in the '70s when there were these UFO groups; I think they were sort of the same. They were amateurs, they weren't trained in science, but they were interested in doing the right thing in investigating.

"That meant, what our culture said, is that you have to be scientific because there is this honorific use of the word *science*. Anything scientific is seen to be better than an alternative. It carries some cachet to it to say you are being scientific even though you may just be pretending and don't have any scientific background. And these ghost hunters are the epitome of pretending to play scientists on TV," Hill laughs. "They've learned how to do what they're doing by watching other people on TV."

She continued, "So 'scientifical' really does mean you are playing pretend, that you are using a lot of the outward language and imagery of science, but if you ask these people to explain it, they can't. And I've done that. I've cornered a few and asked them, 'What do you mean you're scientific?'

"'Oh, well, we're careful and we're methodical and we use equipment,' which to them is objective as opposed to being subjective with a psychic or feeling. They use those objective instruments to justify their subjective feelings about a place being haunted.

"And of course what they are doing is just anomaly hunting with the evidence, finding environmental variables that are weird or wacky—'Oh, that's paranormal!' They default to that position.

"If I can't observe it, it's not science. Peer review, skepticism, being a critical thinker—some of those are really key to things that are missing in the current ghost hunting community. They don't publish the results, they don't share the results regularly, they don't get together and talk about values and foundations and agreed-upon assumptions, so there is no foundation to it. It's really a free-for-all.

"They envy the authority of science that they don't have. And they can't get that by being on TV. They can only get that by doing the work, going to school and immersing themselves in how really hard it is to do scientific work. You have to have a thick skin, you have to be open to criticism, and they *are not*. They don't like to be criticized or questioned."

Hill concluded, "So there is a mirror image of science and scientifical. It's really claim-pretend, is how I would explain it."

Hill even joined a group of paranormal investigators from New Jersey when they did an investigation of historic American Revolution outpost Fort Mifflin in Philadelphia. "I said, 'I'm just going to keep my mouth shut all night long,'" Hill said. But when the group began experiencing what they thought was a ghostly tapping sound, Sharon broke her vow.

"I was like, 'Are you fucking kidding me? This is so stupid.'" She crawled into a small enclosure behind a prison cell where she found a pile of plastic bags and garbage.

"It was water dripping off the walls onto the plastic. I said, 'OK, everyone, wait a minute.'

"*Plink!*

"'Did you hear that? It's water dripping onto an empty bottle back here.'

"They were really just out to have a good time—and that's OK! I don't have any problem with that. It's when ghost hunters go into the public sphere and talk to the media or give presentations or act like they are some sort of authority that I get perturbed by it. I don't care what you do in your free time, but when you portray yourself to the public as being serious and having the answer, then I get angry that you're basically just making shit up."

Skeptical Scene

After finishing her thesis, Hill needed a new project as an outlet for her skepticism and started to develop her site, Doubtful News (www .doubtfulnews.com).

"I wanted to do something different that involved my own interests. I'm a weird news junkie. I love Fortean stuff about weird natural anomalies, and I noticed they were not covered well in the media with any skeptical angle."

Doubtful News is just one of several outlets of the skeptic community. In addition to sites like Skepchick (www.skepchick.org) and podcasts like *Skeptoid*, there are conferences and meet-up groups.

My friend J. Jason Groschopf (most commonly known by just his last name) is a member of such a group. Groschopf, a graphic designer in Portland, Oregon, began his interest in skepticism when he explored the field of ghost hunting. He was a fan of the classic horror-comedy *Ghostbusters* (1984) and saw ghost hunting as a blend of his interest in the paranormal as well as urban exploration. But the "scientifical" methods he encountered soon led him to an interest in skepticism.

After moving to Portland, Groschopf joined the newly formed northwest branch of the Independent Investigations Group (IIG-NW) associated with the skeptic group Center for Inquiry.

The group has meetings and occasionally takes "field trips." For example, the group attended the Body Mind Spirit Expo 2013 on November 2 of that year and offered a variety of psychics, mediums, clairvoyants, and tarot card readers a reward of $100,000—not exactly chump change—if they would prove their abilities by an IIG test. Out of ten, all but two declined the challenge, and the two who said they would accept did not follow up with the group.

"I still love all of the mysteries, puzzles, history, and ambience that came with ghost hunting," Groschopf explained to me. "Difference is, I no longer start with what the answer is to a given question and work backward to support that. Better to begin with a null hypothesis and follow the evidence wherever it goes. When I was a ghost hunter, I'd say, 'A ghost caused that.' Now that I'm a skeptic, I say, 'I don't know what caused that. Let's explore the possibilities.'"

Chupacabras

In 1995 a panic began in Puerto Rico. Livestock were allegedly being found drained of blood, and their mystery predator soon had a name: El Chupacabras, which translated means "the goat sucker." After these reports began to circulate, sightings of the creature were reported. Descriptions varied, but Loren Coleman and Jerome Clark's guide *Cryptozoology A to Z* gives the most common one: "It was said to be hairy, about four feet tall, with a large, round head, a lipless mouth, sharp fangs, and huge, lidless red eyes. Its body was small, with thin, clawed, seemingly webbed arms with muscular hind legs. The creature also had a series of pointy spikes running from the top of its head down its backbone."

After a segment on popular Spanish-language television talk show *El Show de Cristina*, "Chupamania" spread, and sightings began out-side of Puerto Rico in Mexico, Chile, Brazil, and America's southern states, like Florida, New Mexico, and Texas. What was this vicious creature that feasted on the blood of livestock? Theories were quickly brought forward—a cryptid, an alien creature from another planet or dimension, an experiment gone wrong by the US government in the jungles of Puerto Rico, a starving mongoose, or even a minion of Satan himself.

▲ ▲ ▲

Benjamin Radford, a friend and colleague of Sharon Hill, became interested in skepticism after he went on a scavenger hunt for beer in 1992. He recalls that defining moment in his book, *Scientific Paranormal Investigation*:

> While at the University of New Mexico that year I won a regional essay contest (my piece examined the reasons for the 1986 Chernobyl and Space Shuttle Challenger accidents) and as a prize, I was flown to a college town in Utah to present my paper. While there my colleagues and I decided to venture out for a few beers. Because we were unknowingly in a dry county, this turned out to be an arduous and ill-fated venture. But in the process of going door to door and store to store, we came across a tiny used bookstore. Amid the shelves of books on fruit canning and apocalyptic survival guides (Mormon bookstore staples), I found a few old copies of *Skeptical Inquirer* magazine. One in particular, with a cover article on Nostradamus, caught my eye, as that was the first time I'd seen anyone criticize the famed prognosticator.

The author of that article was stage magician and the most famous name in skeptic circles: James "the Amazing" Randi.

"I love Mr. Randi," Sharon Hill told me. "I've met him a couple times. I first met him at a Center for Inquiry conference, I don't remember the year. I got my picture taken with him, because that's what you do—you get your picture taken with the little Darwin-like magician."

Randi worked as a magician for many years and then, like his magician predecessor Harry Houdini, decided he would concentrate efforts on exposing charlatans. His first famous battles were in the 1970s, when he challenged popular mentalist Uri Geller, who claimed the power to bend spoons with his mind. Randi wrote an exposé book titled *The Truth About Uri Geller.* Geller attempted to sue Randi for $15 million. He lost.

Other Randi targets have included televangelist Peter Popoff—Randi revealed it was not the voice of God but a hidden earpiece that was speaking to him—and famous psychic Sylvia Browne.

The James Randi Educational Foundation set up a reward called the Million Dollar Challenge. Starting with growing pots of $1,000, $10,000, and $100,000, the reward reached its $1 million offer in 1996. It's a guaranteed cool mil to anyone who can pass tests set up by the Randi Foundation in a laboratory setting that prove that he or she has psychic powers or another paranormal ability. To date, many have tried but none have successfully completed the test and claimed the reward.

Randi's exposures have made him a hero and mentor in the skeptic community. An annual highlight of the field of skepticism is attending the Amaz!ng Meeting, a conference far removed from old haunted houses and foggy forests in the bright lights of Las Vegas.

To say Randi's article and *Skeptical Inquirer* made an impact on Radford is an understatement—he eventually became the magazine's deputy editor.

▲▲▲

Radford's skeptical interests in the paranormal began when he was a young reader, he told me in an interview, Skyping in from his office in Albuquerque, New Mexico.

"Like a lot of boys of the Tom Sawyer variety, I was always interested by adventurous, mysterious, weird things. Growing up in New Mexico, there were local legends like La Llorona"—"the weeping woman," a ghostly woman said to haunt bridges in a white dress, crying because she has killed her own children. Radford would spend his allowance on books examining these phenomena.

He read "mystery-mongering books from the '50s. Frank Edwards was infamous for cranking these things out. Books with titles like

Stranger Than Science and *Science Can't Explain Blah Blah*," Radford told me, accentuating the titles through the air dramatically with his hands. At first fascinated, Radford soon recognized that the stories were being recycled and not examined thoroughly. Perhaps lending to Radford's skepticism was the fact that his father and both of his grandfathers were journalists.

"No one was actually doing any investigating. These were just stories with no references, no citations. It said 'they said that,' and even from a young age I was skeptical of 'they say.' I lost this natural awe."

After writing a book on skeptical investigation (*Scientific Paranormal Investigation*, 2010) and a book debunking sightings of Lake Monsters (*Lake Monster Mysteries*, 2006), Radford set his sights on the mysterious blood-sucking monsters of Puerto Rico, along with the canine-like creatures with the same name stalking the American South: Chupacabras.

A Strange Species

In his book *Tracking the Chupacabra: The Vampire Beast in Fact, Fiction, and Folklore*, Radford suggests, "The chupacabra is merely a recent incarnation of a centuries-old vampire myth, with a Hispanic twist."

Word had been circulating earlier in 1995 that something was attacking and sucking the blood from livestock, but it wasn't spotted until August of that year. In August 1995 Radford tracked the legend down to Canóvanas, Puerto Rico, where he found the original eyewitness, Madelyne Tolentino. Radford interviewed Tolentino and found her story to be without merit. As he wrote in *Tracking the Chupacabra*:

> Much in her incredibly detailed account is dubious, nonsensical, and contradictory. If Tolentino's account is accurate and truthful, the woman has near superhuman powers of observation; most witnesses would have only remembered a few of the most obvious features, but she spills out detail after detail of description, from its eye color to the number of toes on its feet to its missing anus. You would think she had gotten an up-close, 360-degree

inspection, instead of seeing the creature from one vantage point
(a window) at some distance in the early afternoon.

Tolentino said her mother and a local boy gave chase to the creature, but this was never verified.

"It is amazing the Puerto Rican chupacabra researchers apparently didn't corroborate Tolentino's story with either her mother,
the young boy, or another nearby man who first saw the creature,"
Radford wrote.

The members of the Puerto Rican Research Group apparently
didn't conduct any sort of investigation at all, and instead merely
interviewed Tolentino about her story. Reports of lost pets are
treated with more professionalism and competence. This is not
even amateur investigation, this is non-investigation, with little
or no attempt made to determine the validity or truth of the
report. Yet this account, clearly fabricated (or, at the very least,
heavily embellished), is regularly presented as one of the best,
most important pieces of evidence for the chupacabra.

Radford also found Tolentino's description, which led to the first
sketch of the Chupacabras, had an uncanny resemblance to the alien
in a movie released shortly before the alleged 1995 sighting, *Species*.
The movie featured a spiny-backed alien designed by artist H. R.
Giger that does indeed resemble Tolentino's description. Radford
eventually tracked down an interview with Tolentino where she
admitted that she had seen the movie before her sighting and used it
as a reference to the Chupacabras she claimed to have seen.

Tolentino's encounter soon became a media hit, and sightings in
Puerto Rico and beyond quickly followed.

Chupacabras Type II

Soon there were sightings of a different kind of animal being called
the Chupacabras in parts of the southern United States, particularly

Texas. This animal was not being described as a spiny alien with kangaroo legs and bat wings. It was said to have little to no fur, long fangs, and a sinister, ugly disposition.

Radford and others quickly unraveled the mystery—coyotes, foxes, dogs, and other animals with severe cases of mange.

Chupacabras Type II has been sensationalized and always follows the same story line. Person or persons encounter the mangy animal, sometimes poaching livestock. They shoot it or trap it. Unused to seeing an animal in such a bizarre (and miserable) state, they assume they have caught the elusive Chupacabras. Local media, happy to roll with an unusual news-of-the-day piece with lots of clickbait potential, give it a snappy title—Is This the Mysterious Chupacabras? or something similar. Sometimes a larger media source picks up the story. Toward the end of the story, a token expert—a local game warden or maybe even Radford himself—will comment on the fact that it is just an animal with mange, but that gets buried far deeper than the lead. Repeat cycle.

For example, in early April 2014 I saw a story circulating on Facebook about a couple from Ratcliffe, Texas, who had caught what they claimed was a Chupacabras in a live trap.

"I hunted coons for twenty years with my dogs and I ain't never seen nothing like that right there," Arlen Parma, the man who trapped the animal, is quoted as saying to the local ABC affiliate. "A coon don't make that noise, or a possum. What makes that noise? I guess a chupacabra does."

Strange noises or not, wildlife experts who studied pictures of the captured animal agreed it was a raccoon with mange. After naming it Chupie and giving it a diet of cat food and corn for a few days, the Parmas were told by a DeWitt County game warden that the animal had scabies and it was euthanized. The couple planned to have the body stuffed to sell on eBay.

▲▲▲

"I'm sure in some village in Ireland, you'll find someone who believes in Leprechauns, but for the most part, and if you're over ten years old, Leprechauns and Santa Claus are widely agreed to be mythical. That's not the case with Chupacabras. There are significant numbers of people who genuinely, absolutely, believe this creature exists. I've interviewed many myself," Radford told me, explaining the attraction of debunking the story of the Chupacabras.

"The other thing that attracted me is the fact that it's a vampire. Bigfoot leaves behind footprints, Chupacabras leaves behind dead bodies. *Wow, that's fucked up! This is something that could theoretically kill me."* Radford found that most of these alleged "blood-drained" animals were not scientifically tested and had probably experienced normal blood loss in a predator attack.

"I didn't know where it would lead, and that's what drew me to it, the ability to definitively solve a modern mystery, and a global one."

It's an enigma that Radford says he has unraveled.

"I believe, and many people believe, I have definitively solved the Chupacabra mystery. Now you can argue with that, that's fine. If someone else wants to write a book showing I'm wrong, that's great, I'll be the first to buy it. It's weird, I was thinking about this the other day: in my obituary it's going to mention I'm tied to this Chupacabra thing, which is bizarre to me. I'm proud of the book, proud of the research, but it's weird to me when people talk about me they'll be like, 'Oh, he solved the mystery of that vampire thing . . . what was it called?'"

▲▲▲

Not so fast, says Loren Coleman.

"Ben and I respect each other intellectually, but that also means we can agree to disagree," Coleman told me. "To explain away all two hundred or so incidents of bipedal, short, hairy Chupacabras with his mass-hysteria theory from a movie trailer is just the usual Ben Radford rantings. He and I agree that probably 100 percent of the Tex-Mex findings of four-legged bodies are canids (dogs, foxes, coyotes, wolves) with mange."

When I spoke to Coleman he told me that skeptics, especially those intent on debunking, are the mirror image of the obsession, just as bent to prove something *doesn't* exist as those who try to prove it *does*.

"They're somewhat simplistic," he explained to me. "They look for the one story that is a hoax and try to paint the whole field based on 1 percent of the cases, and try to find one or two explanations. I mean, most of us in the field know that about 80 percent of the field is misidentifications and mistakes. So then the whole field has to be thrown out? Fifteen percent is still unknowns, and 15 percent is enough to keep me going."

Everyone Needs to Be a Skeptic

At first, I was thinking that Ben Radford might be a villain in this book, or at least that guy who likes to pop balloons at parties. But he told me this is "categorically not true."

"I'll give you an example. About five or six years ago, I was at a Bigfoot conference in Pocatello, Idaho, talking about Bigfoot. I was the only skeptic in the room. There were lots of people who had seen Bigfoot tracks, eyewitnesses, and I'm the asshole skeptic in the back. I got up onstage and said, 'Look, I'm trying to tell you why I don't think there is good evidence for Bigfoot, and we can talk about eyewitnesses, lack of evidence, tracks, I'm perfectly willing to go into the details. But you need to understand—I'm on your side.'

"I said, 'I'm not laughing at you. A lot of people out there, outside this convention hall, they think you're crazy. They think you're full of shit and they think it's too silly to investigate. Not me. I'm willing to listen to your story. I'm willing to look at your evidence. I will look at your tracks, your DNA reports. I'm trying to bring scholarship and science to the endeavor. If I was completely convinced Bigfoot or ghosts didn't exist, I wouldn't waste my time. I've spent eighteen years of my life and a lot of my own time and money, and I do it for the intellectual challenge. I do it because I genuinely want to know.'"

▲▲▲

Before talking to Sharon Hill, I watched a video of her giving a talk at a conference. One of the points she made was that "everyone needs to be a skeptic." I asked her why.

"Everyone needs to be a critical thinker and consider the evidence, because if you're not, you're going to go through life getting taken," Hill told me. "People are trying to scam you, fool you, take your money. They're trying to sell you something that doesn't work. You can also invest emotionally in things like psychics and astrologers or hunting Bigfoot or ghosts. It can be harmful."

« 4 »

LAKE MONSTER FEVER

"**Y**OU HEARD ABOUT THE TIME some guys saw Champ try to eat a seagull?" Scott Mardis asked, surveying the lake with a pair of binoculars. I told him "No."

"Yeah, I got a file of that on one of my discs. These people from Maryland were down here fishing, and they saw Champ surface and try to eat one," he said.

Mardis lowered his binoculars from his eyes and set them down on the bench of the deck overlooking a part of Lake Champlain named Button Bay, about a half hour south of Burlington, Vermont. Then he opened his bag of tobacco and removed some rolling papers. He licked one end and stuck two papers together, took a massive pinch of tobacco, spread it over the papers, rolled it up, and licked the paper again. He smoothed it out and lit it up. Then his gaze fell back on Lake Champlain. Birds chirped in the background, but other than that it was remarkably quiet and peaceful in Button Bay State Park.

Mardis was referring to the Lake Champlain Monster, commonly and affectionately called Champ. The two of us and a small band of cryptozoologists were in the park for a Champ Camp weekend devoted to searching for the mystery animal.

What Champ—or, more likely, the multiple Champ creatures— might be, if anything, is the subject of some debate. Champ is described as a fifteen- to twenty-five-foot-long creature with a long neck that has been spotted by many witnesses on Lake Champlain for more than a hundred years. The most common theories suggest a plesiosaur or some unknown mammal. Skeptics scoff at these ideas, dismissing the stories as nothing more than sightings of odd-looking driftwood or other flotsam coupled with human imagination.

Mardis said his research points to Champ being a plesiosaur, an aquatic dinosaur thought to have gone extinct millions of years ago. "If it's not a plesiosaur, it's probably some animal that has evolved to look like one and is shaped like one," he told me. "It could be a giant, long-necked seal or possibly some weird prehistoric whale with a long neck. It's not impossible. But based on what we know, a plesiosaur is the best bet."

Mardis takes his Lake Monster research seriously—he has an extensive archive of historical documents, newspaper clippings, and forms he's filled out detailing eyewitness reports. As a cryptozoologist specializing in the study of Lake Monsters, he says he has to study "a multiple disciplinary field that includes marine biology, folklore, psychology, and limnology [freshwater biology]."

When Mardis was younger he was interested in all sorts of strange things: "UFOs, Bigfoot—but now I got tunnel vision for Lake Monsters," he told me.

It all began with Mardis's interest in Champ's more famous Scottish cousin, the Loch Ness Monster. Nessie draws tourists from around the world each year who squint along the shores of Loch Ness.

Descriptions of Nessie and Champ are very similar. Mardis's theory is that the two cryptids are from the same Lake Monster family tree.

"I think they both sprang from the same ancestral stock in the Atlantic Ocean, and one bunch went east and got into Loch Ness and one went west and got into Lake Champlain. When the land levels rose, they got cut off in both places," Mardis explained.

A fan of Scotland's unknown Lake Monster since a child, Mardis was vigorously researching books on the subject. He had moved to Philadelphia from his home state of Alabama and was a volunteer worker at the Vertebrate Paleontology Center at the Philadelphia Academy of Natural Sciences. While searching the library for books on Nessie one day, he found a book that would forever change the direction of his life. It was titled *Champ: Beyond the Legend* and was written by Joseph Zarzynski. This book, the first written about Champ, became a holy grail to Mardis, and by the time he was finished reading it, he had a severe case of Lake Monster Fever.

In 1992 Mardis decided that he wanted to pack up in Philadelphia and move to Vermont so he could be close to Lake Champlain and look for the creature described in Zarzynski's book. He would spend the next seventeen years carefully scrutinizing this lake. But it was only two years later, in 1994, when Mardis had the moment that made the move worth it. He was sitting at a park bench in Battery Park scanning the lake with his binoculars . . . and he saw it!

"It was a greenish-black, fifteen-foot hump coming out of the water with some kind of appendage that I think was a flipper sticking out sideways. It sat there for a minute and then sank. It reminded me of the color and skin texture of a leatherback sea turtle."

I asked him if this was the highlight of his search. "Oh yes, absolutely. I've been hoping it will happen again. It hasn't so far, but you never know."

Mardis admits spotting Champ is like a needle in a haystack—Lake Champlain is one hundred miles long, bordering on Vermont, New York, and Quebec. Mardis says the deepest part is Thompson's Point off Charlotte, Vermont—four hundred feet deep.

Mardis's move to Vermont was a success at first. A former IBM worker who got laid off after a round of downsizing, Mardis found a job as a clerk at a convenience store in a north Burlington suburb, Winooski. He started a hard rock band—the Black Tryangul—based on the sounds of his favorite bands, Black Sabbath, Yes, and the Allman Brothers.

Mardis bears a striking resemblance to Jerry Garcia of the Grateful Dead. He has a white beard stained by nicotine and long white hair. He has a big belly and walks with a determined Bigfoot-like stride. Besides rocking out and lake watching, he also hosted a cable access show on Channel 15 in the 1990s titled *The Haunted Sea*, in which he updated viewers about his Lake Monster research.

All of this made him into a local character, profiled in local papers as a "Lake Monster expert." While I was walking with him by the lake in Burlington, we ran into a man Mardis recognized.

"Hey, you used to shop at the convenience store I worked at in Winooski," he said to him. The man looked at Mardis and down at his T-shirt, which featured a plesiosaur swimming underneath the words CHAMP EXPEDITION 2008.

"Oh yeaaaaaah," he said, pointing at the shirt. "You're the Champ Guy!"

Hard times later hit Mardis in Vermont. He lost his job at the convenience store and his unemployment benefits dried up, so he moved back to Gadsden, Alabama, to live with his elderly father. During that time, and after forty-eight years of bachelorhood, he met his future wife via a Facebook dating app and soon moved to Bradenton, Florida, to be with her. He tried to talk her into moving to Vermont to no avail, so he agreed to enjoy life with her in Florida with the stipulation that he would try to get to Vermont at least once a year to spend some time Champ hunting.

Mardis and his wife were managing a hotel, but hard times hit them again and they lost their jobs—Mardis blamed a weak economy.

"Now we're barely scraping by," he told me. But where there's a will, there's a way, and Mardis has returned to Lake Champlain again for the first time in two years, joining me and five fellow cryptozoologists for Champ Camp 2013.

As I watched the lake with him, I could see some of the appeal—it's a serene hobby, like fishing or bird-watching. We sat out there as the sun set. Mardis believes the best times to potentially spot Champ are around sunset and sunrise, when fish are busy feeding on insects.

Around 9 PM the birds stopped chirping, the sun had set, and it was quiet except for the humming of insects and an occasional frog croak or fish jumping and splashing.

"Not so much as a tadpole," Mardis said softly, slightly defeated.

"These bugs are eating me up alive!" Mardis declared, and we soon decided to head back to Champ Camp, where Lake Monster investigation would be in full swing the next day.

Believe It!

After I arrived in Burlington, Mike Esordi and Diana Smith, founders of Believe It Tour, picked me up in their Jeep Wrangler. The couple had met twenty years before in California along "Bigfoot Highway," a stretch of Sasquatch hotspots in the Pacific Northwest, where they were both doing Bigfoot research. They were both in other relationships at the time but remained friends until divorce and other circumstances brought them together. Now they're engaged and live in Chaplin, Connecticut, with their horse, goat, four dogs, and six chickens.

Not content to travel and hit your run-of-the-mill tourist traps, the couple organizes trips to search for the unique and unknown. Believe

It Tour officially started in 2007. Esordi said it is based on five points: cryptozoology, classic monster stories, folklore, paranormal investigation, and ufology. They've put in thousands of miles and have been to every weird and eerie place you can imagine, from Transylvania to a Tour of the Crystal Skull in Belize, timed to coincide with the so-called Mayan Apocalypse year of 2012.

At Champ Camp, the couple were excitedly planning their next trip, Alaska—Our Next Frontier, where they planned to look into local Sasquatch stories and Native folklore, and also to sky-watch for Thunderbirds, cryptid birds of prey of unusually large proportions.

Lake Monsters have always been a special favorite for Believe It Tour, although in general the pursuit does not have the same large following that ghost hunting, Bigfooting, or ufology does. Esordi wonders if this is in part because "there is no hit TV show, no *Finding Lake Monsters* or *Lake Monster Hunters.*"

In the past Esordi and Smith have satisfied their Lake Monster Fever by visiting Lake Tahoe in Nevada, home to a cryptid serpent named Tahoe Tessie, and looking for the Flathead Lake Monster in Montana.

Lake Monsters and Sea Serpents have been spotted worldwide. Of course, the most famous of these cryptids is the Loch Ness Monster. Believers point to alleged evidence that Nessie sightings date back to monks in the sixth century, but the first widely circulated modern sighting was in 1933, when a couple saw the creature cross the road in front of their car. The famous fuzzy Surgeon's Photo, depicting a hump and long neck protruding from the water, was taken the following year. Debate still takes place on whether this is a genuine photo or a fake made of modeling clay and a toy submarine.

In addition to Nessie and Champ, the other most famed Lake Monster is Ogopogo, the horned serpent of Lake Okanagan in British Columbia, Canada. There are many others—Sweden's Storsjöodjuret is said to be found in Lake Storsjön, South Bay Bessie in Lake Erie.

Champ Camp is an event Believe It Tour had been hosting since 2009. In the past it has been a more family-oriented affair with activities for kids and adults, like Champ-related craft making, storytelling around the campfire, workshops on Lake Monsters, and lake watching. In 2013, though, Esordi and Smith had been rethinking the camp and decided to rework it as an invitation-only cryptozoological research expedition. Loren Coleman pointed me in their direction after I asked him about any upcoming Lake Monster expeditions.

▲▲▲

Coleman has long been interested in the case. On August 29, 1981, he attended the seminal "Does Champ Exist?" seminar, which Coleman described to me as "the Woodstock of Champ." That day was packed with speakers on the subject, including *Champ: Beyond the Legend* author Joseph Zarzynski, one of the most dedicated Champ researchers at the time; his colleague and rival researcher Dr. Phil Reines; Dr. Roy P. Mackal, a University of Chicago biochemist who went on expeditions searching for the Loch Ness Monster and Mokèlé-mbèmbé; and Sandra Mansi, eyewitness and photographer of one of the key pieces of Champ evidence: the Mansi Photo.

"I can give you Mansi's phone number if you want to interview her," Mardis told me later in the weekend, while rolling a cigarette.

"Sure," I said, pulling my notepad from my pocket. "Do you have it written down somewhere?"

"Oh, I got it memorized," Mardis said, licking a rolling paper and then rattling off the number. I think a clear sign of Lake Monster Fever is knowing Champ witnesses' phone numbers by heart.

▲▲▲

After picking me up, Esordi and Smith swung the Believe It Tour expedition Jeep to pick up Mardis, who was hanging out in front a friend's house in downtown Burlington. Mardis's Lake Monster Fever had become so severe that he packed very few supplies for the weekend camping trip—a duffel bag that had his binoculars, a big bag of rolling tobacco, a stack of printouts relating to Champ, a couple T-shirts, swimming trunks, and that's it. No towel or blanket, no tent or toiletries. Fortunately, Esordi had a spare pup tent, so he had some basic shelter. Mardis asked Esordi if we could swing by the grocery store on the way out of town to get some food for the weekend. We made the stop, and he emerged minutes later carrying a brown paper bag with four items in it—two giant bags of BBQ-flavored potato chips and a couple two-liter bottles of Dr Pepper.

▲▲▲

After looking at a Champ statue in Burlington, one of our last stops on the way out of town was the Auer Family Boathouse, home to Champ eyewitness Christine Hubert. Hubert has lived on Lake Champlain her whole life, operating the boathouse, which is located right where the Winooski River empties into Lake Champlain. There, she rents canoes and kayaks to vacationers and sells concessions like soda and candy. Hubert had an unusual visitor twice in May and July of 1986, she said.

Mardis found Hubert after carefully scrutinizing *Champ: Beyond the Legend*.

"When I first moved to Burlington, I went through the list of eyewitnesses in Zarzynski's book attempting to contact the ones in the Burlington area I could find by phone. Hubert was one of the few I could find that was willing to talk to me," Mardis said. He made arrangements to meet Christine and her brother Charlie, both Champ witnesses.

"She's lived here her whole life and has seen every fish you can imagine pulled out of the lake, but she's insistent that what she saw, and I quote, 'is like a dinosaur.' I showed her a little rubber plesiosaur I had, and she said, 'Yep, that's it.'"

Mardis had been to the boathouse several times to talk to Hubert and her brother. When we walked in, Hubert recognized Mardis.

"Oh, I haven't seen Champ in a long time," she said, almost reluctant to talk about it. But after she dealt with a customer, Mardis asked if she would share her story. Soon Hubert was out in front of the boathouse, retelling her story to us and a picnic table full of elderly

French-Canadians on vacation. She pointed to a concrete boat landing on the lake near the boathouse, underneath a streetlamp.

"This water was much higher than it is now," she started. "I was in that upstairs window," she said, pointing to the boathouse. "If you don't believe me, that's OK. I know what I saw, and you can't take that away from me. The dogs were barking that night and standing up, pointing this way." She pointed to an area by the boathouse where the doghouses used to be.

"It came right under this light and stayed there, and then it went back out to the lake. Its body was bigger than me, and its head was like this," she said, holding her hands about three feet apart, "and there was a body with a hump. It was a big one and a green one.

"About a week or so later my mother was staying with me, and I heard the dogs start barking. I went back to that window, and this time there was a brown one out there. Not a green one, but a brown one. It was smaller. I thought it was beautiful, majestic. All I can think was— *dinosaur*. I thought I was going crazy at first." She tried to get her mother as a witness.

"Well, first of all, my mother had taken her glasses off, her hearing aid out, her teeth were out—she was all of ninety-eight years old! I went and got her out of bed, I grabbed her and pulled her across the floor, I put her head in the window and said 'Look!'

"She said, 'Ohhh . . . what do you think?'

"I said, '*Chhhh Chhhh*'—I was trying to say 'Champ.' I called my brother. I could hardly talk on the phone."

Her brother rushed over and spotted the creature before it slid back into the lake.

"I never saw them before, I didn't see them after," Christine said.

This bay was also where Mardis experienced one of his most solid failures while Champ searching—capsizing a vessel into the bay.

"It was an inflatable raft from K-Mart on sale for twenty-some dollars. It was a real piece of crap, and I got to about halfway out to the middle of this bay here and it sank on me. I guess I felt a lot like Captain Ahab," Mardis said, looking out at the bay.

Champ Evidence Review

After we arrived at Button Bay State Park, I set up my tent. Champ
Camp had reserved three adjoining campsites just a short stroll from
the shore of Lake Champlain. Mardis and I set up our pup tents on
one of the sites. After setup, I joined Mardis, Esordi, and Smith at the
couple's site, where Mardis had loaded one of his discs into Esordi's
laptop, which was positioned on a picnic table. As the sun set, we
crowded around Mardis, as he led us through his huge collection of
Champ evidence.

The first sighting of Champ has often been attributed to the lake's
namesake, explorer Samuel de Champlain, in 1609. He reportedly
said that he had spotted a "serpent-like creature about twenty-feet
long, as thick as a barrel and with a head shaped like a horse."

It's a good story, but as author Robert Bartholomew dissects in
his book *The Untold Story of Champ: A Social History of America's Loch
Ness Monster*, it is simply not true. Champlain's report was of a five-
foot-long creature and was clearly a description of a longnose gar.

The myth that Champlain was a Champ witness is due entirely
to sloppy reporting and one of many fact-checking errors that have
added to the big fish story. The first actual reported sightings began
in the early 1800s. Several sightings occurred in the 1870s, so many
that 1873 was known as the year of the "Great Sea Serpent Scare."
Passengers and crew of a steamship even claimed that they had col-
lided with the creature. Famous circus entrepreneur P. T. Barnum
offered an astronomical sum of $50,000 for "the hide of the Great
Champlain Serpent."

Champ continued to be a legend over the years but had dropped
into obscurity until a famous photo emerged. The Mansi Photo, as
it's called, was taken by Sandra Mansi, on vacation with her family
in 1977. It depicts what might be the neck, head, and back of the
creature. The photo energized a new group of people interested in
studying the cryptid, and although it has been criticized by skeptics,
it remains a key piece of evidence to Champ believers.

CRITICS OF THE MANSI PHOTO

Benjamin Radford's model reconstructing the Mansi Photo as a tree stump. COURTESY OF BENJAMIN RADFORD

SKEPTIC BEN RADFORD thoroughly investigated the Mansi Photo in an article for *Skeptical Inquirer* and later in his book *Lake Monster Mysteries: Investigating the World's Most Elusive Creatures*, which he coauthored with skeptic Joe

Nickell. One of his experiments was re-creating a model of a tree stump that would match the Mansi Photo.

"I haven't seen good evidence Champ exists," Radford told me. "One of the problems is the universally recognized best evidence for Champ was Sandra Mansi's 1977 photograph, later published in 1981 in the *New York Times*. I believe I have well demonstrated—and other people can disagree—I think I've made a strong case that she photographed a floating log. When your best evidence turns out to almost certainly be a log, you got a problem."

Champ researcher Scott Mardis said his viewpoint is different from Radford's.

"So far no one has been able to go back in time and conclusively identify the object in Sandra Mansi's photograph," he said. "It could be anything from a plesiosaur to a floating log.

"A lot of people's perceptions of the credibility of the photo are based on their degree of faith in Mansi's apparent sincerity versus questionable circumstances surrounding the provenance of the photo. These factors include the inability to find the exact location where the photo was taken and the loss of the photographic negative," Mardis said, pointing to common criticisms of the Mansi Photo.

"Mansi says she threw away the negatives to the photo, making further examination of the photo impossible. She also says she can't recall where the photo was shot, making a reconstruction difficult.

"While the tree stump idea is certainly possible, I find it questionable that most of the images from Lake Champlain and Loch Ness are simply floating logs that happen to so greatly look like animals, much less something resembling a plesiosaur."

Other evidence has occasionally risen to the surface. The 2005 Bodette Video shows . . . something . . . swimming by a fishing boat. Mardis played the video of excited fishermen pointing to a large, dark shape by their boat.

In the early 2000s Elizabeth von Muggenthaler of Fauna Research Communications purported to have captured evidence of a large creature echolocating in Lake Champlain. One of her expeditions was captured on the cryptozoology-themed show *MonsterQuest*. Mardis was an assistant for the expedition, and he played us a recording of the echolocating sound on Esordi's laptop.

"That's the sound of Champ supposedly echolocating," he told us, playing a clip of a high-pitched clicking sound. Then he played another clip, with a higher pitch. "That's a dolphin," he said. He played another clip. "That's a killer whale."

Next Mardis showed us a series of photos in which he had over-lapped graphics of plesiosaur skeletons with the Mansi Photo and the Surgeon's Photo, which is the famous grainy black-and-white photo of the Loch Ness Monster taken in 1934. Mardis had juxtaposed the photos and the plesiosaur skeletons from every angle.

"Some nights when I'm working on this, I'll drink two pots of coffee and smoke two packs of cigarettes," he told us. He later sent me a seventy-nine-page PDF he had compiled on plesiosaur anatomy and other items related to Champ.

▲▲▲

When I woke up the next morning, Mardis was sitting at the picnic table, smoking. He had already been up for several hours, Champ watching. "All I saw were a few fish jumping and some loons," he said. Mardis decided to go down for a nap and climbed into his bare pup tent.

"I can't wait to get into a real bed," he said, struggling with the tent zipper. "Only thing that's got me down here is plesiosaurs."

After Esordi and I got back from a canoe ride, we found members of Champ Camp slowly arriving. Jeff Meuse, assistant director of the International Cryptozoology Museum, had driven down from Maine with his girlfriend. William Dranginis, a cryptozoologist from Virginia, had driven straight through in his truck, which had a vanity plate that read VA BGFT. Esordi met Dranginis at a Bigfoot conference back in 2000. Dranginis had a cabin in Virginia that he rigged up with equipment to capture evidence of Bigfoot. He said he has even spotted a Bigfoot staring at him in the darkness at the site.

At this point, Champ Camp was running into a problem: organizers were unable to secure an adequate boat. Mardis knew someone with a boat but was unable to get in touch with his connection, and searching for an available rental for the busy summer weekend was producing nothing but dead ends. The plan was changed to do a night watch on the shore and spend some time socializing around an important tool to storytellers and cryptozoologists alike—the bonfire.

▲ ▲ ▲

"My grandfather introduced it to me at a historical society," Jeff Meuse said, talking about the Gloucester Monster, a Sea Serpent spotted frequently in the 1800s in the harbor of Gloucester, Massachusetts. "One of my goals is to drive around the coast, stopping at historical societies to find what I can on Lake Monsters."

The fire continued to burn and the cryptozoologists talked into the night about different Lake Monster cases. It is a topic for dreamers.

Mardis was there, despite being broke, to continue his pursuit of the creature. Dranginis drove a truck filled with specialized equipment he had built to try to finally find evidence of the mystery creature. They were dreamers in other ways, too. Diana Smith had recently left her job within the corporate world, hoping to pursue things that brought more enjoyment, like art, food, and travel. Meuse said that he saw his boss at the pizza restaurant he worked at covered in grease and pizza sauce, and that, coupled with his passion for cryptozoology, made him dream of a career change. He was in college, hoping to be a teacher.

Today's the Day

The dream is a hard one, though, when it meets stark reality. Finding a boat, for example. All of the leads had dried up on the final full day of Champ Camp, and the cryptozoologists decided to load up in two canoes to brave the choppy waters and install the equipment.

In the morning Dranginis set up his equipment spread out on a picnic table. A friend of Believe It Tour, Bruce Harrington, arrived sometime in the middle of the night for Champ Camp's big day.

"Bruce," he said, shaking my hand. "I'm known as the Creature Seeker." Harrington, from Boston, runs an annual cryptozoological conference in Ohio called Creature Weekend, filled with guest speakers and workshops. Harrington is quite a character and a self-described "ballbuster." Later, while he was grilling the largest steak I had ever seen—it covered the entire surface area of a grill—I commented on a huge knife, almost a miniature sword, that he had hanging off his belt. He told me he was a knife collector. I asked him if he knew how many knives he had in his collection.

"About 312," he answered.

Harrington set up his video camera on a tripod, ready to film some footage of Dranginis explaining his Champ-seeking equipment.

Harrington: "What do you call yourself?"

Dranginis: "A researcher."

Harrington: "Champ researcher?"

Dranginis: "Champ researcher, Bigfoot researcher, anything cryptid."

Harrington: "How about *chicken wing eatin' sumofabitch?*"

Dranginis: "That's even better, I like it."

"That's what I call him! Don't I, Bill?" Harrington said, laughing boisterously. Then he got serious.

"OK, here we go," he said, then paused for a second.

"I'm with Bill Dranginis. He's a cryptozoological researcher. He's going to be talking about some of the technology he's using to investigate the Champ phenomenon."

Dranginis picked up a large, yellow plastic tube with a couple of holes cut into it, attached to a long yellow rope and a white plastic buoy.

"I call it the Eyegotcha H_2O," he said. "What it includes is the digital video recorder right here," he said, pointing to a hole near the bottom of the tube, "and a twelve-volt battery source, which is rechargeable. It's a piece of PVC pipe, with two end caps that are waterproof. These slots are where the hydrophones are. It's submergible down to about fifty feet, although we'll place it about four feet below the water." Dranginis estimated the setup cost him about $250. Harrington asked him if it had been tested before.

"We've deployed it to Lake Champlain before. No evidence whatsoever so far."

Dranginis also showed off a waterproof camera on a pole that could be submerged from the boat and some camouflage-colored time-lapse cameras.

"Why haven't we gotten more evidence of Champ yet?" Harrington asked. Dranginis reflected on the question.

"I think they live at deep depths and don't come up often," he answered.

▲▲▲

The canoes were loaded up with the equipment, Esordi and Dranginis in one canoe and Meuse, Mardis, and me loaded into another. Smith stayed onshore and took pictures of us with her long photo lens. As Mardis climbed into the boat we shook and wobbled violently, and I was certain we were going to tip over, a repeat of Mardis's sinking inflatable raft misadventure. But we stabilized after he sat down and soon were cruising out on the lake.

"Is today the day?" Mardis excitedly asked of the world in general.

"Today's the day we find evidence!" Esordi responded. We began to paddle out, the hot sun beating down on us and reflecting on the metal canoes. We found a spot to place the Eyegotcha H_2O, its white buoy floating in the bay. We cruised around while Mardis listened to a hydrophone dipped over the side of the boat.

"I hear a real faint clicking, like echolocation, in the distance," he told us.

We placed the time-lapse cameras on a small, rocky island in the lake and were floating in the canoes talking and looking through binoculars when a State Patrol boat slowly started chugging toward us.

"Hey there, fellas," the officer called out. "What are we looking for here?"

"Champ," Dranginis said, matter-of-factly.

"You're looking for Champ?" the officer said, gauging if it was a joke. "Seriously?"

"Yes. Have you seen it? Do you think it exists?" Esordi asked.

"Naw, I'm from Missouri—the Show Me State," the officer said, leaning on the boat's wheel. "I've been out here for thirty-one years, on the lake for six. I haven't seen anything."

"Any recent sightings you've heard of?" Dranginis asked.

"Only what I've seen on the Discovery Channel," the officer said. "Well, good luck. If ya catch him—better have a permit." He laughed and began wheeling the boat away.

Later the cameras were collected. No evidence was discovered.

A Visit to Dennis Hall

On the way out of Champ Camp, we made a house call to someone well known in the field of Champ research, a man with a critical case of Lake Monster Fever, Dennis Jay Hall.

A Vermont resident obsessed with Champ, Hall led a group called Champ Quest and wrote the *Champ Trackers* blog on the organization's website. He gave Champ the pseudoscientific name *champtanystropheus* and invented the term *champology* to describe his field. He self-published a guide on Champ, *Champ Quest: The Ultimate Search, 1999 Field Guide & Almanac of Best Search Dates for Lake Champlain*.

Hall has many outlandish claims that involve Champ. He claims that his father captured a baby one when he was a child and that this baby was kept in captivity for a period at his school as a classroom pet. (He says as unique as the creature was, the school later simply "threw it away.") As an adult, he said that he has spotted Champ creatures many times over the years.

After years of interacting with other cryptozoologists and Champ advocating, Hall suddenly disappeared in the mid-2000s, and many of his contacts wondered where he had gone. "He's the Howard Hughes of cryptozoology," Mardis told me.

▲▲▲

Classical music. Back at the International Cryptozoology Museum, Coleman had told me about Champ and the variety of people the creature has attracted over the years. He was familiar with Dennis Jay Hall.

"He's had bizarre behavior sometimes, disappearing, people not knowing if he was alive for three years, rumors he had committed suicide, all kinds of things like that. Very bizarre," Coleman said. He had seen quite a few people overcome by their obsession, becoming isolated and weird.

"I see people intensely interested, and some people give up so much. There's some people in the field you get worried about because they become so obsessed with one part of cryptozoology, they kind of lose sight of living."

▲▲▲

By 2013, Hall was back on the grid, though still reclusive. "He's literally living in a shack, but he has a museum's worth of stuff," Dranginis told me excitedly as we drove out there. He and Mardis had visited Hall a day earlier to see if it might be acceptable to bring the rest of us along as visitors on the last day of Champ Camp. Hall agreed, and after packing up camp we caravanned over.

When we arrived, I found that "shack" wasn't an exaggeration. He lived in what appeared to be a converted equipment shed near a farm. Cows mooed loudly in the background, and about a dozen kittens wandered in and out of Hall's residence, walking around the piles of random artifacts, maps, and stacks of paperwork. A line of photos and other papers was clothespinned to a laundry line stretching across the room.

Hall greeted us happily and took us inside, where we crowded around as he showed us a binder full of photos of what he claimed were images of Champ that he took, some from freeze-frames of videos. The photos were bizarre, heavily pixilated black squiggles that were hard to make out.

Hall began recalling his long history of Champ sightings, beginning with an encounter in the spring of 1978, he said. "My first encounter other than the baby one [the classroom pet] was in that marsh," Hall told us, referring to a marsh we drove through along the way. "It was late at night. I was woken up out of a sound sleep; I had a dog that was barking. Yelp and bark. I went over to the dog and was trying to figure out—it was crying and crying and barking. I smelled something and I thought, *What the hell is that, a skunk?* Then I listened and I heard something in the marsh, and it was a *Splot! Splot! Splot!* Then the same thing, *Splot! Splot!*" Hall was very animated. "*Splot! Splot!* What the *heck* is that?

"There was a bank right behind the house, and it dropped off about eight feet into the marsh, about three feet of water. My car was here and the marsh was there, so I just drove my car up and turned the headlights on. Got out, looked, first thing I think is, *Wow, look at the raccoons out here!*

"Turn, and here's these bright red eyes. *A raccoon? That ain't a raccoon! There ain't a tree bigger than this.*

"I had the lights on high beam, I turned it on low beam and things were more clear—I could see it! Just the head. It came up out of the water and *crash crash crash crash!* It turned and the eyes reflected red, it turned back and it was gray, eyes turned this way, eyes reflected red. Stunk! Musty smell, stunk terrible."

Hall was scared and confused. "I did what every redneck does," he continued, "ran inside and got my gun. I had a two-week-old baby in the house, so I went out with my .22 and *boom boom boom!*" Despite the warning shots, he said, the creature "ignored it, totally ignored it."

Hall followed the Champ creature until it disappeared into the marsh.

As the years passed, the sightings continued. "I just saw one on

Sunday," he told us nonchalantly. He also claimed to have an unprec-
edented knowledge of the Champ creatures and their habits—what
their diet consists of, how long they hibernate (six months), and
where (in the marshes).

"But they probably don't breed in the marsh—they breed out on
the broad lake in mid-June and give live birth. They retain the eggs
in their bodies and wander throughout the winter and give birth
in the spring, early in the spring," Hall told us, as if these were just
commonly known facts.

From Hall's we headed away from Button Bay.

▲▲▲

The previous night we had gathered around the bonfire to celebrate
the last night of Champ Camp with some drinks and stories.

I took the bonfire as an opportunity to ask Dranginis and Mardis
the question of the weekend: Will solid, irrefutable evidence of
Champ ever be obtained? And if so, by what method?

"We got to try to find some way to lure them in, try to find their
hiding places," Mardis said. "If they exist, they'd have hiding places.
I think the best chance is finding a piece of a dead one or, if you get
lucky, get a tissue sample with a biopsy dart [a retractable dart that
can be fired at an animal to collect a small sample of skin or other
tissue], which could be used as a potential type specimen. It would
be a biological sample, and you could do a DNA test on it to tell
what type of animal it is and what it's related to by comparing it to
samples of other animals."

"I think submersibles," Dranginis said. "I think you really got
to invade their territory, but we don't have the technology and the
money to go down."

"You've got to be persistent, not just once in a while," Mardis
added. "You got to get a methodology in place."

The next morning, Champ Camp began to pack up to head out.
Before we left, I brought my binoculars down to the lake to have
one last look.

I guess I had developed a little bit of Lake Monster Fever myself.

5

WHAT WAS THAT?

KNOCK KNOCK KNOCK!

A face peeked from behind the curtain of a window on her door.

"Paranormal Investigators of Milwaukee," Jann Goldberg said, holding up her PIM business card. The woman opened her door and let us in.

Her excessively obscene language aside, Jann cleans up nicely. She was dressed for business and looked like she could be a real estate agent. She was there on a different sort of house call.

Ever since this couple, we'll call them the Smiths, moved into their upper flat on Milwaukee's east side, they had been having unwanted visitors. Jann was there to do what PIM calls a "walk-through," an evaluation of a potential client for an investigation. There are a lot of considerations when doing a walk-through: What type of equipment will be needed and how many investigators? Are there simple explanations for what the client is experiencing, like a broken radiator? Is the client mentally ill? Investigations of peoples' houses, referred to by PIM as "residentials," differ greatly from setting up in a public setting like the Riverside Theater or Brumder Mansion.

"You have a safety issue you have to be concerned with," Noah Leigh explained to me when I asked him about it in our interview. "You're going into someone's house, and you don't know who is there and what their actual intentions are. So we have a process in place before we even go to someone's house. We have an e-mail contact and then a phone contact, and then if there is no red flag from those two things, we do a walk-through, usually during the day so if anything is untoward, it is easier for us to spot."

Once a safe environment is established, PIM examines people's attitudes about their ghosts.

"You get people who are hysterical, you get people who are kind of mellow about it, you get people who are very excited, so it's always very different," Leigh told me. "So you've always got to try to feel them out. You don't know what their religious background is, so you don't want to offend them by saying one thing or another, but you also want to be sure that they know where you're coming from— 'This is how we do this, and if it isn't what you're looking for, you should tell me now. If you want confirmation of what's going on, you're probably not going to get it from us.'"

Some clients don't realize that PIM is just looking for potential evidence and aren't able to do things like throw out ghost traps to capture entities like the characters do in *Ghostbusters*.

"If you want us to get rid of something, we're not going to go do that," Noah said. "How do I go about getting rid of something that I don't know even exists? So we make sure their expectations are lined up with what we can do. I'll just say, 'How can PIM help you?' and see what they say back. That usually gives me an idea of what they're looking for."

And then there's bad housekeeping. I asked Leigh for major challenges on residentials, and he said that at the top of his list are "smells. There was a place that had like twenty cats in their house. The ammonia, your eyes watered when you walked in," he said, wrinkling his nose at the memory. "It was horrible. It was in summer, really hot, and it smelled so bad in there, between animals and smoking. Those are issues we have to deal with."

▲▲▲

Mr. Smith told Jann and me that his favorite thing to do in life is light a fine cigar, put on some classical music, and spend time in the kitchen cooking classic Italian dishes.

"I go over here," Mr. Smith said, swooping his arms in the kitchen, "and I'm in a whole different world. We had a couple clients over a while ago—I made eggplant parmesan, she made chicken marsala, and they said they'll never be able to eat it again, because it was the real deal. Cannolis for desert, I fried the shells myself. They were going nuts!"

Mr. Smith was a large, bald man, and his stature, cigars, and love for Italian inevitably led Jann and me to draw comparisons with Tony Soprano when we discussed the case later. Despite his intimidating comparison, Mr. Smith was frightened. Very frightened.

Since moving in to the remodeled house about five years before, Mr. Smith had been seeing two different ghosts of women, and his wife had had odd experiences, too.

"This is where she'll stand," Mr. Smith said, standing in the doorway to his bedroom, while his wife looked on from the kitchen. "You can hear the footsteps. They'll go like this," he said, backing up and then walking slowly, deliberately, for a few paces, stopping at the bedroom door. "And stop here.

"A couple times only, it comes right to me. It'll stand right here," he said, moving to the side of the bed, "and . . ." he paused, reliving the memory nervously, breathing harder, ". . . and, I'm frozen. I'll get up and it'll go out and kinda," he waved his hand around, "I don't want to say it disappears, but it'll be gone!" He looked at us helplessly, then pointed to a comforter on his bed.

"And this blanket—I sleep with no covers on, and . . ."

"She said you got covered up," Jann said, pointing her thumb at Mrs. Smith.

"This is the freakiest thing!" Mr. Smith said. "I was laying there, awake, and I saw these covers moving up on me!"

"And you were wide awake?" Jann asked, scribbling in a notepad.

"I was awake, and I was wondering what the hell is going on! It got to my neck and I was like, 'Holy shit!'"

"Oh, he was scared," Mrs. Smith added.

"Yeah, I was!" Mr. Smith said, getting scared all over again.

"Well, yeah," Jann said.

There were more ghost stories. Mr. Smith was getting his hair cut at the kitchen counter by a stylist, who spotted a ghost on an upper landing. Both Smiths had been hearing ghostly bells ringing and footsteps marching up and down the stairs to the flat. "Like a herd of people coming to bust down our door," Mr. Smith said, breathing deeply. There had been strange knockings and thumpings and feelings of dread. He said he also saw thick smoke in the kitchen, and when he jumped up to investigate, the smoke dissipated into cracks in the floor.

And just six weeks before, Mr. Smith said, he had been watching a hockey game on TV when he saw a "cone thing fanning out in the air."

The Smiths turned to the Internet and found PIM. "I thought, *We might be crazy to call these people, but we got to find out sooner or later,*" Mr. Smith said.

"You know, everyone says that to us. Don't worry, we don't think you're crazy," Jann assured him. "We're having a meeting this weekend, and we'll discuss your case and contact you," Jann said as we departed.

However, they never followed through with an investigation.

When I asked Leigh about it later, he couldn't recall the exact circumstances but said it was probably one of two things. "Either the people have lost interest, we don't get contact back from them, or they say, 'No, we think we're fine, we feel better after you came here,' especially if we try to give some normal explanations," Leigh told me. He added that trouble scheduling an investigation, especially with clients who flake out, is also occasionally an issue.

▲ ▲ ▲

"We had one lady, she was absolutely off-the-wall unbalanced," John Krahn told me during setup of an investigation. "The first red flag was, I asked her how often things happened, and she said, 'Every day, all day long.'"

"As we're talking to her, she says, 'I see things reaching out to me from the lights.' She says, 'I see something up on the ceiling—what is that?'

"And I said, 'That's the light coming through the window and reflecting off.'

"And she said, 'Well, how do you know?'

"I said, 'Watch this.' And I stood in front of the window and it went away.

"The house was from the '50s, and every mark, every stain, every discoloration, she said was done by an entity.

"She said, 'You can see where something took a sharp knife and was cutting vertical lines in the wallpaper,' pointing to where the seams were. It was old wallpaper and had started to peel back, and we tried explaining it to her, and she wouldn't have it. She said, 'No, no, ghosts did this, I'm telling you.'"

I asked John how he felt about these cases. Were they annoying? Amusing?

"Concerning. I feel bad—as a cop I dealt a lot with mentally ill people. And it's very difficult for them to get help. The majority of the time, the symptoms can be greatly reduced by medication, but the problem is, the more people tell them they have a problem, the more they think it's not them but everyone else that has a misperception of reality. And if you could just get them to go to the doctor and take medications, most of this stuff would just go away."

▲ ▲ ▲

My next walk-through took place in the harsh cold of January. I trudged through the snow down Nineteenth Street, in a largely Hispanic neighborhood. I met Michael "Gravy" Graeve and Randy Soukup as they did a walk-through of a modest townhouse being rented by a young Hispanic couple. We'll call them José and Maria. They were unmarried and lived with five daughters from previous relationships.

The three of us stood in their sparse living room—a couch and flat-screen TV, a plastic Christmas tree in the corner, classic portrait of Jesus Christ—*The Head of Christ* by Warner Sallman—laminated on a piece of wood hanging on the wall.

The couple told us that although they had both experienced things, their major concern was that their oldest daughter, ten-year-old Jasmine, had been having intense experiences spotting the ghost of a little girl in the house.

"She thinks she's going crazy, but we've seen stuff too," José told us. He was wearing sweatpants and a T-shirt and had the word FAMILY tattooed in a loose cursive script on one forearm and FIRST on the other. Maria was wearing black slacks and a Chicago Bears sweatshirt and had her hair pulled back in a ponytail.

The couple led us from room to room. Gravy took notes on a clipboard while Randy swept each room with an EMF detector. (Randy, a pharmacist, would soon be leaving PIM, citing not enough time between work and family. He offered to lend his pharmaceutical knowledge to the team if they needed it for a case.)

In the bedroom, José declared, pointing to his bed, "I woke up in the middle of the night and something was choking me!"

"OK, have you ever been tested for sleep apnea?" Gravy asked, looking up from his clipboard.

"No."

"You might want to do that. It's one possible explanation."

Incense drifted through the room, coming from an incense stick stuck in a nail hole in the wall. A rosary hung from a nail nearby.

"I also heard a whisper from the closet. It sounded like '*Ohhh*,'" José said, pursing his lips.

"She says that she is dressed in a dirty white dress, with black hair hanging in her face," José later said of Jasmine's ghostly companion. We were in a small bedroom that two of the daughters shared. Jasmine had reported seeing the girl standing at the foot of her bed and sitting in the closet.

"Does she watch a lot of scary movies?" Gravy asked, perhaps thinking the same thing I was—that the creepy ghost girl sounded remarkably similar to the starring spirit of *The Ring*.

"She does, but she knows how to differentiate," José shrugged it off.

"Has she ever tried talking to the girl?" Gravy asked.

"No, she's terrified of her!" José replied.

Another of the girls, who had a small bed in the couple's room, had also experienced Jasmine's unwanted friend. "One night I heard her whisper, 'Stop it, no, I don't want to get hurt,'" José told us, fear creeping into his voice. "I asked her who she was talking to, and she said that the girl was laying by her bed, pulling on her hair." José physically shuddered at the thought. "It's giving me the chills just thinking about it!"

"I get the feeling of something watching me while I'm down here doing laundry," Maria later told us. We were in the kitchen, located in the basement level of the house, next to a small laundry room. The couple said that area had been agreed upon by all as the creepiest room in the house. Jasmine spotted the girl ghost down there, too, and the kids refused to go downstairs. The couple's pit bull stared and whimpered.

"My mom and brother get a bad feeling down here, too," Maria said. She was certain that ghosts dwelled there. "I want them gone!" she exclaimed.

Gravy made notes on his Reported Activity sheet.

José said he had had supernatural experiences in the past. He told us that one time he had a job mowing lawns at a cemetery. An empty hearse was parked near a mausoleum, and he spotted three large, black Doberman pinschers barking hysterically at the hearse.

After making a pass on the lawnmower, he looked again and they were gone. When he reported it to his boss, he was informed that the only nearby residents were not dog owners.

"I told him I think he has a black shadow following him from that," Maria told us.

With the claims documented and Randy's EMF readings noted, Gravy tried to get a sense of what the couple hoped to get out of the investigation.

"I need to find out for the sake of my kids," Maria said. "[Jasmine] thinks she's going crazy, and it breaks my heart to hear my ten-year-old girl say that."

"I want to find out if it's me, or something attached to me," José said.

"Reassure Jasmine that she's not going crazy," Gravy said. "Maybe have her confront the girl and tell her to leave her alone. We'll have Missy contact you early next week. Until then, keep documenting anything going on, time, date."

Outside, after the walk-through, Gravy loaded his equipment into his trunk. We discussed the case for a few minutes, our breath billowing in the cold air.

"What did you think?" I asked him.

Gravy had his doubts. He thought the family's home environment might lend itself to the kids seeking attention by letting their imaginations take over. Once there is speculation that a ghost is in the house, the whole family feeds off each other's stories, which makes tricks of the mind easier. Gravy was interested in investigating, but as a skeptical investigator, the couple had not yet convinced him to be a believer.

The Philosophy Student

Gravy was raised in a Catholic family and lived on a farm in Iowa until his father transferred to a sales job in Wisconsin. Gravy went to school in the Milwaukee suburb of Brookfield.

Gravy is unlike most of the core PIM members in one significant way: he is not a believer. "I'm sure you've figured that out by now," Gravy told me when I sat down to interview him in a bagel shop. "It started out, going to church all the time as a kid, I believed everything I was told, kind of like we all believed in Santa Claus. We tell kids Santa Claus exists so they'll behave all year round. Well, we tell adults God exists so they'll behave all year round, ya know? Or at least all week until they go to church again," Gravy laughed.

Gravy attended the University of Wisconsin–Milwaukee, where he settled on studying communications, but it was an unrelated class that would change his life. "When I got to college, I took a philosophy class, and one of the first questions they asked was: 'Does God exist?' And I was like, 'Whoa, whoa, whoa, rewind! You're telling me I can ask this question? Aren't I going to get struck by lightning?' Because I felt something doesn't fit right in this world, this doesn't make sense to me. And after that class it was like a switch turned on. From there, I was like, 'Holy cow, I never really thought of what it would be like if there wasn't a God, and that is an actual possibility.' It all stems back to that basic lecture hall Philosophy 101 class."

From there Gravy took a Greek Mythology class, which further led him to believe that God was a metaphor instead of an actual being. "I am more agnostic than atheist, because I want to believe, I just don't have the answers. It can be depressing when you don't believe there is something out there, but at the same time it makes you cherish life that much more, because if I cross the street and die . . . that's it. I fear death more than anything else in this world," Gravy told me, adding that this was the reason he didn't ride roller coasters.

Gravy found interest in ghost stories as a youth, and this was rekindled when he was working at a local Menards hardware store. One of his coworkers, Tony Belland, was also a future PIM teammate.

"For years I didn't give it much thought. God didn't exist to me, ghosts didn't exist to me, nothing had happened to me, paranormal-wise. I was working at Menards one day, and Tony told me, "You should check out this show *Ghost Hunters*, it's a really cool show."

Gravy found it intriguing. "I thought maybe I could get into this and find answers. Maybe when I die, I do come back as a ghost, and then I can play pranks on my friends and family and have fun," Gravy joked.

Tony signed up for the team, but Gravy's work schedule was too hectic at the time, so he joined about a year later. I asked how his status as a heathen was received by the group.

"I think they've accepted it, and I think it's good to have someone with that mind-set in the group, because I have no bias. I know Noah says ghosts could be anything, but I think there is a little bit of bias if you're religious because you believe in the Holy Ghost. Whereas me, to me it could be anything."

Gravy said his goal with the group has mostly been "to help people understand what they're experiencing." He said he gets satisfaction from showing frightened people that their ghost problems are often mundane, worldly explanations—noisy pipes or uneven floorboards.

Gravy lives outside of Milwaukee in the town of New Berlin with his wife, a real estate appraiser, and his two "future ghost hunter" sons.

"The biggest toll is on the home life," Gravy told me. "Me and my wife have had our share of fights about it. She doesn't like me spending money on it, and 'Oh, I need to borrow the van for the weekend' and stuff like that. Sometimes I have to choose my words and timing very carefully when it comes to my wife and the group. Everyone's spouses handle it differently."

Since he was raised in a religious household, I wondered how his hobby went over with the rest of his family.

"My dad isn't accepting of it, but he's not accepting of tattoos either," Gravy told me over coffee, displaying a forearm covered in a leaf motif tattoo. "Now he just kind of jokes about it—'Got any ghost hunts this weekend?'—then he shakes his head."

Provoking

Perhaps it is this skepticism about spiritual retaliation that makes Gravy comfortable using a technique that some paranormal investigators frown upon and one that PIM uses only on occasion. It's called *provoking*. The idea is that if you anger a spirit enough, it will react to you.

"Our policy is, 'Whatever works,'" Leigh explained to me later. "I'm from the standpoint that if you're doing it nicely and don't get anything you're able to detect, then there's no reason not to go to the next step. I have not come across anything that suggests if I provoke, something terrible will happen. Some groups say these are human spirits and you need to be respectful to them. That's an assumption in my mind, but that's what they believe, and to each their own."

Leigh added, "Maybe the only way to get them out is to say the *F* word six times. Who knows? That's why we do it, unless the client has specifically asked that we don't."

At one PIM investigation (I've been asked to keep the location confidential), I witnessed Gravy launch into a taunting soliloquy to a ghost: "I know I said earlier that we didn't want to harm you or make you leave, but you're really beginning to piss me off. I'm about to throw down! I'm going to kick the shit out of you. I don't know how, but I'll figure a way. I might be punching air, but at least I'll feel better. So I demand you show yourself. Right now!"

Peaceful silence.

"Hit Gravy. He's all talk. Go get'm," Tony suggested.

There was a *click* noise, and then someone in the dark asked the most frequent question I heard during all of my paranormal investigations and expeditions: "What was that?"

"It was me," someone responded.

Gravy continued, "You dead people are alike—dead. I'm right here. You can come up to me and do anything you want to me. You can push me, shove me, punch me, I don't care. There's probably nothing I can do back to you but verbally abuse you, you piece of shit."

No response.

"I dare you to come after me."

Nope.

"You're nothing. You're useless!"

Nothing again.

"Are you going to take that from him? I'd go rip his hair out!" Jann urged.

No response.

"You don't have the nerve," Gravy said, "or the guts—because you're dead."

No response.

"I think when I die, I'm going to come here and kick your ass then . . . unless you do something about it right now."

Silence.

"Kick that table in the room right over there and make that device light up, and I'll stop."

No light.

"Or better yet, slap one of us in the face," Tony said, taking over the role of provoker.

"We asked you to do a few simple things, and you completely ignored us. You're too late now. I think we're going to flatten this place," Tony said with disgust. "We're going to get a bulldozer and flatten [this place]."

Jann let out a burst of laughter.

"That's Jann," Gravy tagged.

"Sorry," Jann said.

"How does it feel to know that no one even knows that you ever existed?" Tony challenged. "No one alive remembers you at all."

The provoking continued for a while but yielded no response.

▲▲▲

José and Maria's case was on the agenda for PIM's next meeting, which also doubled as their annual holiday party in January 2014. It was held at a small bar not far from Leigh's house called the Jock Stop. PIM had done an investigation of the second floor of the building years ago but didn't find it to be active. Since then, the bar had become an unofficial meeting spot, where members of the team gathered to share drinks and discuss business and pleasure. Besides paranormal investigation, the team had other shared activities that some members enjoyed. They occasionally got out and played Frisbee golf together, and a favorite show among the team was the raunchy cable sitcom *The League*, about a fantasy football league.

An array of pizzas, bought with money in the PIM account, snacks, and homemade desserts was spread on a table next to the pool table. Gravy, Krahn, and Missy Bostrom brought their spouses; Tony, Chris Paul, Leigh, and PIM's friend Professor Marc Eaton were also present. Eaton was working on a thesis about paranormal investigations and had joined PIM on several investigations. The plan was to eat, go through PIM business, then drink and play team darts.

As the group gathered around Leigh, having drinks and pizza, he went through his agenda. A new webmaster who wanted to join the team had fallen through because she was "experiencing hard times." Recent investigations of the Milwaukee Public Library and a farm residence in Fredonia, Wisconsin, were reviewed.

José and Maria's was mentioned as having an investigation date of January 24. Upcoming investigations of the Times Cinema theater and a hotel in Pembine, Wisconsin, were discussed, and the investigators marked their calendars.

Jann was missing from the party—she was visiting family for the holidays. From Florida, she was exchanging a testy string of e-mails with Gravy, who was complaining about her not turning in an evidence review from the Milwaukee Public Library investigation. She was also firing off texts to Leigh about an upcoming media appearance, and tension was building between them. I would find out details on this soon, and the situation would come to a head. But for now, people were enjoying some social time.

The last entry in my notepad from the night was a quote from Missy and reads: "Tea, quit taking notes, this is a party!"

I complied and got a drink.

▲▲▲

"OK, time is . . . seven thirty-seven and eight seconds. Milwaukee residential," Gravy said. Leigh didn't hear back from José, but it happened that on the same date that the investigation was supposed to take place, another request for a residential came in, not far from José's house, on Eighth Street.

Leigh and a new member—Denys Blazer, who had actually been a guest at the Brumder Mansion investigation—went out to do the walk-through, and a follow-up investigation was booked for that same night with Gravy, Denys, and me.

When we arrived, the client, Sarah, talked to us briefly about her claims, before packing up her cats to go stay at a friend's house while we investigated.

On the second floor, in the bedroom she shared with her boyfriend, Sarah said she had felt a ghostly presence sit down on the bed next to her. She had also seen a shadow walk past the bathroom door and now refused to go upstairs. In the basement, Sarah reported that a ghost tugged on her hair and that a randy ghost pulled her teenage daughter's bra strap and poked her buttocks.

Sarah had two suspects for potential ghosts. Her boyfriend's grandfather, Tom, died in the house in 2001. Her ex-boyfriend, Jessie, died of a drug overdose, and she suspected his spirit might have an attachment to her and was following her.

After Sarah left, my job assignment was to walk around the house, blacking out anything that emitted light, so I placed black electrical tape over the clock on the coffee maker and glowing power switches. Gravy and Denys set up equipment and time-stamped it.

Gravy decided to put an array of trigger objects on the couple's bed upstairs and made note of them on a sheet—cigarettes, an airplane bottle of whiskey, an issue of *Playboy*. He opened that last item to the Miss January centerfold, hoping the vices might elicit a response from Tom or Jessie or whatever other entities might be around.

The initial investigation was uneventful. We moved from the upper floor to the living room to the basement, conducting EVP sessions, the same usual questions, the usual silence in response.

"That's me," I tagged, after coughing.

With not much more to go on, Gravy decided to invite Sarah back to sit in on a session in each room with us to see if she could stir up anything.

The H1 picked up Gravy's phone ringing Sarah, and a train in the background.

"Hey, it's Gravy. Hey, we are . . . it's pretty quiet here, so we wanted to see if you would come back here and sit on each floor for about an hour and see if anything else happens while you're here. How long? OK, it's completely up to you if you want to do that; I don't want to make you uncomfortable. OK, then we will . . . I'll leave the front door unlocked and we will be upstairs."

Sarah showed up about fifteen minutes later.

"Nothing, huh?" She asked me.

"I don't know," I told her. "I don't think so."

Gravy went over EVP rules with her, and she took a seat next to me. She told us that she had had a psychic do a walk-through of the house, and she had only added fuel to Sarah's fears.

"She told me my ex-boyfriend was staying in the bathroom; that's where he spent most of his time before he died. He'd lock himself in there, and I guess he was getting high. He had drug problems, so he'd be in there for hours. When she walked into my house, right off the bat she pointed to the bathroom and went off about this thing that was in the bathroom and *da da da da da*," Sarah told us nervously. "She told me all kinds of stuff; she told me that the spirits are trying to talk to me and I should listen."

Gravy decided to get the EVP session rolling. "We've got Sarah here. Maybe now that she's here, you'll feel more comfortable talking to us. Could you please tell us your name?"

Silence.

"Why do you stay here?" Gravy asked.

No reply.

At around 1 AM Gravy said to Sarah, "I'm going to call it unless you have something you want us to try."

Sarah paused for a moment in the dark. "No. Can I talk shit to it? I'm kidding."

"If you want, go ahead," Gravy said.

"I mean seriously, dude!" Sarah sputtered out angrily, all of a sudden. "Can you please do something? This is the last chance you have!" There was so much emotion in her voice, I was afraid she might have a breakdown. She took some deep breaths.

"You've brought me to tears," she said, sounding more sad and frustrated than angry now. "I feel like you're trying to give me a message . . . please . . . please, say something now, or don't bother me anymore! Don't make me look like a fool! Oh, *mm-mmm*."

We waited in the silence.

"I would like to help you, I don't mean to shout at you. I'm sorry, I'd really like to help you. I'd like to help myself." She sighed loudly. "Maybe next time."

We sat in silence for a minute.

"End investigation," Gravy stated.

As Gravy drove me home after the investigation, he concluded that the last session, where Sarah was able to vent, was a therapeutic moment. Denys, Gravy, and I reviewed our audio and they reviewed their video, but nothing unusual turned up.

Poltergeist

The last residential I investigated was one with some significantly strange claims of poltergeist activity. PIM had originally adhered to the thought that poltergeists were not caused by ghosts or malicious spirits but by a "human agent," usually a girl going through puberty with psychokinetic powers. Upon further research, the group changed its stance on the subject. As posted on the PIM website:

> Update!: PIM has recently found additional information through research that poltergeist cases are most likely all hoaxed, mainly by the "human agents" themselves. Upon questioning most of these individuals (usually children) admit to causing the activity when adults weren't looking or were not present in the room. The reason for why the hoax was conducted was always some need for attention. As such, it is the official PIM stance that there is no such thing as poltergeist hauntings.

As such, when Gravy and I showed up to do a walk-through, we weren't sure what to make of the incredible claims. The woman living downstairs had called PIM, although the majority of claims came from the tenant living in the small upper flat. There, he claimed he had twice found a framed picture of his daughter upside down, discovered his television moved to the middle of the room and turned upside down, heard ghost footsteps, and seen a shadow moving in one of the rooms. Most strangely, his dishes had been moved from the sink and placed into his oven.

The woman's reports about the downstairs flat were much milder. She claimed to have heard the ghost footsteps when she was certain no one else was home.

"And there's no cats?" Gravy asked.

"No."

After the walk-through, Gravy and I conferred outside by his car. Our suspicions fell immediately to the upstairs tenant's eight-year-old daughter, whom the tenant had partial custody of. The sparse, small apartment seemed to be almost abandoned—no food in the cupboards, a mattress and TV the only furnishings. Certainly a ploy for attention was a possibility. But because of the unusual claims, PIM decided to arrange an investigation.

After coordinating with Missy, we set up an investigation for two days later with Missy, Tony, Denys, and me as investigators.

▲ ▲ ▲

"Eight thirty-one and fifty-four seconds. We are at the Tosa home [referring to the Milwaukee suburb of Wauwatosa] on April 11, 2014," Tony time-stamped. "Game on."

PIM began setting up cameras, audio recorders, and other ghost detecting equipment around the house. I was given the task of walking around the rooms taking "baseline photos" with my digital camera. These photos are taken as a reference in case any object does happen to move during an investigation. I wandered room to room, and while I was in the upstairs tenant's bathroom, I noticed that the medicine cabinet was missing a slat of the door, so I could see inside the cabinet. I spotted a couple of prescription bottles. My curiosity getting the better of me, I opened the cabinet door.

"Tony, come up here," I called down the stairs. He bounded up the stairs and gave a wide-eyed look to the open medicine cabinet. There stood a long row of tall, translucent orange plastic bottles.

"Holy shit," Tony said.

There were heavy medications for pain, like oxycodone, antidepressants, and meds like Lunesta for insomnia. All potent and with a wide range of possible side effects.

"Well, I guess we can pack our stuff up and get out of here," Tony said while the rest of PIM laughed. "Debunked! He's on a drug cocktail that would kill a horse."

Speculation was that the pharmaceuticals could easily have led to sleepwalking, which could explain things like pictures being turned upside down and dishes being moved from the sink to the oven.

Although the drugs were a likely explanation for some of the goings-on in the house, PIM decided to continue the investigation as usual, because there were the claims of the downstairs neighbor hearing ghostly footsteps when the upstairs tenant was not at home. The equipment was set up, and an EVP session started in the downstairs living room.

"Nine nineteen and nineteen seconds," Tony time-stamped. "Is there anyone in this house that wants to make themselves known? Could you make a noise for us and let us know you're here?"

Later, we spread out in the upper flat. I was sitting on the kitchen floor. "We're only curious as to why you're staying here. Can you help us out and interact with us, make loud noises, talk to us, slam doors, anything to let us know you're here?" Tony questioned.

"It's like regular hunting," Tony explained casually. "You're not going to get a trophy every single time."

At somewhat of a loss for what to do next, we decided each team member would spend some time alone in the client's bedroom to do his or her own EVP session while the rest of the team stayed in the downstairs living room. Missy stayed upstairs and Tony, Denys, and I headed downstairs.

"Whaddaya say, ten minutes or so, Missy?" Tony called over as we approached the stairwell. As we sat downstairs, we could faintly hear her muffled voice, asking questions to the spirits alone in the dark upstairs. Tony went next. Then it was my turn.

I walked into the upstairs tenant's dark bedroom and sat on the floor next to his bed.

"Hello, my name is Tea Krulos. I'm a writer, actually. I'm here with my friends the Paranormal Investigators of Milwaukee, and I'm really just trying to have an understanding of who you are, so if there's any information you want to pass to me, please do so."

Ten seconds. No information.

"Can you tell me what you think of this place? It seems kind of depressing to me."

Ten seconds. No thoughts shared.

"I'm working on a book, so if you have a message for me, I'll share it in my book. Just let me know what you want to communicate."

No response from a potential ghostwriter.

Like most of the PIM investigations I went on, there was nothing. Just silence and darkness. I had come to find ghost hunting to be a relaxing experience, sitting in the dark, thinking about life and the hereafter in often old and intriguing environments. I was to encounter things with PIM that I couldn't explain, but in cases like this, the reality seemed to be all too mundane.

▲▲▲

I was interested in hearing PIM's discussion of the case at their meeting, but I was out of town on that date. Leigh recorded their discussion for me to listen to later.

"Basically he was on knockout juice—everything that can take you down, he was taking," Tony explained to the rest of the team.

"About fifteen bottles of newly prescribed medication," Missy added. She was tasked with writing the report on the investigation for PIM's website. "On the refrigerator he had a list of appointments with his psychiatrist."

"Our theory is, he's sleepwalking, getting up and not knowing what he's doing," Tony said, explaining the drug-induced poltergeist behavior. He added that the only thing that didn't fit the theory was the downstairs neighbor hearing ghost footsteps.

"But that could be her feeding off his claims and misperceiving building sounds as footsteps," Krahn interjected.

"There's a lot of building sounds, pops and cracks," Missy agreed.

PIM discussed how to present the findings and decided to write the report sans drug references but to present that information privately to the house owner who called PIM for the investigation.

Leigh wrapped up the item. "In conclusion, we didn't find evidence there," he told the team. "We think the majority of claims are caused by a medication-induced state that this person is not realizing in some shape or form. I'll also say—I'm sure it already says it in the report—continue to journal things that happen. If things pick up, we can look into it further, but please make sure that the gentleman upstairs notifies his doctor of these happenings, because his doctor might say, 'This is common with the drugs you are on. Don't think you're getting haunted.'"

6

INTERNATIONAL UFO CONGRESS

A FTER SOME ZIPPY SPACE MUSIC and splashy graphics rotating around a CGI planet, the camera settled on a young man and woman sitting at a table, coffee mugs in front of them.

"Greetings, everyone, and welcome to *Spacing Out!* I'm Jason McClellan," said the man wearing a two-tone gray long-sleeved shirt. He had a bleach-blonde half-Mohawk flopped over his head and some black-framed glasses.

"And I'm Maureen Elsberry. Thanks for joining us," added the woman with shoulder-length brunette hair, wearing a plaid button-up shirt and sensible glasses. These two represented the young, hip new face of ufology, a paranormal field that dates back to the 1950s. It's the study of unidentified flying objects and their potentially extra-terrestrial pilots.

"UFO enthusiast John Podesta was recently appointed to serve as one of President Obama's senior advisors," McClellan said. The camera switched to a close-up of his face.

"Podesta was Bill Clinton's chief of staff and assisted with Obama's transition to the White House in 2008. He's also known to be a sci-fi enthusiast. He's been involved with efforts to get the government to disclose all it knows about the UFO phenomenon."

Elsberry and McClellan are founding members of Open Minds Productions, a multimedia company that produces web series, pod-casts, a website, and a bimonthly print magazine. As the company's name suggests, it's open to the different schools of UFO beliefs, offer-ing a voice that tries to be objective. Both Elsberry and McClellan attended Arizona State University in Phoenix, where Elsberry studied journalism and McClellan studied media production. But the two didn't meet until they both signed up to work for a media production company.

"I saw him walking down the hall for his interview wearing a zoot suit, and I was thinking, *Who the hell is this joker?*" Elsberry recalled. "But once we met, we pretty quickly developed a really harmonious work relationship and friendship."

Elsberry and McClellan were approached in 2009 by the owner of the production company with a ufologist dream offer: would the two of them be interested in starting a media company that focused on evidence of UFOs? The two jumped at the chance, founding Open Minds and developing programming like their show *Spacing Out!*

▲▲▲

Elsberry filled in some details on Podesta's career, then McClellan spoke up again.

"Podesta is a known sci-fi buff and made headlines during his tenure in the White House when he had an *X-Files*–themed birthday party. How cool is that?" McClellan smiled. "His sci-fi interest aside, the depth of his interest in UFOs was revealed when he spoke at a press conference at the National Press Club in Washington, DC, asking the government to release its secret files on UFOs so that scientists can determine the nature of the phenomenon."

Speaking of *X-Files*, I later asked McClellan which one of the pair is Agent Fox Mulder, the believer, and which is Agent Dana Scully, the skeptic.

"I think me and Maureen are both more aligned with Scully, actually," McClellan replied. "We love science. We love evidence. But at the same time, we're both optimists, and I think we're far more willing to entertain incredible possibilities than Scully."

On *Spacing Out!*, McClellan and Elsberry moved on to other recent news related to UFOs and life from beyond the planet Earth. They discussed a new study by an astrophysicist on the potential for life elsewhere in the universe and the video of a mysterious light circulating online that turned out to be the image of an airplane caught using a slow shutter speed, among other reports.

At the end of the show, Elsberry and McClellan wrapped up the stories with some candid analysis.

"Do I think it's great that somebody who wants UFO disclosure is in a high position? Yes. But that doesn't mean we're going to see any sort of changes from this," Elsberry reflected on Podesta's appointment. Closing out the show, she gave this pitch: "Also, don't forget to register for the 2014 International UFO Congress. This is the largest annual UFO conference in the world, and it's all happening February 12–16 in Fountain Hills, Arizona."

▲ ▲ ▲

As I cruised in a shuttle bus through the desert of Arizona toward the Radisson Fort McDowell Resort and Casino, located on the Yavapai Nation reservation near Fountain Hills, I looked out the window and reflected on the lore of "UFO Country." The American desert is the site of some of the most famed chapters of ufology.

First and foremost is the story of the UFO crash of Roswell, New

Mexico, known to novice and expert alike. The short version of the story is that a UFO crashed on a ranch outside Roswell in 1947. The government came in to clean up and, some say, recovered extraterrestrial bodies. Officials reported that it was simply a weather balloon—a cover story, ufologists say, with too many holes to be true. Roswell now revels in this lore by hosting an International UFO Museum and Research Center and an annual UFO Festival.

Across the desert, Nevada holds a mystery base, famous as being a symbol of government secrecy and alleged to hold alien technology. It's located on Groom Lake and is commonly known as Area 51. Goings-on at the base are kept classified, and some ufologists insist that besides the human aircraft held and tested on the base, vessels from another world are also in the collection.

And right where I was shuttling at that moment was part of the site of a mass UFO sighting from 1997 known as the Phoenix Lights. On March 13, 1997, hundreds of people witnessed a triangular formation of lights slowly cruising over Mexico, Nevada, and Arizona.

Later, I talked to two of the sound guys for the International UFO Congress, who recalled seeing the Phoenix Lights in their youth. One recalled standing in a grocery shop parking lot with other strangers, "like this," he said, pointing up to the sky, his mouth agape in surprise.

I began to learn about lesser-known lore and current UFO news by absorbing as much media produced by Open Minds Productions (based out of Tempe, Arizona) as I could. I watched new episodes of *Spacing Out!* every two weeks. I subscribed to the bimonthly *Open Minds* magazine, until it folded with the June/July 2014 issue. I also regularly perused the Open Minds website, which has UFO news roundups and podcasts.

The UFO stories were on my mind as my bus wound through a landscape of looming saguaro cacti and brown and red mesas, before pulling up to the Fort McDowell Resort and Casino, where the IUFOC had kicked off earlier that morning.

▲▲▲

Elsberry, looking a bit frantic, was at the registration / merchandise / general help desk of the conference scrambling through paperwork and handed me my press pass and conference program. Eager to jump into it, I walked around the corner to catch a lecture titled "My Secret Life Comes Full Circle," by Kim Carlsberg. I grabbed a chair in the resort's ballroom, where all of the speeches and screenings were to take place.

Screens flanking a stage with a podium with the IUFOC 2014 logo on it showed a computer animation of UFOs flying over a city filled with happy, amazed people looking skyward. The Carpenters song "Calling Occupants of Interplanetary Craft" drifted over the speakers.

"Calling occupants of interplanetary, most extraordinary craft, you've been observing our earth and we'd like to make a contact with you," Karen Carpenter's voice crooned. "We are your friends," the Carpenters harmonized together.

Oh boy, I thought. *Here we go . . .*

About three hours later, I walked quietly out of the conference center and stood blinking in the bright Arizona sun. I had just been thrown into the deep end of ufology. Kim Carlsberg's speech had been a disturbing recollection of her history of being abducted by aliens. She described being strapped to a cold metal table while bobble-headed Grays (the common depiction of the stumpy, big-headed, black-eyed aliens) performed intimate experiments on her. She claimed that in one instance she acted as an incubator for an alien fetus, which later grew up to be her "hybrid" son, whom she can telepathically communicate with.

Carlsberg's mentor, hypnotherapist Yvonne Smith, also gave a talk at the IUFOC and led an "experiencer session" twice a day, in the morning and evening, throughout the conference. This was sort of a support group for abductees. I respectfully followed the "no press" policy for these sessions but later talked to a man named Avril, who was at the conference with his friend Sarah. Avril's main motivation in driving to the conference from his home in Oklahoma was to be part of the experiencer sessions.

He agreed to talk with me about his own abductions. "About three years ago, I started having these dreams and weird things turning up on my body," Avril told me outside the convention center, in the twilight of the desert.

He told me about one of the dreams: "There was this one time, I was on a spaceship. Everything was smooth, metallic. I was buckled down to something and I had this device in my ear with a micro-phone, like a Bluetooth. Then all of a sudden, the whole room shifted up, like *crash!*"

What happened next was a blank. The next thing Avril remem-bered, "I was being escorted by two people—humans—in military uniforms through a bunker, and I caught my thumb on a door and cut it. One of them said, 'That'll hurt,' and the other replied, 'No it won't; he won't remember it.'"

Avril looked at me intensely and held up his hand. He had a circu-lar scar on the base of his thumb, below the second knuckle. Other strange things happened to Avril. He awoke another morning with a headache and a black mystery mark on his head. Another time he was doing a job canvassing, when he experienced missing time—several hours just disappeared from his memory—which, along with strange markings, is said to be a telltale sign of abduction.

Avril told me he greatly benefitted from the conference's experi-encer sessions.

"It's so great to meet these people," he said, guessing there were seventy to eighty people in a typical session. "People from all over the US and Canada, and the stories are so often the same, it's amazing."

▲▲▲

Skeptics commonly agree that stories of alien abduction (as well as some stories of ghost or demon visitation) are generated when the abductee experiences sleep paralysis, a disorder also known as Old Hag Syndrome, as it was thought to be the work of a witch sitting on the victim's chest.

I spoke with Dr. Susan Blackmore, a researcher who has studied alien abduction cases in the past, from her home in South Devon,

England. She didn't want to try to diagnose Avril, explaining that to do so properly would take a thorough questioning and analysis, but she told me of another case she looked into.

Dr. Blackmore told me, "This person might be like someone who I know locally here who had abduction experiences again and again and again starting with one off A38, which is our main road out here, and the aliens came down. He painted me loads of pictures, which I still have, of the people who abducted him, the places he was taken, and so on."

Later, Dr. Blackmore e-mailed me pictures of the paintings. They depicted a Gray with a probing device grabbing the abductee's feet, a strange, wobbly UFO hallway, and a giant saucer illuminating the English countryside with giant lights.

"Now, he suffered from narcolepsy, and it very clearly was sleep paralysis experiences," Dr. Blackmore explained. "He was one example where he was very ambivalent about the explanation. In a way he was pleased to know there was an explanation, but in another way not at all because he made friends with these aliens, they all had names, and they had jobs on their planets. It was so much a part of his life, it was a mixed blessing."

▲▲▲

I caught another speech by Mike Clelland, not as intense as Carlsberg's. I'd say it was the most delightfully eccentric talk I've witnessed to date and was titled "Owls, Synchronicity, and the UFO Abductee."

Clelland paced the conference stage wearing a blue dress shirt and suit coat, Chuck Taylors, and blue jeans as he showed slides and led the audience through the various twists and turns of his own apparent abductions and his startling conclusion that owls might be acting as alien agents.

After a dramatic encounter with owls himself, Clelland has been recording stories of people's strange experiences that involve owls and UFOs crossing paths.

"I feel like the owls were an alarm clock and they were screaming . . . wake up," Clelland concluded.

Day 2

After the speeches, I retired to my hotel, which was attached to the conference center. Desert surrounded the area as far as the eye could see. The next morning I decided to explore the conference's show floor. It was a bizarre market, crowded with IUFOC attendees perusing the aisles. People had come to the conference from all over the country and as far away as Switzerland and South Africa.

Some of it was just good fun and a good place to purchase a few unique items. There was jewelry modeled on actual crop circles, Native American artwork, self-published books and UFO magazines, and a table selling detailed busts and sculptures of bug-eyed aliens.

Other stuff made me imagine my friend J. Jason Groschopf's skeptic group having a field day challenging the validity of the items. There were "aura reports" for thirty-five dollars and a man enthusiastically hawking "instant pain relief with simple oriental medicine." His products included "herbal pack miracle salt" and an acupuncture device that looked like a gold-plated pinecone covered in spikes. I also found a table selling "orgone energy generators," little silicone pyramids with metallic bits stuck in them, advertised as "transmuting negative energies into positive ones!"

Crossing the aisle, I spotted an elderly gentleman about to place some earphones on at a booth with a banner that read, ET MUSIC HELPS SHIFT CONSCIOUSNESS!

"Oh!" the man exclaimed, yanking the headset away from his ears.

"Oh, I'm sorry," the woman at the booth apologized. "Was that too loud?"

After a few days of people-watching, it was also evident there was an eclectic conglomeration of people from different corners of UFO thought. Ufology draws a lot of extreme interpretations. I could tell by some people's appearances and a flier I found for PrepperFest AZ that there was a contingency of doomsday preppers at the conference. Conspiracy theory overlaps with ufology in some quarters, to varying extents. Some allege the government is simply withholding information on aliens; more extreme conspiracy theories hold that key politicians are actually Reptilians, sinister reptile-like extraterrestrials bent on world domination.

After spotting a woman in what looked like a psychedelic nun outfit, I was sure that members of various UFO cults might be in attendance. These were not given stage time or recognition at the conference, but UFO cults remain active. Scientology is sometimes listed as a UFO cult, and another popular one is Raëlism, founded in 1974 by French race car driver Claude Vorilhon, now known as Raël.

Another odd presence on the conference floor were black-suited, bow-tied members of the Nation of Islam. The group has long had an interest in the phenomenon, and some of the most heavily attended speeches on the subject have been delivered by Louis Farrakhan, who describes a "Mother Wheel" that will "rain down destruction on white America but save those who embrace Nation of Islam." In a sermon series, he also asked President Obama to open up Area 51 to scientists.

Fitting into this topic of distrust and conspiracy, the next speech I saw was by Don Schmitt, titled "Inside the Real Area 51: The Secret History of Wright Patterson." After speeches about abduction and hybrid star children and alien messenger owls, it was a nice change of pace to hear about some good old-fashioned government cover-up.

Schmitt was a prominent researcher of the Roswell crash, coauthoring a popular book on the case, *UFO Crash at Roswell*. More recently he worked with the Mutual UFO Network (MUFON), the world's largest organization dedicated to UFO research, to do an archaeological expedition of the crash site. It was documented in a film, *The Roswell Project*, which screened at the conference's film festival, a showing of five short documentaries and a short fiction.

The Roswell Project followed Schmitt and MUFON's effort to map and cordon off sections of the crash site and then sweep it with metal detectors, hoping to come up with an extraterrestrial nut or bolt, any evidence that a UFO had crashed there. The project has so far yielded nothing but is ongoing.

Schmitt's latest research has been into Wright-Patterson Air Force Base in Ohio, which he alleges was the recipient and storage area for the Roswell wreckage. Popular myth said this storage area was Hangar 18, of which there is no record, but Schmitt did find evidence of *Building* 18, divided into sections A–G, the foreign technology division, and in this case Schmitt was convinced "foreign" was an understatement.

▲ ▲ ▲

To offset the talks about conspiracy and abductees, Open Minds worked hard to incorporate a third group of speakers for that year's IUFOC lineup: legit scientists with an interest in life beyond our planet. I saw a fascinating presentation by astrophysicist Jeffrey Bennett titled "Beyond UFOs: The Scientific Search for Extraterrestrial Life and Its Astonishing Implications for Our Future." I also sat in on a presentation by former NASA Inventor of the Year Richard Hoover titled "Is Life Restricted to Planet Earth—or Is It More Widely Distributed Throughout the Universe?"

I had spotted Hoover earlier in the day. Wandering from the convention area to my hotel room, I passed a man sitting on a bench outside while another man performed what I would guess to be Reiki on him. A punk rocker smoking a cigarette stood near the corner of the building, excitedly talking about the conference on her phone. I walked by Mike Clelland, barefoot and stretched out on a patch of grass, talking to a friend, about owls no doubt. And then, walking through the hotel lobby, I spotted a bespectacled man showing off his gold trilobite-shaped belt buckle to a journalist. This was Richard Hoover, astrobiologist.

Hoover has led expeditions from Antarctica to Sri Lanka searching for evidence of the littlest of aliens, scanning meteorites to look for microfossils that might prove any life at all is out there.

"I'm not talking about little green men here, I'm talking about blue-green algae," Hoover explained in his presentation. Hoover's work studying extremophiles—organisms that can live in extreme conditions, such as inside ice glaciers, volcanic lava, and outer space—has made him certain some kind of life must exist outside of Earth, even if it's not the classic image of Gray aliens cruising around in a UFO.

Day 3

The next day I decided to hang around with Maureen Elsberry, who was on the flight of a bumblebee, multitasking a whirlwind of details.

She walked quickly to the show floor and spoke to Ben Hansen, former FBI agent and host of the show *Fact or Faked: Paranormal Files*. Hansen was set up at a table with a line of new night-vision binoculars and telescopes and was letting conference attendees try them out in a stargazing session that night.

Elsberry was trying to sort out the details but then remembered that the tech people needed a DVD of a film that would be featured in the evening as part of the IUFOC's film festival. She dug through a large Tupperware container filled with supplies underneath the registration table, found the DVD, and carefully inserted her pointer finger into it, balancing it on her finger as she walked to the backstage area.

I tried to keep up. Behind the stage and screens, there were tables full of computers and soundboards and cords wrapping around the floor. Open Minds' setup was so elaborate that DVDs of the conference speakers were quickly produced, packaged, and sent out to the merchandise table so attendees could buy a DVD of a speech they had just seen less than a day before. Jason McClellan and Alejandro Rojas were backstage talking to volunteers about technical setup when Elsberry handed off the DVD to Rojas.

Rojas, along with Elsberry and McClellan, is the face of Open Minds Productions, and was acting as the emcee of the conference. Dressed in a baggy suit, with a small soul patch and a few gray hairs but still youthful-looking, Rojas resembled a vaudeville comedian. He took a moment out of his hectic schedule to sit down and talk to me in a small conference room near backstage that was being used for media interviews.

Rojas first developed an interest in ufology after he attended a 2000 event on the UFO phenomenon at the National Press Club in Washington, DC. Instantly hooked on the topic, he began researching, eventually joining the Mutual UFO Network as a director of education and PR. Rojas moved to Irvine, California, where MUFON was headquartered at the time. Later, he had his own UFO sighting while traveling. It was at a place called the UFO Watchtower, an observation deck, campground, and gift shop near Hooper, Colorado, overlooking the San Luis Valley.

Rojas signed on with Open Minds in 2010.

After delivering the DVD, Elsberry was on the move again, locating an extension cord and bringing it out to the area where Hansen planned to conduct his stargazing session, then talking to the hotel people about getting a couple tables moved out there to put the equipment on.

"It's hard because while we're here, we're also trying to run a business," Elsberry told me over her shoulder, power walking down the hallway. "I've got like eight million unanswered e-mails. My phone dies every half hour."

Elsberry, svelte and doe-eyed, has attracted several UFO aficionados who have made attempts to woo her. As we walked, we encountered a smitten French man who asked her if she had had a chance to try the chocolate-covered strawberries he'd brought to the conference as a gift for her.

"Uh, creepy," she said under her breath after politely rebuffing him and leaving him behind, gawking after her quickly accelerating figure.

"I'm super adventurous," she later told me about what little time she has outside of working for the company. "I love the outdoors, so the more time I spend hiking, camping, traveling, the happier I am. And the way to my heart is through wine, cheese, and Harrison Ford."

Exhausted with power walking to keep up the pace with Elsberry, I wandered around the conference floor and stopped to talk to Aaron Sagers, pop culture guru who starred on the Travel Channel show *Paranormal Paparazzi* and had a popular paranormal entertainment website, ParanormalPopCulture.com. Sagers was at IUFOC to deliver an entertaining talk titled "Celebrity UFO Encounters: True Stories of Famous Names and Their Famous Sightings." Sager's celebrity anecdotes included everyone from Elvis Presley to Shirley MacLaine and Dennis Kucinich (Kucinich's sighting was later used to ridicule the politician in an election primary), to *Jersey Shore*'s Deena Nicole Cortese.* David Bowie, John Lennon, Fran Drescher, Jimmy Carter, Russell Crowe, and Billy Ray Cyrus are also all UFO spotters.

After talking with Sagers, I attended Ben Hansen's demo for his Generation 3 (the best quality) night-vision equipment. After Hansen explained the various devices and described things we might spot— like run-of-the-mill airplanes and satellites—people lined up to have a turn looking through the binoculars and telescopes. I closed an eye and squinted through one, amazed by the bright green illuminated desert sky above me, millions of stars spreading out forever. Just looking at such magnitude inspired the imagination. There must be something else out there, right?

While at the night-vision demo, I got a text from Elsberry: "We're hanging out by the fire." Wandering over to a fire pit in the resort's courtyard, I found Elsberry, McClellan, Sagers, and some other young Open Minds Productions personnel. It had been a long, hectic day, and the group decided to celebrate by smoking cigars and drinking whiskey.

"We really need to get a sponsorship for these," McClellan said, lighting up Elsberry's cigar.

"Yeah, I know someone. I think we could make it happen," Sagers said, puffing on his. The talk turned to the reality TV show biz. Besides Sagers and his *Paranormal Paparazzi* show, both McClellan and Elsberry had recently signed up for reality shows. Elsberry was cast as part of a quartet of UFO researchers on the show *Uncovering Aliens* for the Discovery Channel. At the same time, McClellan had signed up for a show called *Hangar 1: The UFO Files*, which costarred members of MUFON, for the History Channel. They relayed various UFO cases in each episode, which were then reenacted.

Cigars cost money, and these youthful paranormal researchers had limited routes to take if they wanted to turn their passion into a

---

* Who has one of my favorite quotes on a UFO sighting, via Twitter: "I just friggin saw an asteroid UFO. The thing looked like a friggin ball, red and green stripes, and it was like 'Merp!'"

paying gig. They could either become prolific, bestselling authors on the subject or get paid to do a reality TV series. Choosing the latter also added the rush of fame, but as the whiskey flowed, the would-be reality stars shared that taking direction from show producers was somewhat equitable to an unwanted probe from an alien.

For now, though, Elsberry and McClellan had lucked out. Open Minds Productions members have a dream job—the media venture and its employees are all bankrolled by a backer.

"John," Elsberry told me, mysteriously pointing to the second floor of hotel rooms at the resort, sipping her whiskey. She described him as someone very interested in the UFO phenomenon, and not much else was said about him. Open Minds Productions was registered as an LLC in 2010 by John Rao, who also founded Secure Medical Inc., a medical technology company.

"Within the medical field, Mr. Rao is an accomplished entrepreneur, innovator, and strong patient rights advocate, including his involvement with the American Telemedicine Association and his current patents relating to remote health kiosks and glyph identification," a 2008 press release from a medical company hiring Rao as a consultant states.

No mention of UFOs.

Day 4

The next day I saw a couple more talks. Rob Simone gave a rundown of "UFOs in the Headlines: Real Reporting on a Real Phenomenon," a slide show of newspaper clippings of classic UFO cases, like the Washington, DC, flap of July 1952, when fleets of UFOs were spotted buzzing around the US Capitol. I also caught part of the talk "Closer Than Ever Before" by Jaime Maussan, the leading UFO researcher of Mexico. But my main focus was on one of the conference's most interesting—and to some the most controversial—members of the speaker roster: retired colonel (and doctor) John Alexander, returning to the IUFOC to deliver a talk titled "UFOs: Science or Science Fiction?" After his talk, I caught up with him on the conference floor.

"Half of these people are glad I'm here, and the other half wants to burn me on a bonfire," Colonel Alexander told me, gesturing across the room, where he was selling his book *UFOs: Myths, Conspiracies, and Realities.* Colonel Alexander has a polite but intense military posture, and when you try to crack humor with him, he doesn't respond by smiling but by raising his eyebrows a few millimeters at you.

Colonel Alexander has spent much of his career researching nonlethal weapons as well as subjects like near death, out-of-body experiences, remote viewing, and UFO encounters.

"The first line of my book is 'UFOs are real,'" Colonel Alexander told me, pointing to the cover of his book. But despite being a proponent of UFO research and organizing some of the few government efforts to look into the subject, he is viewed as a villain by the fringes of ufology. Some say he is a government "spook" and an "agent of disinformation" on the topic. He was a member of the clandestine group known as the Majestic-12, they whisper, a group that believers say is a government black ops group that controls information; it's a story that skeptics say is nothing but a hoax.

"If that's true, please tell them to send me a paycheck," Colonel Alexander scoffed.

"It's difficult in a field where people have so many extremely strong beliefs," Elsberry later explained to me on similar accusations she'd heard about Open Minds. "If you say something they don't agree with, well then . . . you're a debunker, a disinfo agent, a government stooge. . . . I could go on. The truth is, most sightings can be explained; it's important to explain them to weed them out so we can focus on the truly anomalous cases."

Besides giving a talk, Colonel Alexander was featured on a heated panel discussion titled "Is There a Government Cover-Up?" which included Stephen Bassett, founder of the Paradigm Research Group. Bassett led the 2013 Citizen Hearing on Disclosure in Washington, DC, demanding the government turn over UFO evidence. British researcher Timothy Good sided with Bassett in asserting the government was withholding secrets, while Robert Powell, director of research at MUFON, agreed with Colonel Alexander that the government had little interest in the phenomenon.

"Given Robert's answer, though," panel moderator Alejandro Rojas said, "that they see nothing, do nothing, hear nothing—I think that's a little hard for people to swallow, because why wouldn't they do anything?" He gestured to Colonel Alexander, holding a microphone. "Why would they bury their heads in the sand? Your experience in the military, you have more insight in that. Why would you say that's the case?"

Colonel Alexander explained that the air force did spend time researching with Project Blue Book, which was concluded with the (admittedly flawed, as Colonel Alexander details in his book) Condon Report that gave a bottom line that UFOs were not a security threat.

"The question then becomes, from an institutional perspective, what amount of resources are you going to expend on a situation that is a) not a threat," Colonel Alexander said, looking across the panel to Rojas, "and b) one you have very little probability of resolving. Economically as well as time, it's a rabbit hole. And so the air force got exactly the answer they wanted—make this go away, not our job." Colonel Alexander added that with ongoing trillions of dollars spent to fight wars in Afghanistan and Iraq, health care reform, and myriad other issues, the government doesn't have the time and resources to grab flashlights and go look for UFOs.

While Colonel Alexander was talking, panelist Stephen Bassett was furrowing his eyebrows and aggressively rubbing his forehead.

"OK," Rojas said. "Steve is showing mannerisms in which he is showing me he maybe wants to respond." The audience laughed.

Bassett pointed to Roswell as being the starting point for the end of the "truth embargo" and said that research definitively points to the government having UFOs in an undisclosed location. The debate rages on as it will, probably, forever, unless a major disclosure or undisputable body of evidence is found.

▲▲▲

Saturday night was concluded with an evening of anecdotes and a Q and A session with paranormal star George Noory. "I don't know about you folks, but the idea that we're alone in the universe is just too damn depressing for me," Noory—host of long-running show on all things supernatural, paranormal, conspiracy-driven, spooky, and just plain weird, *Coast to Coast AM*—told the audience.

Noory began his career in broadcasting, despite his father's hope he would be a dentist, in 1972 in his hometown of Detroit. His first radio interview ever was with influential ufologist Stanton Friedman, perhaps the most widely recognized researcher and author on the topic of UFOs. Noory did the report on his own time and brought it to the local WCAR-AM radio station he worked for. Noory took over *Coast to Coast* hosting duties from longtime host and paranormal king Art Bell in 2003.

Noory is a showman and a crowd pleaser, and most of his presentation is a Q and A with the audience. He showed good humor and kindness to his questioners. After one man stepped up to the mic and told Noory he needed him to establish communication with the Pleiadians via a microchip hidden in his body, so they could have a meeting to discuss the fate of the universe, Noory asked the audience, "Well, all right, do you people want to meet these Pleiadians?" Appreciative applause. "Then I say, bring them on!"

Noory later hosted a fancy-dress awards dinner and presented awards to Stephen Bassett, who won the Researcher of the Year Award for his work with the Paradigm Research Group, and ufologist Dr. Bruce Maccabee, who won the Lifetime Achievement Award.

Day 5

Sunday was the last day of the conference, and I packed up to leave early. I had spotted a handwritten note taped to a wall near the conference's show floor from a guy named Mark who was looking for people to share the cost of a shuttle bus back to Phoenix Sky Harbor. I called him, and we met in front of the resort. A young woman dressed in a black suit and glasses pulled up in the shuttle and helped load our baggage.

"Look, it's the Men in Black! Or should I say . . . the Women in Black!" Mark said to me, pointing to the driver and laughing heavily at his own joke. The driver smiled politely. An elderly gentleman from South Carolina also joined us in the shuttle.

I asked the two what their favorite talks had been. The man from South Carolina said that it was Jeffery Bennett's talk on astrophysics. Mark said it was leading UFO author Timothy Good. "Did you see his talk?" he asked me, swiveling his head from the passenger seat to look at me as we cruised through the desert.

"No," I said. I had been conducting interviews during the speech.

"He told this story: He was in a hotel lobby—he's a violinist for an orchestra, and he was giving a performance. In the lobby he saw this attractive blonde who was staring at him, and he got the overpowering sense that she was an ET. So he sent a telepathic message," he explained, touching his fingers to his temple. "If you're an alien, touch your nose right now. And right then, she touches her nose!" he said, touching his own nose to emphasize.

He looked at the shuttle van driver. "She must think we're totally crazy! It's OK."

"Yep, we're crazy," the passenger sitting next to me said.

Realizing the talk had turned to her, the driver turned to Mark. "Oh, I was only half listening. I'm in my own little world here," she said.

▲▲▲

How many people believe in UFOs? A 2013 poll by the *Huffington Post* showed that 50 percent of Americans think that there is life on another planet, another 33 percent weren't sure, and a quarter of those polled believed aliens had visited Earth.

Elsberry told me that a night out with her friends often includes them prompting her to tell people they meet what she does for a living.

"'The surprising bit about this is I cannot tell you how many people, whom I would never expect, look at me and say, 'Oh my gosh, I had experience when I was growing up . . .' or 'This is my experience with that,'" Elsberry said. "More people than you realize have had pretty incredible sightings of unexplained things."

« 7 »

THE TERROR AND SUBSEQUENT PRIDE OF POINT PLEASANT

IT'S A STORY WELL KNOWN in the small town of Point Pleasant, West Virginia. Late on the night of November 15, 1966, two couples—the Scarberrys and the Mallettes—were joyriding in an area outside of town, a rural stretch known as the "TNT area."

The former site of a large dynamite factory, the plant was abandoned after World War II and had become a popular spot for the bored youth of Point Pleasant to socialize, drag race, or make out in the dark. The area contained numerous abandoned factory buildings and about a hundred empty "igloos"—storage buildings that formerly stored dynamite, mostly hidden by trees and brush to disguise them from potential enemy bombers. The couples were cruising around in Roger Scarberry's '57 Chevy looking for friends, but on that fateful night they encountered something else, something they would never forget.

While cruising by the old generator plant, they saw something that Linda Scarberry would later describe as being "about six feet tall with large wings on its back. It has the shape of a man . . . a wing spread of 10 feet . . . it was a dirty grey color . . . fiery-red eyes that glow when the lights hit it."

Terrified, Roger wheeled his car and took off as fast as he could. The creature gave chase. The couples claimed they were speeding at 100 mph while the strange being effortlessly kept up, following them down Route 62, scratching at the roof of the car and occasionally making a bizarre sound.

"It squeaked like a big mouse," Mrs. Mallette reported.

Approaching town, they turned around near the gate of a farm, where they spotted a dead dog by the side of the road. The creature flew out at them again, and the car raced to Tiny's Drive-In, where the terrified couples called the police. The police first suspected they were high, possibly on the famous psychedelics of the 1960s, but after seeing their genuine terror, they investigated and had the couples separate and write reports of the encounter.

Sheriff George Johnson called a press conference the next day, and the story hit the newspapers.

COUPLES SEE MAN-SIZED BIRD . . . CREATURE . . . SOMETHING! the *Point Pleasant Register* reported on November 16, 1966. RED EYED "WINGED MONSTER" SIGHTED IN W. VIRGINIA, the *Columbus Dispatch* announced two days later. Soon, a clever anonymous copywriter came up with the name Mothman, inspired by the campy *Batman* TV show popular that year.

It turned out that the Mallettes and Scarberrys weren't the only ones to spot the red-eyed monster. Reports of the Mothman began to pour in from all over the Point Pleasant area.

▲ ▲ ▲

"This is the road they were on when the creature was flying on top of the car," Ashley Watts said, speaking with a smooth southern drawl over a PA system to a minibus full of tourists eager to relive the story. They gazed out the windows at the rainy stretch of street. We had just exited the TNT area and were heading back to downtown Point Pleasant.

"They were going 100 mph in their Chevy Bel Air. Dad says he remembers that car, and [Roger Scarberry] was always washing it and taking care of it." Ashley was referring to her father, Jeff Wamsley, who as a child was a neighbor of the Scarberrys. In 1966 and 1967 Mothman terrified residents of Point Pleasant. Doors were locked at night in the small town. Men patrolled the TNT area with rifles. But 2013 was a different year, and Wamsley had become a key figure in transforming Point Pleasant's most infamous resident from something that goes bump in the night to the town's beloved star.

Wamsley first heard the Mothman story when he was in junior high. "I picked up John Keel's book and realized a lot of the places and people in his book were people here in Point Pleasant, and I knew a lot of those people from it being a small town," Wamsley told me, referring to a definitive chronicle of the events, Keel's 1975 book *The Mothman Prophecies*. "I just thought it was cool that it had happened to people that lived on our street."

John A. Keel (d. 2009) was a Fortean researcher and ufologist, author of several books now considered classics on the topic, and a contributing writer to early publications devoted to UFO reports, like *Saucer News*. He sometimes stopped by the Pentagon and had snippy exchanges with air force officials about getting copies of UFO reports that may or may not have existed. Keel had received a book advance and used the funds to travel to various UFO hot spots. After a call from fellow ufologist and colleague Gray Barker, he made Point

Pleasant a destination and traveled there five different times from his home in New York City in 1966–67, as the events surrounding the Mothman were unfolding.

Although the Scarberrys and Mallettes' sighting is often listed as the first Mothman encounter, Barker reported to Keel that he had interviewed a Newell Partridge, who had a terrifying experience the night before the couple's sighting in the TNT area on November 14, 1966.

Partridge said his TV reception began to act up and he heard a high-pitched hum. His German shepherd, Bandit, began wailing. When Partridge went outside to investigate, his flashlight fell on what he said were "two red circles, or eyes." Bandit snarled and ran in the direction of the red eyes. Overcome with fear, Partridge retreated indoors. Bandit never returned, and Mothman lore says that the dead dog the Mallettes and Scarberrys saw on the side of the road was Bandit's body.

After arriving in Point Pleasant, which he described as "a town of six thousand people, twenty-two churches, and no barrooms," Keel quickly collected other stories of Mothman sightings.

On November 24, he reported, two adults and two children were driving past the TNT area when they saw "a giant flying creature with red eyes." On November 25 a shoe salesman named Thomas Ury was traveling along Route 62 when he spotted a tall, gray figure standing by the road. It suddenly spread a pair of wings "and took off straight up, like a helicopter."

On November 26 a housewife in a suburb of Charleston, West Virginia, "found Mothman standing in her front lawn."

The bizarre encounters weren't limited to the Mothman. Point Pleasant was also experiencing a flap of UFO sightings. Two nurses driving a Red Cross Bloodmobile reported a UFO pursued them up Route 2. And then there were the Men in Black, mysterious men in black suits (government black ops or extraterrestrial spies, or both, depending on whom you talk to) who crept around Point Pleasant, interrogating UFO witnesses.

Reports of this high strangeness continued throughout the next twelve months.

▲▲▲

Wamsley now works as a high school graphic design teacher, but in 1989 he was pursuing being a rock 'n' roller and opened his own small chain of record stores, Criminal Records. He still sports a long mane of curly hair, sometimes tucked out of the way with a baseball cap. He found that passers-through at the Point Pleasant location frequently asked about the Mothman story.

"A buddy of mine was a graphic designer," Wamsley explained. "We did a couple T-shirts to sell in the store, and I saw the interest was there. I had been talking to Linda Scarberry, one of the original witnesses off and on, and I thought it would be cool to do a book that was mostly archives of early newspaper reports. She offered to let me use a lot of the stuff that she had kept."

Wamsley and his friend Donnie Sergent Jr. started a website, www.mothmanlives.com, and released a scrapbook-style book under their own Mothman Press imprint in 2000. It was titled *Mothman: The Facts Behind the Legend*. The timing was good. A film adaption of Keel's *The Mothman Prophecies*, starring Richard Gere, was released in 2002.

"The 'true story' part involves the possible existence of Mothman," acclaimed film critic Roger Ebert noted in his review. "The human characters, I believe, are based not on facts but on an ancient tradition in horror movies in which attractive people have unspeakable experiences."

Interest in the Mothman story rose, and Wamsley and Sergent Jr.'s book got a good bump from it.

Loren Coleman says he encouraged Point Pleasant to take advantage of the Hollywood spotlight. "I kept going down there before the movie," Coleman told me as we paused to look at his small Mothman display in the International Cryptozoology Museum. "I met with the people from the [Lowe] Hotel and Jeff Wamsley, and I said, 'You don't know what this movie is going to do for your town. You've got to do a museum or a festival.'"

Wamsley decided to spearhead both.

Mothman Festival

Arriving in downtown Point Pleasant, one of the first spectacles I ran into was a team of clog dancers who were clacking out a dance routine to Will Smith's bouncy hit "Men in Black," from his action-comedy of the same name. The women were wearing the MIB's signature black suit coats, ties, and sunglasses, enthusiastically clogging away. Joining them was a bug-eyed, tongue-lolling, tap-happy Mothman.

The cloggers were just one of the great moments of people-watching I had at the annual Mothman Festival held in downtown Point Pleasant. It was a mix of paranormal conference and small-town festivity. Vendors were selling everything from Mothman pancakes to Mothman-shaped wind chimes. At an old theater on Main Street, a lineup of cryptozoologists and paranormal experts were giving lectures on Mothman and his strange kin.

The Mothman Festival, which started with a few hundred people in 2002, had grown to an estimated five thousand attendees for the weekend, usually in mid-September. Wamsley estimated about 85 percent of people were there from out of town and were there because they were intrigued by the strange tale of Mothman.

Downtown turned into a strange dimension. I spotted a guy with a huge gut and a Harley-Davidson T-shirt smoking a pipe, arm-in-arm with his biker babe, who was wearing antennae and fairy wings. A few guys were dressed as the Men in Black, and a cheerful young blonde ambled by wearing a tiara and a sash that announced she had won the title of Miss Mothman Festival Princess.

The best photo opportunity for the festival was in a small plaza downtown with some park benches and flower beds. In the middle of the plaza, where you might expect to find a statue of a city's founding father, was a statue depicting a more hideous likeness: the red-eyed Mothman, reaching out his claw hands to grab you and pull you into another dimension. Kids posed stoically in front of the statue, a teenage girl climbed halfway up the statue and swooned in Mothman's arms while her friends laughed and took a picture. Although the monster has become the town's lovable mascot, the story was a much more frightening tale in 1966.

▲▲▲

Keel settled in a hotel across the river from Point Pleasant in Galli-polis, Ohio, in 1966. He was soon knocking on doors of Mothman witnesses, cruising the TNT area often, and stargazing, hoping to spot UFOs. He soon had a companion in his search, local reporter Mary Hyre, who authored a column called Where the Waters Mingle for the *Athens Messenger*.*

Hyre assisted Keel with his research and investigation. Hyre claimed she was visited by the Men in Black, who badgered her for information about her interest in Keel and the case. Keel also wrote that on one occasion they both witnessed a UFO.

He was later in Loren Coleman's circle of correspondents, with Coleman contributing reports that were sometimes used in Keel's writing. They later met in person, and Coleman wrote about him in his 2002 book, *Mothman and Other Curious Encounters*:

> Keel acted almost like an anthropologist, getting to know the local people and gaining their trust. Through these contacts, Keel became a lightning rod for reports and was able to gather accounts that would have been unavailable for a more conven-tional journalist. His gentle personal style was endearing and people were delighted to share their stories with him.

Returning to Point Pleasant in November 1967 to continue his research, Keel wrote in *The Mothman Prophecies* that he was picked up at the airport by Mary Hyre. "As we drove to Point Pleasant, she told me about her own dreams. 'Just before I got your letter,' she said, 'I had a terrible nightmare. There were a lot of people drowning in the river and Christmas packages were floating everywhere in the water.'"

---

* Another reported member of Keel's Point Pleasant entourage was local businessman, edu-cator, stage magician, and mentalist Ben Franklin IV. "Keel, Franklin, and newspaper writer Mary Hyre quickly joined forces and engaged in round table meetings and discussions con-cerning the UFO, Mothman, and Men in Black activity here in Point Pleasant," reads a display in the Mothman Museum that features a poster advertising Franklin's magic act.

On December 15, 1967, thirteen months after the initial appearance of Mothman, tragedy struck Point Pleasant. The number thirteen eyebar pin gave out on the Silver Bridge, which connected Point Pleasant to Ohio over the Ohio River. The bridge collapsed, killing forty-six people, some who had been Christmas shopping. It appeared Hyre's prophetic dream had come true. Urban legend later spread that Mothman himself was spotted at the scene, though there was nothing to substantiate any witnesses giving that report.

And then, for a time at least, the Mothman was gone. But what was it?

A Paranormal Rosetta Stone

In addition to the Mothman Festival, Wamsley is curator to "the world's only" Mothman Museum, located in an old storefront attached to the Lowe Hotel. There you'll come face-to-face with a giant rubbery Mothman suspended by wires, gliding across the ceiling. Several pages of Keel's original *Mothman Prophecies* manuscript are on display under glass, and props from the film version, Mothman art, and vintage newspaper and magazine pieces are spread throughout the room. Wamsley has collected most of the items and is always on the lookout for more.

It was a perfect setting to ponder what exactly the mysterious creature might be, and people have many theories. Coleman, in his book, argues that "the Mothman belongs to cryptozoology." Ufologists say that Mothman was most certainly an extraterrestrial and point to the flux of UFO sightings that occurred at the same time. Others say it was a spirit or demon.

"I have a theory, and you probably never heard this one, but it's the only one that makes sense to me," Ashley Watts told the tourists as we pulled into the TNT area. "It is more of the religious side of things. In Greek mythology, there's three different types of fallen angels. And it also talks about them in Genesis and talks about them in Revelations, the end days and the return. Basically it is a demonic presence that is half-human, an offspring between humans and demons. A tall figure with wings. Sounds just like Mothman," she said into the PA system.

"The second fallen angel of Greek mythology was a round object with eyes that go all the way around it, which sounds like UFOs. The third fallen angel—which freaks me out the most—is a presence that comes to you as a man that smells like sulfur." Watts says the Men in Black fit this description; they're associated with the same foul odor.

Later, when leaving the festival, I grabbed a taxi driven by a woman named "G.G." according to her card. G.G. believed another theory about Mothman—that it was some kind of secret government program that went wrong, possibly a mutant. She said she had also seen Point Pleasant's UFOs, one even above the factory where she worked third shift (when she wasn't caregiving or operating her taxi), "sucking the energy out of it."

"There's a lot of strange things that go on in these here hills," she drawled as she drove us to our hotel. "There's also these things called Devil Dogs. They're big, black dogs almost naked with no hair, a head like a Tasmanian devil, except with a real long snout and burning red eyes."

Skeptics, of course, almost immediately dismissed the reports as a mix between misidentification and mass hysteria. They said the probable suspects were the red-plumaged sandhill crane, which can grow to be quite tall, or a barn owl seen at a funny angle.

After the original witnesses had their avian encounter in the TNT area, skeptics said that new witnesses were retrofitting odd things they had seen in the past or any out-of-place thing and immediately crying "Mothman!"

Furthermore, Keel's definitive work is not without flaws. An immediate bad connection is his association with ufologist Gray Barker (d. 1984), who coined the term Men in Black, writing about them for the first time in his 1956 book *They Knew Too Much About Flying Saucers*. Along with his colleague James W. Moseley (d. 2012, publisher of *Saucer News*), Barker was considered a UFO reporter who wouldn't let facts get in the way of a good story.

"He hawked his books and magazines by embellishing stories and

encouraging others to fabricate more," wrote John C. Sherwood, for
the *Skeptical Inquirer*. Sherwood collaborated with Barker on a hoax
report for *Saucer News* in 1969, written under the pseudonym Dr.
Richard H. Pratt. "He launched hoaxes, joined others' deceptions,
and manipulated people's beliefs," Sherwood said, adding that Moseley once told him that Barker mostly viewed ufology as "a joke."

Keel understood this and even suspected that Barker was responsible for some of the bizarre phone calls and reports that he received
while working on *The Mothman Prophecies*. Originally hoping to col-
laborate on a Mothman book, the two split paths, with Barker publishing his own book on the Mothman saga, *The Silver Bridge*, in 1970.
In a heated letter from March 15, 1969, Keel tells Barker:

> I made every effort to cooperate with you characters and devoted
> a lot of valuable time to writing for the various fan magazines.
> I have been repaid by groundless gossip, rumors, and maniacal
> nonsense. You and Moseley are directly responsible for much of it.
> It is little wonder that the subject has acquired such a disreputable
> aura. I don't pretend to understand your motivations, but I do
> wish you would adopt a more mature approach to the situation.

"Everyone's entitled to their opinion," Wamsley generously said
when I asked him about skeptics. "I've run into plenty of skeptics.
Some of them come in the museum and kind of laugh about it, but
then we have people who stay and look around for four hours. All I
can say is, I know there was something people were seeing, too many
people describing the same thing, too many witnesses."

Whatever the Mothman was—cryptid, alien, demon, sandhill
crane—he has certainly become intertwined with the identity of
Point Pleasant.

Local Legends

Although Lake Monsters and Bigfoot (and cousins, like the Yeti) are
spotted around the world, several pockets of the world have their
own specific cryptids.

The Jersey Devil has been reportedly spotted in the Pine Barrens forests of New Jersey for more than a hundred years, with a wave of sightings in 1909. It was described as a horse-faced, bat-winged, flying animal with a devil tail. It is still occasionally reported, although *Cryptozoology A to Z* notes that any mysterious sighting in that area is lumped under the "Jersey Devil" title. A New Jersey group calling itself the Devil Hunters did field investigations to search for evidence, but the last entry on its website is a field report from 2009.

The village of Mawnan, in Cornwall, England, was home to a flap similar to the Mothman story in 1976, with the appearance of a red-eyed, beaked, and winged humanoid referred to as Owlman. It reportedly appeared twice lurking near a church in 1976 and was spotted again in 1989 and 1995.

One of the interesting talks I saw at the Mothman Festival was by cryptozoologist Lyle Blackburn, who was promoting his book *The Beast of Boggy Creek: The True Story of the Fouke Monster.* It's about a cryptid that allegedly terrorized residents of Fouke, Arkansas. Described as being similar to Bigfoot, although some tracks had only three toes, the Fouke Monster's heyday was in the early 1970s. One witness, Bobby Ford, even claimed that the creature grabbed him on his porch and threw him to the ground.

Blackburn is a part of a certain Texas school of cryptozoology that included his colleagues Ken Gerhard, British transplant Nick Redfern, and *Cryptomundo* blog founder Craig Woolheater. They are a little bit more metal than your average cryptozoologist.

Blackburn paced the stage of the State Theater in downtown Point Pleasant wearing ripped-up blue jeans, a wallet chain, black button-up shirt, and black cowboy hat. His arms were sleeved in tattoos and he had a black mustache and beard. He writes a column for horror magazine *Rue Morgue* called Monstro Bizarro and sings and plays guitar in a band named Ghoultown.

Rolling through his PowerPoint presentation, Blackburn pointed out similarities between the Fouke Monster and Mothman cases. In both, residents were scared, and both the TNT area and the bogs surrounding Fouke were crawling with armed hunters, hoping to bag the monster.

SPRING-HEELED JACK

Illustration from *Spring-Heel'd Jack: The Terror of London*, a story serialized as a "penny dreadful" in the 1860s.

REPORTS OF ODD LOCAL LEGENDS go back much further than Moth-man's manifestations in 1966–67. One bizarre early case took place in the streets and fringes of London in 1837–38. In the cold winter of 1837, reports began to circulate of an odd character soon dubbed Spring-Heeled Jack. The devilish man was often described as wearing a cloak and a "suit of bronze armor, equipped with clawed gloves." Some stories said he had the ability to transform into a white bull or bear.

Spring-Heeled Jack targeted women, jumping out of the shadows and terrifying them, then allegedly making his escape by leaping and bouncing over fences and walls with his spring-powered boots.

Newspapers at the time were dismissive of the reports, with one commenting that the stories were "a gross species of humbug."

One definitive Spring-Heeled Jack story was reported in 1838 and says that a woman named Jane Alsop answered a late-night knock on her door on Bearbinder Lane to find a cloaked man who told her, "For God's sake, bring a light, for we have caught Spring-heeled Jack in the lane." She handed him a candle, and the man threw off his cloak and "vomited forth a quantity of blue and white flames from his mouth." Alsop reported he wore a helmet and skintight clothes like "white oilskin." He leapt off into the night.

Who was he? A demon, a ghost, an alien, a pervert with spring-loaded shoes?

In 1907 speculation on the identity of the culprit turned to the Marquess of Waterford, "an aristocrat with a reputation for cruelty and practical jokes." In an article for *Fortean Times*, writer Scott Wood writes that the manifestations might have been the work of one or more aristocrats, looking to have fun at the expense of lower-class servant girls.

"Guising was popular in the seventeenth and eighteenth centuries, and dressing up as a ghost and walking the night, looking to frighten people, was an almost common adult pastime," Wood writes.

By 1888 the spring-heeled devil had disappeared and London had a new Jack to worry about stalking around in the night—the notorious and brutal serial killer Jack the Ripper.

"That's what they did on the weekend," Blackburn said. "Get your gun, get your beer, and go hunt the Fouke Monster."

Blackburn summed up the appeal of such local legends: "It's cool, it's fun, it's a mystery, it makes a good T-shirt."

Mothman Lives

Mothman did not disappear completely in 1967. Sightings have still occasionally and allegedly occurred in Point Pleasant and beyond.

My cab driver, G.G., told us that a couple she knew had an encounter with Mothman as recently as 2009. They told her that Mothman jumped on the hood of their car near Point Pleasant, temporarily hypnotizing them with its huge, red eyes.

Mothman was also the subject of an episode of the Destination America reality show *Mountain Monsters* in 2013. The show follows hillbilly monster hunting team Appalachian Investigators of Mysterious Sightings (AIMS). The group is led by mountain man / cryptozoologist John "Trapper" Tice, along with teammates Huckleberry and Wild Bill.

For this episode, after seeing what was alleged to be a new video of Mothman on top of an old bridge, the team decided it was time to build the nuttiest monster trap ever—a gigantic bug zapper that they hoped to lure Mothman into.

"It's actually the biggest bug zapper ever built," said Willy, the team's engineer. "That'll produce an electrical force that will fry his little ass."

"He'll think the ol' Fourth of July has come early," his assistant Wild Bill agreed. "Plan on having some moth *wings*."

The trap was hoisted up on the bridge, and later in the night something apparently triggered it, but no Mothman was found. Like everyone before them, the group collected no tangible evidence.

▲▲▲

Jeff Wamsley sees himself as someone trying to preserve and research his town's interesting lore. In addition to his museum and festival, he followed his first book with a similar second book in 2005, *Mothman: Behind the Red Eyes*, and was working on a third book at the time of our interview. He admitted that, despite all his research, it was all a mystery he didn't have the answers to.

"I'm still searching, just like everyone else. I know there was something that people were seeing," he told me. "But I don't know what it is."

Whatever it is, it deeply impacted the lives of the people who saw it in Point Pleasant in 1966–67.

"None of us have ever been the same after the first sighting," Linda Scarberry told Wamsley in an interview for *Mothman: The Facts Behind the Legend*. "I still look over my shoulder. I feel like there's something behind me, or in the room with me. I still dream about it after thirty-five years."

Loren Coleman, cryptozoologist and founder of the International Cryptozoology Museum. TEA KRULOS

Noah Leigh time-stamps a PIM investigation at the Modjeska Theater in Milwaukee.
COURTESY OF JENNIFER JANVIERE

Michael "Gravy" Graeve (walking) and John Krahn set up PIM's equipment.
COURTESY OF JENNIFER JANVIERE

Missy Bostrom records data. COURTESY OF JENNIFER JANVIERE

PIM investigators in the Modjeska's main theater, L–R: John Krahn, Denys Blazer, Chris Paul, Noah Leigh, Tony Belland, Missy Bostrom, and Michael "Gravy" Graeve.
COURTESY OF JENNIFER JANVIERE

Scott Mardis scans Lake Champlain, hoping to spot Champ. TEA KRULOS

Champ Camp prepares to launch out on Lake Champlain to install cameras.
COURTESY OF DIANA ESORDI / BRITE YELLOW

BFRO member Jim Sherman at camp at the investigation site known as Isabella. TEA KRULOS

Jim Sherman "call-blasts" Bigfoot howls into the woods, hoping to get a response. TEA KRULOS

Mothman statue in downtown Point Pleasant, West Virginia.
TEA KRULOS

Jason McClellan and Maureen Elsberry, two of the organizers of the International UFO Congress and hosts of *Spacing Out!* COURTESY OF OPEN MINDS PRODUCTIONS

Heated debate: IUFOC panel "Is There a Government Cover Up?" features (L–R)
Timothy Good, Stephen Bassett, Robert Powell, and Col. John Alexander.
COURTESY OF OPEN MINDS PRODUCTIONS

The author attempts to recreate the scene at Bray Road. COURTESY OF LACY LANDRE

Dave Shealy outside of his Skunk Ape Research Center. TEA KRULOS

Rev. Bob Larson hams it up with a "Satanist" and his friends at a Chicago seminar. TEA KRULOS

PIM at the Bobby Mackey's Music World investigation. L–R: tour guide Wanda Kay, PIM members Jann Goldberg, Noah Leigh, John Krahn, Missy Bostrom, and Michael "Gravy" Graeve. TEA KRULOS

The author looks at the scene of the Waukesha Slender Man stabbing incident.
COURTESY OF WENDY OTT

« 8 »

DRAMA WITH THE DEAD, PROBLEMS WITH THE LIVING

CINDI MUNTZ SAYS SHE HAS A GIFT: she can see dead people.
She can hear them, and feel them, too. "You should all know that coming out here at night is not a good idea; the police will arrest you," Muntz told a group of curious ghost seekers. We were standing

139

on a median in the middle of the Midlothian Turnpike, waiting for traffic to clear so we could cross the street. We were near the Rubio Woods by the Chicago suburb of Midlothian. "They don't ask questions; it closes as soon as the sun goes down."

Traffic zoomed by, and Muntz led the group down a battered asphalt path into the forest. After a few minutes of walking, we stepped through the entry of a ripped-up chain-link fence into a small plot of land, legendary in ghost lore—Bachelors Grove Cemetery.

Established in approximately 1840, the graveyard is surrounded by forest on three sides and a small lagoon overgrown with bright green algae on the other. The out-of-the-public-eye location has made the site a target of vandals—several headstones are missing or knocked over. Such behavior, we can speculate, is not appreciated by the cast of ghosts said to haunt the land, stories that make the cemetery a perennial favorite for people cranking out ghost guides.

Some of these stories are classic—a sad woman dressed in white and crying, a typical ghost archetype. Here she's known as the White Lady and the Madonna. Adding credence to this story is an unusual picture taken by old-school ghost hunters Ghost Research Society, a Chicago group founded in 1977 by Dale Kaczmarek that is still active today. In 1991, using infrared film in her camera, GRS member Jude Huff-Felz snapped a photo in broad daylight of what appears to be a forlorn woman in a white dress sitting casually on top of a squat, cube-shaped grave marker with a checkerboard pattern engraved on the sides. I soon found myself standing next to the site, staring at a fresh lily someone had placed on top of the grave. The *Chicago Sun-Times* published the photo, and it was considered a sensational find by paranormal investigators.

There are other stories, too—Al Capone was said to hide bodies in the lagoon; thus it is said his ghost is wandering around. There are the expected stories (a ghost of a former cemetery caretaker) and the bizarre—a ghost of a two-headed monster seen patrolling the lagoon.

Inside Bachelors Grove, Muntz, still recovering from a leg surgery, sat on a rectangular tomb. "Usually, if I were walking around more, there's a few more places I could point out—there's a few places here that usually have more of a bump in energy in the cemetery proper. The first one is, you see where the guy in the red shirt is standing?" Muntz asked me, pointing across the cemetery. "There is a husband and wife couple buried right there; they like to sit on top of their headstones a lot of times and hang out."

▲▲▲

Muntz, along with her husband, Brian, runs a paranormal investigation team called Researchers Investigating the Paranormal Midwest (RIP Midwest). At a cursory glance, it has several things in common with Noah Leigh's group, PIM. The Muntzes' home base is Naperville, Illinois, a suburb of Chicago about 106 miles away from Noah's home in West Allis, a suburb of Milwaukee. Both RIP and PIM were founded in the year 2007. They both have a membership that fluctuates between six to ten members. Both teams do "tagalong" investigations—I joined PIM at the Brumder Mansion, and here I was at Bachelors Grove Cemetery with Cindi, her husband Brian, and team members Pat and Dave. Both teams also investigate residentials for clients. They both conduct workshops and classes on paranormal investigation and use some of the same equipment, EMF detectors and audio and video recording equipment.

Photo of an alleged ghost sitting on a tomb in Bachelors Grove Cemetery, taken in 1991. JUDE HUFF-FELZ / COURTESY OF GHOST RESEARCH SOCIETY

PIM and RIP both have prize pieces of EVP—remember PIM's recording at Willow Creek Farm that says, "I don't want her to crawl up the ladder like that."

Muntz sent me an audio file RIP recorded at a residential that stands out clearly. The clip is apparently of a disembodied voice saying, "None there right now. Through energy, through energy he came and then he didn't come home."

Both teams have also created the same humorous holiday video greeting featuring themselves as cheeky elves via JibJab, the online e-card and humor site. But the similarities between the groups, both teams agree, end pretty quickly.

▲▲▲

There are various terms for those who claim abilities like Muntz's. *Psychic*, which implies the ability to see into the future, isn't what many ghost hunters call themselves anymore. They prefer terms like *medium, clairvoyant,* or *sensitive.*

"What I'm told," Muntz explained, "the technical terms of what I do, I'm clairvoyant, which means I can see spirits; I'm clairaudient, which means I hear them; and then there is something called clairsentient. That one is hard to explain, but it is like they just give you information. For me it's not something I turn on and off, it's how I live my daily life. So I could be at Walmart and see somebody telling them who's around. My husband says he can't take me anywhere without making somebody cry!" Muntz said, chuckling. "At Subway he was like, 'For God sakes, do you have to have the girl behind the counter crying about her grandfather?' There's a lot of people around, but it's more about people who come to you that have something to say that is important."

Muntz said her gifts arrived at birth. "As soon as I was born, I was able to see people on the other side and to talk to them, just as if you and I were sitting next to each other, talking to each other, having a cup of coffee," Muntz explained. "That's literally how I see them—they're tangible, no different than you and I. And when I was younger it was really difficult because I didn't notice the subtle differences, so it was confusing to me when I was younger, about who was where. As an adult now, I've figured that part out, obviously."

This ability soon got her in trouble with her Roman Catholic parents, Muntz explained to me, especially after she had a psychic vision of an incoming phone call her mother received.

"My mother was so freaked out from the situation that when my father got home from work they took me to the rectory and did their first quote-unquote exorcism on me," Muntz explained. "There were several after that. As the years progressed, the church ended up telling my parents they didn't think it was negative."

Muntz told me she felt a calling to use these abilities to help people who were frightened and confused with their hauntings. Although you can hear pride in her voice when she talks about these cases of acting as mediator of the drama between the dead and the living, she still faces obstacles in what she does on occasion.

"A pastor told one of my college friends that she shouldn't be friends with me because I was like a human Ouija board, and those are demonic, and so I must be evil. People think because I'm a medium I don't believe in God. I think that is hilarious, because it's very much the opposite. I know the other side exists, I know I'll have a life review, and I know I'll probably need a gin and tonic while we're doing it," Muntz laughed. "I have a strong belief."

Muntz is a hearty, jolly woman with an infectious smile and dark brown features. I found her to be a warm person. She loves to talk and gabs away, punctuating her thoughts with the word "literally" for emphasis and "know what I'm saying?" and "know what I mean?" to make sure you are keeping up with the words flowing out of her mouth. She throws in a lot of "LOL" and smiley-face emoticons in her e-mails and online postings.

Muntz has tapped into her proclaimed talents in a number of ways. Besides working with her team on paranormal investigations and workshops, she lists herself as also being a clairvoyant and offers one-on-one reading sessions, as well as being a Reiki master and teacher, energy healer, and shamanic practitioner. She works as a medium hosting séances from time to time, and she was invited by the Chicago Paranormal Detectives (CPD) to be a medium for the team.

She has developed quite a devoted clientele, and about thirty people have thrown down $5.50 to join her group and their expertise at the Bachelors Grove Excursion, as it was billed. As she sat in the graveyard, she chatted away with various people who had signed up and were excited to be out in the field looking for evidence of the afterlife.

Not everyone is such a fan of her work, though.

"I got a notice you were talking about another team, and I don't want to give them publicity, so I'm not going to mention any names, but there's a group in your area that charges for investigations," said Jim Malliard to Noah Leigh. Malliard is the host of the Internet radio show *The Malliard Report* and had Leigh on his program on June 11, 2013, to discuss RIP Midwest. On the other end of the line, his guest sighed deeply.

"Yes, there is," Leigh replied. "I recently found out about this, and I wasn't happy, to say the least." Leigh discovered what he feels is an unethical practice—RIP charges its clients for services. There is a fee for mileage, lodging (if the investigation is more than one hundred miles away) and a three-tier investigation lineup, with tier two being a $100 donation and tier three being $200. These tiers include progressively more detailed investigation options, such as EVP review, copies of evidence, and a longer investigation time.

PIM does do annual fundraisers, like the event at the Brumder Mansion, but it does not charge clients to investigate their home or business, and the team believes paranormal investigators shouldn't charge because of the difficulty of proving what they do.

"At first I was like—how should I react to this?" Leigh told Malliard. "Should I act like I never saw it? Should I say, 'Well, I guess that's their thing, you know'? But I actually kind of got pissed off. And because this group is not too far from us and they've been around a long time and are supposedly *so great*, if you read their website they say they're *so fantastic* and apparently they're doing things *so differently* than everyone else, it validates their charging for these services and recouping for costs and so on. So I said, 'You know what, I'm just going to put a little question on their Facebook page.'" Leigh posted this question to RIP's Facebook page on May 29, 2013.

"It was a simple question, an innocent question—I basically said, 'Can you explain to me how you charge for investigations, question mark.' That's all I put."

The response on Facebook was: "Literally how? Usually via Pay-Pal! Or . . . is this more about the reasons of why?"

"I mean, ethically how?" Leigh challenged. A long series of

exchanges from various paranormal investigators followed. Leigh made a mini-media blitz on the topic. On June 4, PIM updated its Facebook page:

> R.I.P. Midwest is a group based out of Naperville, IL. They are run by a woman named Cindi Muntz who claims to be a medium. They charge for investigations, a minimum of $1.95/ mile and up to $200 depending on how long the investigation lasts and other parameters which you can see in the post below. PIM thinks this practice is vulgar and would encourage its followers to spread the word about this group and its founder Cindi Muntz. Taking advantage of people is wrong.

Leigh appeared on *The Malliard Report* on June 11 and on another paranormal-themed show, *Prove It! Live*, on June 19 with hosts Chuck Manning and Don Ford. He sent information to a website called Paranormal in Review, which posted screencaps of the Facebook debate.

Leigh was calling Muntz out, big time.

I spoke to Muntz over the phone before attending the Bachelors Grove Excursion, and she defended herself from her critics by saying she does something well and should be paid for it.

"I hear that I shouldn't charge for my services—not from my clients, obviously, but from people that are more than skeptical. Which is kind of confusing, because I still have a mortgage. I used to work in the corporate world, and I had my job there, but then what happened is that more and more people wanted me to help them. So I started having to have to make a choice—*Do I fly to Canada to help on this case of a little boy that's missing, or do I go to work today?* Do you see what I'm saying? Eventually I had to make a decision—see what I mean?—because it wasn't working. So I jumped into this full-time and allowed it to be my life."

Muntz argues time and money should be reimbursed.

"It's still a service. I don't charge for police cases," she told me, alluding to another of her claims: success in assisting law enforcement with her abilities.

Another member of PIM and a vocal critic of Muntz is former police officer John Krahn, who finds her claim to be dubious. He told me he was not aware of any precedent where a psychic actually helped police solve a case.

"I asked her what police departments she has helped and she said she has solved a lot of criminal cases as well as helped to find lost children," Krahn told me in a Facebook message. "She said she won't say what departments she's helped because she didn't want to put her family in jeopardy. You know, because the families of missing kids found would come after her," he added sarcastically.

"For our team, some people think we're horrible," Muntz said, alluding to PIM. "But whatever. We do have donation levels, we have sets for different things we do for people. We've never turned anyone away because of payment, ever, in our history, but we also acknowledge the fact that when we're driving to Washington State, that takes gas and car money or flight money to do that. There's a bunch of flash drives and batteries and expenses, and we feel we should at least recoup the costs that we're taking on. You're talking a lot of time and devotion with no money."

Leigh's opinion differs. "Some people say it's your time—well, OK, it's my choice to do it," he explained to me. "If you ask me to do it and I don't want to, I can say no. No one has a gun to my head, no one is twisting my arm. The majority of people in this field have day jobs and they have this thing they do at night. It's called a hobby."

Leigh also says that there is nothing to prove for the services you are providing.

"The example I always give is that if your toilet is clogged, you call in a plumber and pay him a fee for service. You had a problem, he fixed the problem, and you had to pay him. We come in and yes, we may be more knowledgeable about the paranormal than the average person, but I don't have a degree in paranormal investigation or a hundred cases where I was able to expel spirits from a home and everything was hunky-dory—there is no such thing as that. There is no proof of what we do. As such, it is hard for me to say, 'Well, I know there's no proof we've done anything, but I want to charge you money for it.'"

▲ ▲ ▲

"Have you heard of this thing, Paranormal Unity?" Jann Goldberg asked me while I was interviewing her. I told her no.

"Oh, fuck me," she replied, rolling her eyes. "Um, OK. There's even a Paranormal Unity conference and all this bullshit." Jann described an effort within the paranormal community to unite groups with a scientific (or in some cases "scientifical") approach with those that are psychic based, ghost whisperers, hunters, researchers, all under one banner.

Jann doesn't think it's such a hot idea, and Noah Leigh agrees.

"I don't believe in that," Leigh told me. "I believe people should be rational, and the issue the paranormal field has is that we aren't critical enough. There's too many people who are more than happy to accept your explanation without any evidence to back it up."

Jann told me that it becomes difficult to tread on the same turf as some of these groups.

"If you're a group like ours that goes into a place after these groups that have already been there and told all this bullshit and you have a family that's scared—there was some group that told a family they had a portal to hell in their house—that is shit you have to deal with. And I mean, shame on them for believing it, but you don't know what someone's mental condition is, and for them to go in and say this, it's like, *What are you doing?*"

Paranormal Unity is a cause, and one that PIM appears to clearly say "no thanks" to.

In addition to charging, the other big difference between PIM and RIP is that RIP uses Muntz's professed abilities as a medium for a guide in investigating and employs related equipment that a group like PIM frowns upon. Muntz set her equipment case on a tombstone in Bachelors Grove and demonstrated some of these devices to her excursion attendees.

One piece of equipment RIP Midwest uses, she explained, is called the Ovilus. The device is programmed with a long string of random words, and ghosts supposedly can manipulate the word catalog to speak through the Ovilus. The machine will click away and begin to blurt out random things—"ceiling," "mortgage," "Mindy," "ice cream"—and the investigators interpret the words from there.

"Someone tried to explain to me how this is supposed to work, and it made no sense to me," Leigh told us in his Paranormal Investigation 102 class.

Another device RIP uses and PIM doesn't are ghost-detecting dowsing rods. Muntz pulled a pair of these—L-shaped wire from coat hangers with Bic pen tubes as handles—from her case.

"This is a metaphysical tool, and you have to watch how your hands are; they have to be really still," Muntz said, telling the group crowded around the gravestone that dowsing rods can also be used to find water. Then she addressed the ghosts: "For our purposes, though, can you guys show them what 'Yes' looks like?" The dowsing rods slowly moved outward. "Thank you. Bring them out to ready, and can you show them what 'No' looks like, please?" The dowsing rods crossed inward. "Thaaank you. What? Who are you talking about?" Muntz said to the air, then turned to us. "Oh, my one guy was just saying hello."

▲▲▲

When PIM was first established, Leigh's goal was always to take a scientific approach, but when he first started the team, he wanted to be inclusive, so those who claimed to be "sensitive" were allowed to be investigators. PIM reports used to have a special section that relayed "impressions" that the sensitives picked up.

"We don't take those notes anymore," Leigh told me when I interviewed him. "I initially used them. My reasoning was, 'Well, I don't know that it doesn't exist, so any information might be useful on an investigation.'" But Leigh soon changed his views.

"The more I read about sensitives, the more I found they are not really right about things, and there is no way to independently verify what they are getting. We just don't do it anymore, not in an official capacity," he said. One current member of PIM identifies as a sensitive, but I've chosen not to identify whom. This person is sometimes casually asked about his or her impressions, but it isn't an official part of the investigation.

"I took that all out [of the reports] because I thought it was unnecessary and made us seem less scientific," Leigh explained.

Muntz, on the other hand, believes her techniques are a success story. In our conversation, she told me of several things she'd put in the "win" column.

"For example," she said, "there was a team in Washington State that was dealing with a client who was having ashtrays flung at the back of her head on a fairly regular basis.

"A team had already been in there and investigated. They got some voices, nothing that big, but the client was in distress. So we drove out there, and literally, I was there for twenty-five minutes; I barely got my coat off. Turns out there is an old guy there, he's talking to me, it ends up being her grandfather. He tells me he gave her this house, which she confirms, and he ends up telling me he's throwing the ashtray at her because she's smoking pot in the house and he doesn't allow that in his house.

"It's something she hadn't told the team, what she was smoking or anything like that. It was kind of funny, and she said, 'Yeah, I am,' and he told her, 'Well, that's what the porch is for,'" Muntz laughed.

"She started smoking out on the porch like he told her to, and the ashtray hasn't moved since and everything has been fine."

Rosabelle, Believe!

If any of this conflict sounds familiar, it should: it's been going on for about a hundred years now. Ehrich Weiss, better known by his stage name, Harry Houdini (d. 1926), devoted considerable time and money during the latter stage of his career to debunking psychic claims. Early in his career Houdini did mediumship as part of his stage act, but he said he soon found he couldn't bear the guilt of shamming his audience.

"I was brought to a realization of the seriousness of trifling with the hallowed reverence which the average human being bestows on the departed," Houdini later wrote. "I was chagrined that I should ever have been guilty of such frivolity and for the first time realized it bordered on crime."

The death of Houdini's mother left him heartbroken—he actually collapsed when he received a cable that she had died. He approached Spiritualism with an open mind, hoping there was a genuine case of someone able to communicate with the dead. What he found was a long road filled with charlatans associated with the Spiritualist movement.

One of the strange friendships-turned-rivalries of history was between Harry Houdini and Sir Arthur Conan Doyle (d. 1930), Spiritualist and author of the Sherlock Holmes stories. Doyle became heavily involved in Spiritualism after losing his son Kingsley, his brother, and other family members during World War I.

Although he was responsible for creating the highly deductive Holmes, Doyle's own detective skills were at times clouded by his desire to believe. He was a proponent of the Cottingley Fairies, a hoax propagated by two young girls who carefully copied illustrations of fairies from a children's book* and posed with them near a brook by their house.

Looking at the photos now, it's hard to see how anyone could fall for such a stunt, but for many years people thought they were real. Doyle wrote magazine articles arguing that the photos proved there was a doorway to another world.

Doyle's wife, Lady Jean Doyle, also a Spiritualist, was an acclaimed medium. The Doyles held séances almost nightly, and would communicate with a spirit named Phineas, who often warned the Doyles that the world was facing impending doom and that the end times were near. After Doyle met Houdini, he was convinced that the magician had actual unearthly powers and hoped to recruit him to the Spiritualist movement.

When Houdini came to visit the Doyles, they staged a séance for

---

* The 1915 book, an anthology titled *Princess Mary's Gift Book*, ironically had one of Doyle's own stories reprinted in it.

him, as recalled in the book *The Secret Life of Houdini: The Making of America's First Superhero* by William Kalush and Larry Sloman. Houdini accepted, but as the séance began he quickly became disappointed. Lady Doyle claimed that she had channeled Houdini's beloved mother.

Houdini had not told the Doyles a simple but important fact about his mother—although she could speak four or five languages, English was not one of them, and yet now Lady Doyle was delivering a message in the Queen's English. Other subtle mistakes convinced Houdini that Lady Doyle was a failure as a medium. Doyle and Houdini's relationship quickly soured over one sentence Houdini wrote in an article for the *New York Sun*: "I have never seen or heard anything that could convince me that there is a possibility of communication with the loved ones who have gone beyond."

Houdini and Doyle began to trade criticisms of each other openly in newspaper reports and in lectures and stage performances.

After their falling-out, Houdini stepped up his campaign against Spiritualists, and it became a full-out battle. He kept a huge collection of files on fraudulent mediums and employed a circle of spies who attended hundreds of séances and gave field reports. Houdini would use this info to bust the mediums when he came through their towns on tour. He would sometimes attend séances disguised as an old man, bringing along reporters and/or undercover police, who would charge the mediums with "obtaining money under false pretenses" and "fortune-telling."

Houdini wrote a 1924 book exposing fraudulent medium practices titled *A Magician Among the Spirits* and offered a forerunner of the James Randi Educational Foundation's Million Dollar Challenge, a $10,000 reward Houdini offered to any medium who could pass his tests. No one ever successfully claimed it. Needless to say, Spiritualists who had their money flow disrupted viewed Houdini as public enemy number one. He began to receive a steady stream of death threats and frivolous lawsuits.

Authors William Kalush and Larry Sloman even speculate in their Houdini book that Houdini's death might not be the simple accident often portrayed. Houdini claimed he had "an iron stomach" and after a man punched him in the gut, he died of complications from a burst appendix. Kalush and Sloman believe this incident could have been set up by Spiritualists, since the investigation was rudimentary at best. Houdini died a few days after the punch to the stomach, on Halloween 1926.

Houdini and his wife, Bess, had a phrase arranged for Houdini to say to her if he came back to her from the dead: "Rosabelle, believe!"

Houdini séances are still held in various parts of the world every year on Halloween, hoping to have his spirit manifest. There is no credible evidence that the world's greatest magician has ever returned to our earthly plane.

Problems with the Living

There are other, more earthly dramas that paranormal investigators face. Common human drama is the cause of many rifts in paranormal groups. In addition to his falling-out with the first group he was part of, the Greater Milwaukee Paranormal Research Group, Leigh had a divisive team split within PIM in 2012. Things got ugly.

"In 2012 we kind of hit a snag," Leigh told me. "When you start out with a group, you want to be friends with them, be nice, you don't want to have disagreements. After a while, that honeymoon phase fades away. When we're doing this, we're spending money, time, effort, time away from your family, so you want to do this in the best way possible. I was finding there were people on the team that I would consider deadweight. They didn't do a lot."

Leigh began to implement some rules that were voted on and accepted by the rest of the PIM team. Most of them had to do with attendance. "This isn't a placeholder group that fills your need when you have an inclination to do it. There are plenty of groups out there that are like that, but we're not one of them."

Members of the group who weren't following the guidelines were voted out, but Leigh found that the issues ran deeper, stemming from a couple of members, including one woman the team has given a derogatory codename who Leigh said was responsible for the 2012 exodus of PIM members. The team refused to call her by her real name, and I once witnessed team member Tony slap himself across the face after accidentally uttering it. I've given her my own pseudonym here, Mrs. X.

"[Mrs. X] came to us from [another research group]," Leigh recounted. "She got kicked out of that group in the same manner I got kicked out, about a year and a half after I did. She was an integral part of the group—she was my number two. I did a lot of planning with her, setting up investigations, did interviews with media with her. She was important. She did a lot of things for the group. But her personality, the best way to describe it, was immature."

▲ ▲ ▲

I met up with "Mrs. X" for coffee one afternoon to get her side of the story. She agreed to meet me if I assured her I wouldn't use her name in print.

"There's good and there's bad," she told me. "I'll start with the good. I know when I first joined, it was early in my learning about how to do investigations properly, and during that time [with PIM] I began looking at things from a scientific perspective. There was definitely a lot of training in relation to how my mind-set was with that, and I still attribute that with a good investigator. There was one episode where I did almost want to quit as an investigator, but then Noah did push me to get past those fears, and it ended up helping a lot, so I do give him credit for that."

But she also shared a laundry list of complaints. She found her expected workload of contacting and interviewing clients "very stressful."

"After a while there would be constant e-mails from Noah asking me to contact this person or this person or this person, and I felt like with the timeline he wanted it done, I didn't have any personal time for myself."

Mrs. X shared a story that Noah also told me, although, as expected, their perspectives vary on the incident. Noah maintained it was lighthearted joking, but she saw it differently.

"The one other big thing I had was a lot of sexism. I was a joking female, I would always throw it back at them, but after a while the sexist comments started to dig at me too much. I reread one of Noah's last e-mails he sent, where he said I had 'juvenile outbursts.' I admit they might have been outbursts I should have handled differently. The last investigation I did with them was Mansfield Reformatory in Ohio. Being on extremely little sleep and constantly hearing all the way there and back how bad women drivers are—and I'm the only woman in the car—it put me a little over the top, and I yelled at everyone in the car and refused to talk the rest of the way home. So I know I didn't handle that situation well."

"The comments weren't directed at her but the actual women who were driving," Leigh told me. "The topic lasted no more than ten minutes each way. I'm fairly certain we spent more time making fun of Jarod [a former PIM member] for hitting a squirrel and feeling bad about it than talking about women drivers."

Shortly after that incident, Mrs. X decided to circulate an anonymous survey around the team to do a poll on Leigh's performance as team leader.

"My first thing was, why do we need a survey? If someone has an issue, why don't they just bring it up?" Leigh told me at our interview. Just recalling the incident was making him flustered. As the surveys circulated, drama escalated.

In a short space of time, five members of PIM either quit or were kicked out of the group. And then Noah found out that Mrs. X had been planning on forming a new group while she was still in PIM. Two other ex-PIM members also joined, making it a team composed of seven former PIM investigators. About a year and a half after forming, the new group disbanded. Mrs. X told me the key members just didn't have enough time to conduct investigations. I asked her if she missed paranormal investigation.

"Not really. I had a lot of personal stuff happen this last year. I had a tragedy happen to me, and then both of my parents passed away. After all that, it made me think—*What's more important in life? Is it looking for something that we may or may not ever prove, or is it living life in the moment?* I'd rather focus on what's most important at this point. Will I miss it? Maybe. Will I do it again? Maybe. We'll see how time goes by."

Leigh has had no contact with the ex-PIM members involved in the 2012 split. "It was the drama I was trying to avoid," Leigh said. "It was a turning point for PIM, because at that stage we could either crumble because I was sick of the bullshit, or I could say, 'Fuck you, I'm going on to bigger and better things.' So with John and Gravy's help, that's what we did. Jann and Missy joined shortly after that, and these are the core members, people I could count on to get things done."

Leigh paused to reflect on the 2012 situation. It was obviously a bad memory for him.

"It was painful, and it still irritates me, it gets my ire up when I think of it, because I think it could have been handled so differently. It could have been better for everyone involved, but in the end it was good for us because we cut the fat off the group and kept the people that were useful, and that's where we are now."

« **9** »

SQUISHES

G HOST HUNTERS AREN'T THE ONLY ONES with a field plagued with high drama. Conflicts occur in different schools of UFO research and among cryptozoologists. For instance, cryptozoologists who research Sasquatch—they're sometimes referred to as "Bigfooters"—often possess a seething hatred for one another. Whether it is their deep passion for Bigfoot evidence or too much fresh air, the rivalries within this group are deep.

There was a quartet of classic Bigfoot researchers known as the Four Horsemen of Sasquatchery: Peter Byrne, the Irish big game hunter who discovered the Pangboche Hand during a Yeti expedition and later looked for Bigfoot in the Pacific Northwest; Canadian journalist John Green; pipe-smoking Canadian (by way of Switzerland) Bigfoot tracker René Dahinden (d. 2001); and anthropologist Professor Grover Krantz (d. 2002) of Washington State University.

These four are considered among the earliest noteworthy Bigfooters, who helped popularize the field through research, books, and media appearances. By all accounts they also shared an occasionally heated dispute. As Byrne once said, "There are a number of rivalries in the Bigfoot field. Their principle basis is of course the belief that at the end of the Bigfoot rainbow there lies a pot of gold . . . had they over the years projected a fraction of the time and money that they spend on vilifying each other on Bigfoot research [they] would surely have solved the mystery by now."

Bigfooters have feuds over many different things—territory for research, expertise, information sharing—but a major point of contention is how to definitely prove that the mystery hominid exists.

Bigfoot: Pro-Kill or No-Kill?

The most divisive philosophy between Bigfooters is whether the creature should be shot. On one hand is the "pro-kill" position, which states that in order to certify the status of Bigfoot from invisible monster to actual fact, at least one specimen must be "harvested" for scientific analysis. Supporters of this position argue that a body is needed, not more blurry pictures and questionable video clips. These people's gun sights sweep the woods, hoping to zero in on the cryptid to take it down and prove it exists once and for all.

The majority of Bigfooters, though, are of the "no-kill" school of thought. They believe shooting the hominid entity is a cruel and outdated philosophy.

"In the 1970s there was a big breakdown between the kill and no-kill factions," Loren Coleman explained to me, when I visited him at the International Cryptozoology Museum. "People literally hated each other." Coleman himself is a strong advocate of no-kill. I asked him to explain why, and he said he had two reasons, one being that "scientists are not primitive Victorian zoologists anymore."

Coleman said the other reason is simply that he is a pacifist by nature. "I was Decatur, Illinois's first Vietnam-era pacifist, based upon being a Fortean. My whole notion is even though Charles Fort didn't want us to think of him as a religion and didn't even join the Fortean Society because he said he wouldn't join his own club, I think if you look at it as a philosophy, it's really holistic, really anthropological. Look at other people's point of view through their eyes, not just your own.

"There was no way during the Vietnam War I was going to go and kill Vietnamese. Politics aside, there seemed something really off about it. So I refused the draft, I got arrested by the FBI, I had to go to court, I got an ACLU lawyer, all of that. As I was going through the courts, the Supreme Court made a decision that summer that you could become a conscientious objector based on nonreligious points of view, so it worked out for me. I already volunteered to do two years of alternative service during the war, working with juvenile delinquents. So it was easy when I started writing about the kill versus no-kill philosophy. I'm already a pacifist—why would I change it?"

Coleman told me about one group where he had served on the advisory board, the Texas Bigfoot Research Conservancy. After another board member told Coleman he was resigning because he discovered the group had a pro-kill position, Coleman followed suit.

"They made a statement they were out to kill Bigfoot and brought guns on expeditions. I didn't know they had that philosophy or I would have resigned earlier. They got all upset with me because I resigned and made a big deal of it, but you know, more people should have known that were on the board of advisors."

▲▲▲

Although there are many different Bigfoot groups coast-to-coast, some pro-kill, some no-kill, the largest Bigfoot group around is the Bigfoot Field Researchers Organization (BFRO). Founded in 1995 by love-him-or-hate-him Bigfoot researcher Matt Moneymaker, the group rapidly expanded membership throughout the country with the power of the Internet.

BFRO's public profile was raised considerably when the group launched a successful reality show for Animal Planet called *Finding Bigfoot* in 2011. Starring Moneymaker, along with field researchers Cliff Barackman and James "Bobo" Fay, the cast is rounded out by skeptic Ranae Holland. The effect the show had was similar to the impact *Ghost Hunters* had on paranormal investigators—a flux of new Bigfooters entered the field.

Finding BFRO

Eager to get into the field and see if I could spot hide or hair of Bigfoot myself, I began perusing BFRO's website, which listed a page of upcoming 2013 expeditions that would-be Bigfooters could sign up for to join BFRO members in the field across the country.

To my delight, I found one in Michigan's Upper Peninsula. The UP, as it's known, was not too far of a voyage for me and is a delightful north woods area with a lot of character. I wrote down the dates and e-mailed BFRO, explaining my intentions to go on the UP expedition.

But the next day I got a message from Moneymaker himself. "We don't allow journalists on the expeditions for a variety of reasons," he wrote to me. "The main reason is that it could make the other participants nervous. It would also make our nondisclosure agreement (partly for protecting the names of other participants) seem a bit hypocritical."

Moneymaker went on to say that he would help in a different way, though, by getting me in touch with Jim Sherman, an active BFRO researcher in Michigan.

"[He's] actually onto something—a habituation situation—where some sasquatches have been coming around a farm house for the past few years," Moneymaker wrote. "I've been to the location myself and camped there a few nights. I got screamed at around 3 AM one of those nights. It's a good spot."

Before I met Sherman, my vision of the typical Bigfooter was of someone bearded, unshowered, spitting angry and muttering about a rival Bigfooter, sneaking through the forest in safari gear and a well-worn fedora, glancing around wildly for the mystery hominid.

No description could be further from Jim Sherman. Sherman is an extremely nice person. He's a high school history teacher in Bloomfield Hills, a suburb of Detroit. He has a passion for military history, the Revolutionary War, and World War II. His wife is a high school science teacher at the same school. She received an award for excellence in her field and used the cash prize to buy a tandem bicycle and a new grill. They have a young daughter, and Jim enjoys sharing anecdotes about her antics.

Besides teaching, the couple is athletic. Jim coaches his high school girls' cross-country team, who have twice been league champs. He has a tattoo on one leg celebrating his victory winning a triathlon and another on his other leg commemorating his finishing a Half Ironman competition. His wife is an avid cyclist. Jim is a voracious reader, in particular books on history. He also enjoys fishing and deer hunting but quickly points out to me that he eats what he kills and is not a trophy hunter.

And then of course, there's his other hobby: Bigfooting. Jim's wife views this with some amusement and calls it "unicorn hunting." Jim has long had an interest in Bigfoot, especially because he's had some questionable experiences in the past. In 1989 he went on a fishing and camping trip with his dad and heard a large creature in the woods that approached his tent.

"It was walking near the back of my tent, and then it stood there breathing. I was strangely powerless to move or speak and felt frozen in my sleeping bag separated from whatever was out there by the thinnest of nylon walls," Sherman told me. The creature pushed on his tent near his head, and Sherman backhanded the beast through the tent wall. Whatever it was grunted and stomped away. "It sounded like a man walking," Sherman said. The incident led to a fear of the forest at night, which Sherman says he overcame by signing up for a BFRO expedition in Michigan. Jim found the excursion to be an enjoyable trek, and he made new friends and entered the Bigfooter community.

Jim was eventually told by the BFRO that it needed more boots on the ground in Michigan, and the group asked Sherman if he wanted to be a representative. Sherman agreed and was soon fielding a stream of reports of Sasquatch sightings from all over the state. Some of these were compelling, he says; some were dead ends.

Sherman began coordinating with BFRO to lead expeditions in Michigan. And then he got a case that was like a dream come true for a Bigfooter: Isabella farm, the location Moneymaker had alluded to in his e-mail reply to me. Isabella is surrounded by about eighty acres of woods and, I was told, had many telltale signs of Bigfoot habitation—odd vocalizations howling in the night, footprints, mysterious knocking coming from the woods, rocks being pelted at the farmhouse, items oddly moved around the farmyard. Sherman met and befriended the farm owners and began visiting on a regular basis. He began recording some of the odd sounds and sent me a link to some of them, which he had cataloged on a SoundCloud page.* I followed the link and listened to the eerie howls, grunts, screams, and whoops recorded coming from the dark woods surrounding Isabella.

After about a year of coordinating schedules, Sherman and I finally found a few days in early July 2014 to meet up for an expedition exploring Isabella, which was his fifth trip investigating the property.

"This place gets scary for me even, so get ready," Jim warned me in a Facebook message shortly before I left.

▲ ▲ ▲

Sherman picked me up in Mount Pleasant, Michigan, located somewhere in the middle of the state. From there, we drove about thirty

---

* soundcloud.com/jim-sherman

miles to the property. The couple who own the property value their privacy and don't want to attract uninvited guests, so I won't give exact coordinates. The nearest town is miles away and is simply named Lake. The land is located in Isabella County, hence Sherman's naming of the site. I've changed the names of the couple who own the farm to Samantha and Ivy. We arrived and found them attending to the horses on the property.

Jim immediately put on a tactical vest and began gearing up with the tools of the trade. He had some practical camping needs—bug sprays, bear mace, a knife, a 9 mm (at the request of the landowners), and flashlights. He also had gear specifically for collecting Bigfoot evidence. His parabolic microphone looked like a ray gun, with a dish attached to a trigger handle. A microphone in the dish picked up remote sounds, which could be listened to through a set of attached headphones. An equipment case contained a night-vision telescope, audio recorders, a camera, and a video recorder.

After checking in at the farm, Samantha and Ivy joined us in Sherman's Jeep, and we set out on an extremely bumpy journey across an old cornfield that had now become a sprawling meadow. The Jeep headlights illuminated the sedge grass parting in front of us.

"What's going to be great is the sensation of falling into a pit!" Sherman laughed as the Jeep lurched across the field.

We found a spot on the edge of the meadow near the forest. This was the same spot where Sherman, off camera, had camped with Matt Moneymaker and one of the cameramen from *Finding Bigfoot* for a Michigan episode of season 3 of the show titled "Bigfoot and Wolverines."

"C'mon, Sasquatch, I know you're out there," Moneymaker told the camera as he walked through the dark forests of Isabella. Sherman later appeared in a season 5 episode of the show, "Super Yooper Sasquatch," where he shows Moneymaker and company a spot from his UP expedition where they saw unusual eyeshine glowing at them in the dark.

We set up tents in the headlights of Sherman's Jeep and walked down into the field, where Samantha and Ivy had set up a small bonfire. As we sat gazing at the flames and swatting at mosquitoes, I asked the couple to relay their experiences to me.

"We kept hearing, every time we did chores, we thought they were coyotes," Samantha said. "We had a friend up here, and we said, 'Listen to this, this is crazy because we've never heard a coyote sound like this,' but it was the only thing I could think of.

"And he said, 'No, it's not a coyote.' For about two years we heard it just about every night, every other night. It was pretty consistent, but they calmed down a little bit starting last year. There's been a lot of changes, with cutting down forests," Samantha said, gesturing to the distant edge of the field. Encroaching development had already caused a patch of trees to be leveled.

"So they might have moved on. But I still hear some things in the middle of the night, just not as vocal," she continued. Samantha and Ivy said they started letting an audio recorder run to try to capture these sounds. One night they left a recorder near a horse pen, and they captured something opening the heavy gate and then walking around the pen, sniffing heavily. They also found footprints near the edge of the dirt road that leads to the farm.

"The Squishes threw a rock that hit that metal building," Samantha told me. "It wasn't there at the time—it was by the chicken coop. We heard them; they were really close that night. There was knocking in the woods all around us."

"Wait, what did you call them?" I asked, not sure I had heard her right.

"Oh, you caught that!" Samantha laughed. "Squishes. That's what I like to call them instead of Sasquatches."

"We haven't had them come up and knock on the windows or anything, because we really try to respect them and not piss them off," Samantha told me.

"Doesn't make a lot of sense to do that," Ivy agreed. She shook her head at the idea of a pissed-off Bigfoot rampaging on the farm.

There was one time they had an angry Squish on their hands, they had told me earlier. Sherman was also present for that one. They were walking from the farm toward the field when they heard a loud growling from behind a nearby tree.

"It sounded like someone starting up a snowmobile," Sherman said. "Like a loud *RRRRRR!*"

"It was deep, guttural," Samantha added. "You were like, 'Oh, it's a snowmobile,' and I was like, 'No it's not!'" She laughed.

Then something hit his chest, Sherman said, bringing a fist up to his ribcage. "It was . . . disconcerting. It felt like someone pushed me!"

The trio sitting by me at the campfire told me there was a telltale sign the Squishes were on the move. They told me that you would hear dogs going crazy, barking and howling way down the road. Then you would hear dogs closer to Isabella reacting, and closer. Then Samantha and Ivy's own pack of dogs would start going nuts barking, and their horses would snort and run wildly in their pen. That meant the Squishes had arrived.

▲▲▲

Nothing unusual happened that first night at Isabella. The next day, we decided to take a couple of long hikes around the property. Sherman explained that this might help to "stir things up."

The forests of Isabella are varied—we walked through a dense grove of bright white birch wood; our feet squished in the muck of the cedar wood swamp, complete with a pond overgrown with bright green algae. There was a section of pine forest and open meadows. We swooshed through the sedge grass and milkweeds, bumblebees buzzing and pollinating. As we walked through a field toward a small pond, I asked Sherman if he was a pro-kill or a no-kill guy.

"I think it'd be a tragedy to shoot something like that. It'd be like, 'Oh, there's a passenger pigeon over there, I'm going to blow it away.' That is unconceivable for me. There are things you just don't do. I wouldn't even think of shooting it."

We often found remnants of deer hunting. There were quite a few deer stands of varying size and quality sitting vacantly in the trees.

We found deer bones and ancient cans of Budweiser and a full-size deer decoy, eaten away by the elements.

Between hikes we took a lunch break, and Samantha's parents stopped by to visit. They got out of their pickup truck wearing matching sweatshirts with a camouflage tree bark and leaf print on them. Samantha's mom wanted to tell Sherman a story, but she wanted to do it out of earshot of her husband, because he would ridicule her, she said. Samantha led her father to cut some stalks of rhubarb off the land to use for a pie later.

Samantha's mom told us of a sighting she and her kids had. Samantha was there, too, but just four years old. It was at a park outside of Shepherd, Michigan, in 1977 or '78, late afternoon, she said.

"I do remember, very well. There was a creek that ran along the property there, and one of the kids looked and said, 'Hey, what's that?' There was something there; it was tall and it was hunkered over like this," Samantha's mom said, hunching over and swinging her arms. "And it was really going. It went down to the side and disappeared in the swamp."

"How long did you have an eyeball on it?" Sherman asked her.

"Oh it was . . . probably an eighth of a mile it had to go down before it was out of sight."

▲▲▲

After the day of hikes, Sherman and I were invited to the farmhouse for a dinner of goat meat burgers, and then the four of us set up a bonfire near camp again. Besides the crackling fire, there were only a couple other noises in the night: the ricocheting call of bullfrogs (*GRINK grink*) and the call of the whip-poor-will bird (*whipPOORwill, whipPOORwill, whipPOORwill*).

But then we heard something else, off in the distance. There was a higher-pitched chattering that almost sounded like a hyena laughing hysterically. We strained our ears and my mind tried to think of the solution. *People laughing and yelling?* Sherman and the farm owners did not strike me at all as being hoaxers, but the thought crossed my mind that someone could have seen Jim's Jeep (complete with BFRO stickers) and gear at camp and decided to alleviate boredom by doing a Bigfoot impersonation in the distance.

What else could it be? Coyotes? Birdcall?

Bigfoot?

"Did you hear it?" Sherman whispered. I nodded. Crickets chirped. Then we heard it again, a high-pitch *whoop* and then a deeper growl sound.

"There was the higher pitch, and then did you guys pick up on the lower pitch?" Sherman asked.

"Yeah, that's what was creeping me out," Samantha said.

"It sounded kind of like a person," Sherman said. Then another high-pitched howl rang out.

"What was that?" Samantha asked in a hushed tone.

Then there was nothing in the night air except the call of the whip-poor-will again: *whipPOORwill, whipPOORwill, whipPOORwill.*

Sherman later sent me an audio clip of the incident. The sounds last about two and a half minutes, and although I can't say they are Bigfoot, they do sound pretty bizarre.

▲▲▲

The next day, Sherman and I hit the road to travel about forty-five miles north. Sherman wanted to meet up with his BFRO colleague Kim Fleming, a science teacher who lives a bit east of Traverse City, Michigan.

Fleming had originally used the Bigfoot as a fun example for her science class to discuss how a scientific investigation could be executed in theory, but the more she read on the subject, the more fascinated she became. Soon she contacted the BFRO about becoming one of its Michigan field researchers. Sherman told me the BFRO has nine Michigan field investigators, although two of them are mostly inactive.

Fleming had been studying a case of a man—we'll call him Ted—who lived in a trailer outside of a small town, located within the Pere Marquette State Forest. Ted had been reporting frequent visits by the "Forest People." Fleming had been out to his trailer several times to hear about his encounters and to look at his evidence. She wanted Sherman's opinion, but Sherman was already apprehensive about Ted's wild claims of Bigfoot encounters.

Samantha and Ivy had seemed like sane, salt-of-the-earth people, but as soon as Sherman and I pulled up to Ted's trailer, I knew we were dealing with an odd duck.

"They're watching us right now," is one of the first things he said to us, nodding his head to a patch of trees between his trailer and another trailer down the street.

Ted was wearing a denim do-rag with a long strand of braided hair hanging out of the back, jogging pants, and a stylized muscle shirt with a crucifix on it. His shoulder also revealed a tattoo of a crucifix with a pair of hands displaying stigmata and rays of sunlight at the base. He stared at us wide-eyed through yellow-tinted sunglasses. He had a mustache attached to his sideburns.

We sat in lawn chairs by a fire pit, and Ted threw a bundle of wood in, hosed it down with lighter fluid, and lit it up. He sat down in a chair by a makeshift coffee table he'd made out of a big cardboard box for a HYPOALLERGENIC 4 MEMORY FOAM MATTRESS TOPPER. His table had a pack of Marlboros and a coffee cup that read HAPPY BIRTHDAY on it, with floating slices of cake, gifts, balloons, and confetti decorating it. He took a sip of coffee, then lit a cigarette and stood near the bonfire.

"I know there's things in the world we aren't told about; I hear them every day," he told us, his eyes shifting around. The bonfire flared up, and he turned to it. "Hey, it's getting a little warm!" he scolded the fire.

Ted began talking nonstop about his experiences, as Sherman and Fleming listened politely. The drone of his voice, the lack of a good night's sleep from camping, and the warm sun and fire made me start to fall asleep in my lawn chair. I started to nod off and then jerked awake suddenly.

After talking for more than an hour we went inside Ted's trailer to eat a lunch Kim had packed for us. Ted's wife was sitting quietly in a recliner, watching *Star Trek*. Ted showed off several Bigfoot shrines he'd made. One had a mass of plaster casts Ted had made of various footprints he'd found around his trailer and the nearby woods. They ranged in size quite a bit; some were tiny baby-sized Sasquatch prints, and another was comically big—it covered Ted's entire torso when he picked it up.

Another display had a shrine of "gifts" Ted said the Forest People left him on his property—a knotted-up tangle of weeds, a small animal skull, other bits and pieces. He had all these collected in an empty pizza delivery box, underneath a poster of an illuminated cross breaking through the clouds.

After lunch, Ted took us to his yard to point out recent evidence. "Here's a footprint," he told us, and pointed to a spot in his lawn. Sherman and I looked at the ground, then looked at each other. I saw absolutely nothing resembling a footprint in the lawn. Ted got down on his hands and knees and outlined it for us, tracing a seemingly random outline in the dirt. "Probably an eighteen-incher," he said. "Here's another one," he said, walking a few steps and pointing at another random dirt patch in his yard.

Eventually, we slowly managed to back away from Ted, get into our vehicles, and leave to take a look at another one of Kim's cases. As we drove, Sherman told me he found Ted's foot casts to be interesting but was all-around skeptical about his claims.

We drove another fifteen miles, where Kim led us down a dirt road through the forest, peppered with No Trespassing signs. Kim told us that she had received reports from a man, Walt, who owned a vacation cabin there and was experiencing Bigfoot activity. Walt spotted the creature on one occasion, and another night, he claimed, his cabin was pelted with stones. He found a large handprint on a camper he had parked on the property. Kim had been out to look around the property a couple times. She let Walt know we'd be taking a look around, and the man called his brother, Bill, who lived nearby, to stop by and corroborate his story of finding the handprint on his trailer.

We heard a truck driving down the road and met up with Bill on the property near the cabin. His first line was, "You guys have any luck?" By his tone, it quickly became clear that Bill hadn't stopped by to corroborate anything but had showed up to give the Bigfooters a sharp dressing-down. Although he admitted he saw the handprint, he was not a believer, and we soon found out that he thought his brother was deluded in thinking Bigfoot is real. He also appeared angry that BFRO had shown up to add fuel to the idea. Bill was joined by two of his friends—a bald guy grinning and squinting in the sun, and a heavyset, red-haired man with a pistol openly strapped to his belt. It seemed obvious that Bill wanted to put the Bigfooters in their place and brought his good buddies along for the spectacle.

"I think the world of the guy, I do," Bill told us about his brother. "We never saw eye-to-eye on the whole Bigfoot thing, but I said, 'Yes, Walt, I will absolutely go talk to those folks,' but I have no information for you. I come up here, I spend more time than most, certainly more than Walt, and bears, yeah, I've seen bears, but other than that, not so much. So tell me, is there any credible evidence?"

"You know the bulk of the pictures now is people super-zooming in to the woods and thinking they see something and they don't," Sherman explained. "Easily 90 percent or more of everything that comes in to me is misidentification of a known something. That's why I like audio. It's harder to hoax."

The conversation started cordially, but as it went on—it lasted about forty minutes before Bill grew tired of it and walked off—it became more and more heated.

Kim: "Do the research if you want to know the truth."

Bill: "Oh, I think I do."

Kim: "There's a lot still to learn, but when you have people who are professors at universities studying this and looking at handprints . . ."

Bill: "Means nothing to me. Let's look through the camera roll on my phone, and I have no Bigfoot. Show me yours."

Kim: "I don't have any either. "

Bill: "Then I made my point, I already proved it."

Kim: "Well, you can't say that."

Bill: "I just did. I've been in these woods and swamps for twenty years and I've never seen *a thing*."

Skeptics: "Just a Myth"

Bill is not the lone skeptic when it comes to the topic of Bigfoot. In fact, hammering Bigfooters is a pastime for skeptics.

"Does Bigfoot exist?" skeptic Sharon Hill asked, repeating my question back to me. "Do ghosts exist? Does Santa Claus? It depends how you want to define that object. Bigfoot is a tremendously large iconic American thing, part of our culture. We all know him when we're kids, from TV, cartoons. He's a symbol. And that to me is what he is: he's a symbol but not a real animal. He fits the pattern of a legend, a myth. And I think it is a beautiful myth, I love it and I wouldn't want to give it up, but to accept it is a real animal out there in our backyard, it makes no sense."

As such, it shouldn't come as a surprise that Hill isn't impressed with BFRO and its efforts. "I don't have any respect for the BFRO," Hill said. "They call themselves scientific; I don't see it. Matt Moneymaker—we've had some exchanges on Twitter where he's extremely rude. He acts like the guru, where he's saying, 'Well, you don't know what I know because I've experienced it.' And, 'I know Bigfoot does all these things.'"

A good example of what Hill is talking about would be the *Finding Bigfoot* episode Sherman was on, where he showed the cast the spot where he and an expedition member saw a bizarre eyeshine. They saw the glowing eyes even after they covered their headlamps with their hands. Moneymaker immediately had the answer.

"I think we can eliminate all other possibilities based on one reason alone—they covered up their light and that light was still there. That means there was light coming out of the eyes, and only a Sasquatch can do that," Moneymaker explained to the camera, waving his hand. "They can actually make their eyes glow—it's called bioluminescence, and they use it to signal each other in the dark."

"Well, how do you know? 'I just know.'" Hill continued. "*Unsatisfying* for me. Frankly, I think you are full of it if you say something like that. I think this is his career, and he is trying to forward it in a way that I don't think is really genuine."

The group's show especially raises Hill's ire.

"I'm not a fan of *Finding Bigfoot*. I think it's a stupid show and it does a disservice to people, especially kids, who are watching it. They think that's how science works, these people are playing pretend scientists," Hill said. "It's a garbage show."

▲▲▲

I decided it was time to seek out an opinion from someone not heavily involved in cryptozoology or skepticism, so I contacted the acclaimed Zoology Department of Michigan State University. The department referred me to Jim Harding, herpetologist, wildlife outreach specialist, and instructor.

"My impression is that most animal biologists probably would take a skeptical view of cryptozoology, while at the same time maintaining an open mind about accepting new data that is gathered and reported in a responsible and professional manner," Harding responded to my inquiry. "Scientists have a prescribed way of seeking and analyzing data and reporting their research in peer-reviewed outlets. From what I've seen, mostly on TV, people calling themselves cryptozoologists often skip the steps that would legitimize their research in favor of snap judgments, instant publicity, and self-promotion."

"Cryptozoologists say we are discovering new animals all the time," skeptic Ben Radford told me. "Well, hold on there. Most of them are about this big," he said, holding a pen cap. "Or smaller. And these are genus of already existing animals, not new animals. So it doesn't have any relevance to finding Bigfoot. It's apples and oranges."

▲▲▲

Sherman says dealing with skeptics isn't a major issue for him. "I am skeptical myself," he told me. "I will often reply, 'I know something is out there making noises that I have heard and recorded, but is it an eight-foot-tall monkey thing? I don't know, but I really enjoy looking and listening in the woods for it."

For the last night of camp, Jim decided to pull out all the stops for tempting out the Squishes. Bigfooters have a wide variety of techniques for luring out the cryptids.

After setting a bonfire, getting comfortable, and turning on our audio recorders, Jim started to use these techniques.

"I'm going to go out there and do a knock, and then, Tea, why don't you do two knocks to reply?" Jim said, picking up an ax handle. Jim had carved the tool's name, YETI GETTER II, on the handle. (The first one was made from a flimsier wood and didn't last.) Jim carried this multipurpose tool for the duration of the trip. He used it to part brush while hiking, and the tool had inches marked off down the side so he could provide a measurement reference if he found any potential evidence worth taking a picture of. It was also the perfect instrument for "wood-knocking." This method supposes that Bigfoot creatures communicate with each other by knocking on trees. Bigfooters will try to elicit such a response by finding a big tree with lots of resonance to whack with a stick. Each night Jim had tried the method, knocking once or twice. While on our day hike through the woods, he handed over the Yeti Getter II to me so I could take a crack at it. I struck a solid elm tree three times. So far there had been no noticeable response.

"I'm going to hit the tree once, over there," Jim said, pointing to a tree down the field. "Wait about five seconds, then do two knocks with those," he said, gesturing to two pieces of firewood I held in my hands. I walked over by the tree line.

Jim hit the tree. *Tok.*

Tok, tok, I responded.

Everyone was still, listening. I thought I heard a snorting sound in the woods. I strained to hear and heard another snort, like a bull. What was it? An animal? A mind trick?

When I walked back to the bonfire, everyone was excited. They had heard two knocks in response to my knocks. I had not heard them.

Later, Jim tried another method.

"This is the Ohio howl," Sherman had said the previous day,

flipping through the playlist on his iPod during a break between hikes. It was attached to a small guitar practice amp, pointed at the forest. He pressed play, and a bloodcurdling, long howl blasted out of the speaker. Jim had played some of his recordings for me as I sat in a lawn chair in the hot sun to show me the technique of "call-blasting." The theory was that if the Bigfoot creatures heard this yowling and screeching, they would respond in kind.

"This one is strange," he said, playing a singsong of howls that sounded like perhaps a bird from another planet. He blasted another one that sounded like the cartoon Tasmanian Devil growling.

Besides recordings, many Bigfooters have learned to mimic these calls, and letting loose to fill the forest with a loud Bigfoot whoop is seen somewhat as an art form. Sometimes at Bigfoot conferences there will be a Bigfoot call competition to see who can earn bragging rights with their skills. Cupping his hands to his mouth and screeching isn't Jim's style; he prefers to let the recordings do the work.

So as we sat around the campfire, he let the weird singsong howl call-blast into the dark woods. There was no immediate response.

Other than the knocks, there was nothing, so we decided to try what Jim dubbed Operation: Tea-as-Bait.

"Wait, what?" I asked when he announced it.

Jim's plan for when I was ready to sleep was to hide discretely in his jeep, stay awake, and monitor the tent area on the sly to see if he could spot anything curious that came around to investigate.

So around 1:30 AM, after Samantha and Ivy had gone back up to the farmhouse, and with the fire now just glowing embers, I crawled into my tent. I took my boots off, got into my sleeping bag, and zipped it up. About twenty or thirty minutes later, tired from all the hiking and sun, I began to drift off.

Then I heard a loud howl close to my tent. I was instantly wide awake. Before I had time to think, I heard a second loud howl, similar to the first. It sounded like it was extremely close by. I was paralyzed with fear, afraid to move. After the howls, I heard a *thump, thump, thump, thump* on the ground outside my tent, near the forest. I peeked through a mesh window near the bottom of tent, kneeling down and looking at the dark outline of the forest. I didn't see anything. I waited about five to ten minutes, just sitting in the tent in darkness, listening. Then I quietly put on my boots. I had bought a novelty GONE SQUATCHIN' trucker hat, and Jim had lent me a headlamp to strap to it. I put it on and turned on the light. And then, the most frightening moment for me—unzipping the tent door to go outside. What if the howler was waiting for me out there?

I exited and quickly walked to Jim's jeep. He was in the backseat, looking at his phone, trying to text me to tell me the coast was clear. He didn't notice me, even though I was shining the headlamp into the Jeep. I tapped on the window and he jumped in his seat, then opened the door.

"Sorry," I said. "Did you hear that? What was that!"

"I don't know!" he said. He had heard the howling clearly through the car windows. "Do you want to get in?"

"Yes!" I said, and climbed in the passenger seat. We speculated on what it could have been and agreed it was very close. Jim had not heard the thumping I described to him. After a few minutes, I began to calm down. But then the freaky factor went through the roof.

I was staring out the passenger window of Jim's Jeep, looking for any sort of dark shape moving through the meadow or trees, when something odd caught my eye: I saw a star bouncing up and down and wobbling in the sky. At first I thought I must be experiencing post-fright shakes, but I noticed the rest of the stars were clear and twinkling and stationary. The star was moving, and then I saw the tree line in the distance get illuminated by a white light.

"Jim," I said. "Do you see this?"

"Yes," he said. We both got out of the Jeep, and he grabbed his binoculars.

Looking through them, I found a white light in the sky with a vortex of red and green lights swirling around it. It looked like someone creating a pattern with a laser pointer. The lights would form a ball and then swirl in loops, and the conglomeration would dip up and down and side to side. Every once in a while, the illuminating flash would light up the tree line.

Jim got his camcorder and filmed a couple minutes of it as best he could, struggling to focus the camera and keep up with the object.

"I got it!" He whispered. "I'm standing as still as I can, trying to zoom in. Come on . . . there it is. Wow, I can't follow it."*

"Every once in a while, there's a blast of light behind the tree line," I told him.

The object hovered and bounced but did not move in any direction.

We got back in the Jeep, and I watched this object out the window for about a half an hour. Exhausted, I leaned my head back on the passenger seat to take a break for a couple minutes. When I looked again, the object was gone.

▲▲▲

At the International UFO Congress, I had gone through the event program and put an X next to the talks I wanted to see. "Ha! Bigfoots and UFOs—this is too much," I said, marking a talk by someone named Kewaunee Lapseritis titled "Interdimensionalism: The Secret to the Bigfoot/UFO Connection." It was a trippy talk. Lapseritis, with his eyes magnified by his glasses, gray hair in a ponytail, and earth-tone suit, claimed that two different races, the "Ancient Ones" and the "Sasquatch People," were beings that could pop back and forth through eight different dimensions, which explained why it was so dang hard to catch one.

"Many people refer to me as the Sasquatch whisperer," he told the audience, adding that he had often communicated with them telepathically. There are others who have promoted the connection between Bigfoot and UFOs, pointing to case studies where both are claimed to have appeared in the same place. Some say that Bigfoot creatures are extraterrestrials themselves.

Earlier in the trip, I was walking through one of the fields at Isabella, swooshing through the sedge grass. I asked Jim for his take on the "Bigfoot as extraterrestrial" theory. He told me that BFRO doesn't

---

* Footage of the odd object is available on YouTube: www.youtube.com/watch?v=ztuuv6-Otck.

like to entertain those theories, as its members are convinced it is an unknown primate. But he himself is open to any theory, he told me.

"You get a lot of different camps in the Bigfoot community," Sherman said. "We have no idea who is right. How could we? I like to leave all options open, because if I come in with too many preconceived notions, then I might block out evidence because it doesn't fit with what I'm thinking."

▲▲▲

"Do you want to sleep in the Jeep?" Jim asked. I looked at my small pup tent. I imagined an eight-foot, thousand-pound hairy hominid ripping it out of the ground with one massive hand. Then I thought of a swirl of white, green, and red lights hovering above my tent, sending a blast of radiating light into the tent, illuminating my skeleton.

"Yes," I said.

Jim reclined a backseat and slept curled up in the space between the backseat and the trunk. I reclined the passenger seat and unfurled my sleeping bag over me. I didn't sleep much that night.

The next morning, I walked up to the farmhouse to take a shower before we took off, while Jim began to break down the camp. I told Samantha and Ivy what had transpired the night before and they seemed relieved, not because I had been frightened, but because I had been able to experience what they had for so many nights at Isabella. The howls were common, they said, and they had seen the mysterious UFO lights on several occasions in different parts of the sky, too.

Jim drove me to Mount Pleasant for my trip home. He told me he would process the video of the UFO and would have the audio of the howls we heard examined by a friend who was a "crypto-linguist" and an expert at sound identification. I told him I looked forward to hearing any possible explanations of what had transpired that frightening night.

I boarded the bus to Milwaukee in Mount Pleasant. I was heading home with a plethora of bug bites and briar scratches—and one of the weirdest experiences of my life.

« 10 »

WE COME TO WHUP DEMONS

"The great dragon was hurled down—that ancient serpent, who is called the devil, or Satan, who leads the whole world astray. He was hurled to the earth, and his angels with him."
—REVELATIONS 12:9

AFTER STEPPING OFF THE BLUE LINE in Rosemont, Illinois, just outside Chicago, I walked down River Road, a corridor of convention centers and hotels. Entering the Hilton, I asked the concierge, a bit awkwardly, "Can you tell me where the curse-breaking seminar is?"

He pointed me to the elevators, instructing me to take them to the second floor and hang a left. There I found a small lounge with a square of couches and chairs. I stood near a young couple across from a middle-aged woman who looked very worn and tired. But there was a glimmer of hope in her face.

"Have you ever been to one of these?" she asked in our direction. The young couple and I shook our heads. "Oh, you are in for an experience. Yes. Yes. The best thing to do, if you feel them manifesting, is go with it. Just go with it," she told us, shimmying her shoulders.

A couple minutes later, the elevators went *ping ping* and a man walked out, followed by an entourage. "We're getting a little bit of a late start, but we'll get going in just a minute here!" said the seventy-year-old Rev. Bob Larson, dressed in a tan suit, blue shirt, and striped yellow tie. There was gray showing through an orange dye job on his thin hair and beard. He and his staff disappeared into a conference room down the hall.

Rev. Larson calls himself "the Real Exorcist" and says that just the mention of his name can bring the fear of God into demons. He claims he has done thousands of successful exorcisms, casting out demons and sending them hissing and scurrying back to the bowels of hell. He has a devoted following in his current home city of Phoenix (he was based for a long time in Denver), where he is head of the Spiritual Freedom Church, as well as satellite groups, the Do What Jesus Did ministry, around the country. He also has an active ministry in war-torn Ukraine.

Others say Rev. Larson is not a great religious warrior but a con man who preys on the vulnerability of emotionally disturbed people. I made several attempts to e-mail Larson, followed by a phone call to someone who said I needed to e-mail, then I sent another e-mail and got no answer. I had subscribed to Rev. Larson's newsletter by this point, and it mentioned he was touring and would be in Chicago on May 9, 2014.

▲▲▲

"Thank you, we had a little delay. Come on in, folks. How are you?

God bless you, good to see you." Larson was in the doorway, shaking our hands as we entered. "Thanks for waiting. God bless you, good to see you. How are you?"

Inside the room were several rows of chairs with an aisle dividing them down the middle. Loud, soaring Christian rock was pumping out of a single speaker. As people settled, Rev. Larson walked to the front of the room. I had worried I might stand out, so I had dressed in the most nondescript business casual clothes I could find. As it turned out, the focus would be not on me but on three young people in the first row. They were all wearing a heavy Goth style. One of them had a swoop of dyed black hair, lots of piercings (including some kind of animal vertebra hanging from his ear), lots of jewelry, leather pants, and a Blood Ceremony (a Canadian doom metal band) tank top. Tattoos from the Egyptian Book of the Dead ran up his arm. Larson approached them.

"You look like you're all together," he said, staring at them and smiling sharply. "Whose idea was this? Your idea? What are your names? Adam, Jerome, and Ashley. How do you know about me? YouTube? Can I ask you something? Are you a Satanist? You are? He's with you. She's with you. Are they with you?" Larson asked, pointing at a couple a few rows away. They had a punk rock look and smiled sheepishly at being pointed out.

"They're not? How did you find out about me?" he called over to them.

"YouTube."

One of the Biggest Mega-Churches in America

Moments after starting his seminar, Larson asked for a show of hands of how many people had seen him on YouTube. Most of the room, about fifty people, raised their hands. There was an interesting mix of people—a middle-aged Ukrainian couple and their elderly parents, an entire Asian family, a wide age range of African Americans together in a group, and a few lone individuals. They were the tired, the poor, the huddled masses yearning to breathe free.

"I tell people I have one of the biggest mega-churches in America. I call it YouTube. We've reached over three *million* people with our videos. So technology has an upside and it has a downside."

I stumbled across Rev. Larson when I was searching for a news report I had seen about the Vatican stating that the Catholic Church needed to train more exorcists. An Internet search for "Exorcism School" brought up Rev. Larson, who is the founder of the International School of Exorcism®, an online correspondence course that will train you in the art of demon fighting at three different levels: Apprentice Level ($995), Warrior Level ($1,795), or Exorcist Level ($2,495).

Larson's website also advertised Bob Larson's Exorcism Channel, and I soon found myself sucked in, stupefied by the spectacle in front of me. The first video I watched was titled *The Demon of Hate Didn't Have a Chance with Exorcist Bob Larson*.

The video opens with a man in glasses and a white button-down shirt, identified as Jeff, held by his arms by two men. Larson stands in front of them, staring at Jeff intently, with a large silver crucifix and a Bible in one hand and a microphone in the other. Three young women, also armed with crucifixes, flank Larson and Jeff to the right. These are the Teenage Exorcists, Larson's eighteen-year-old daughter Brynne and her friends, sisters Tess Scherkenback, seventeen, and Savannah Scherkenback, twenty.

"I do have a very adventurous life!" Brynne wrote on her profile on the trio's website. "Between casting out demons, keeping up with demanding schoolwork, and travelling all over the world, I have had some crazy experiences!"

Larson assembled this *Charlie's Angels*–style squad to give a young, photogenic face to exorcism; there were hopes they would get their own reality show, but an attempt by a production company to launch it fizzled.

"Satan, you keep toying with this man," Larson says on the video, shaking his head while looking at Jeff. One of the Teenage Exorcists holds her crucifix to Jeff's forehead.

"I don't like it. He really wants to get free." Larson whacks Jeff in the chest with his Bible. "I strengthen the spirit and I smite you with it! You let him go!"

Jeff begins to writhe around and hiss. "Who are you!" Larson demands, and Jeff flails his arms, trying to break free of the grasp of Larson's assistants. "*Hate!*" he growls.

"Well, what age did you get him, Hate?" Larson demands. "When? When did you get him!"

"I'm not going to tell you," Jeff whispers hoarsely, a whistle in his voice obscuring the words.

"What?" Larson asks, turning to the Teenage Exorcists.

"He won't tell you," one of them interprets, disgusted.

"You won't tell?" Larson says, stepping backward and tilting his head back to gaze down the microphone at Jeff in defiance.

"Put Bibles on him," he says to the Teenage Exorcists, with a swooping motion. The three women press their Bibles against Jeff. Larson swings around and joins them, and Jeff is no longer visible in the tangle of exorcist arms and Bibles. "We torment you," Larson says into the mic in his free hand. "We torment you with the word of God."

Jeff grunts, growls, and hisses.

I watched more videos, people thrashing and hollering, screaming and writhing, growling in demon voices, their faces contorted.

I clicked on a video titled *Bob Larson Faces Jezebel and Lucifer Head On!* and watched as a young woman named Tamara snarls at Larson, then screams at the top of her lungs. A little tired of all the screaming, I hit the mute button and watched as she collapses to her knees, still screaming, apparently pushed down by the might of Larson's crucifix on her forehead.

I tried to weigh the options as they pertained to what I saw on Bob Larson's Exorcist Channel, and I came up with three of them.

One: Larson and certain members of his church are "in on it." They have discussed the staging of the exorcism, and although it may be improvised instead of literally scripted, it is a premeditated performance.

Two: Larson's congregation believe they are possessed or believe that demon possession and subsequent exorcism is how they must fit in to be a member of the group. It is a group manifestation that has become real in their minds. The ritual is part of their fellowship.

And, I suppose, to be fair . . . Three: Larson's congregation is actually getting possessed by demons at an alarming rate.

▲▲▲

"Great to be here in Chicago!" Rev. Larson told us, speaking into a microphone turned up a little too loudly. The room was hot and stuffy.

"Before we get started, let's take a minute to give a hug and a handshake to someone sitting next to you." Loud music blared on the PA again, and Larson quickly walked to his staff to confer with them, looking toward the Satanist in the front row.

"Nice to meet you," I said, shaking the hand of a young blonde woman sitting to my left.

"Nice to meet you," I said, shaking the hand of a middle-aged woman in a sweatshirt, jeans, and baseball cap sitting directly behind me.

Larson returned and decided to call up two women he had had personal exorcism sessions with in Chicago to deliver testimonials. One of them was named Michelle, the woman out in the waiting lounge who had asked if we had attended previous seminars.

"Now, when I talked to Michelle, I was thinking, like with a lot of African Americans, that the curse might go back to African witchcraft. That makes sense—that's where your ancestors are from." Larson believes demons are passed down from generation to generation, an ancestral curse that can go back hundreds of years. Larson will sometimes match this idea to race. A Hispanic person, he'll say, might have an Aztec or Mayan curse on them. African Americans are cursed by voodoo or African witch doctors. Even more controversially, he received a lot of negative press when he banished the "Demon of Homosexuality" from a person.

Sometimes when these demons manifest, they'll even give Larson their age when he demands it. "How far does this curse go back? *How far!*" he would scream at a possessed person. "Ten generations," it would hiss back.

"Wherever this thing was hiding, it was causing me a lot of pain,"

Michelle explained to us solemnly, while Larson stood next to her, his hand on her shoulder, his microphone tilted toward her. "Every time I went to the doctor, they said, 'No, you're OK.' So I was like, *The devil is stealing my money, because every time I go, I have to pay out a copay*. There was nothing wrong with me. Well, except the demons."

Larson then got into the exorcism itself. "This started out fairly calmly, and then this thing comes out and screams in my face! It startled even me!" he said. "Do you remember what it said?" he cued Michelle.

"It said, 'I don't like you,' but it didn't say it nice like I am now," she said, smiling and letting out a short laugh.

"It told us it went back *one hundred* generations," Larson said slowly. Audience members murmured in awe. "I said the word 'Egypt,' and about twenty minutes later we're talking to a whole host of angry Egyptian gods."

"I wouldn't even have thought of that," Michelle said, shaking her head.

"Ra, Horus, Osiris, Isis . . ." Larson said, listing the visiting Egyptian deities.

"I just want to encourage people," Michelle told us. "I didn't know what was in there, but I knew I needed to let it go."

▲ ▲ ▲

Larson was about to get into the meat of his seminar, but on taking another look at his Satanist contingency in the front row, he decided to make a spectacle of the situation.

"I know you're sitting there and I want your full, undivided attention," Larson said, waving his hand across the room. "I know some of you can't resist staring at my slightly strange friends here in the front row. I'm going to give you one chance to stare, and then you can't stare anymore. C'mere!" Larson gestured for the young trio to join him. "This is Adam—my friend Adam—and Ashley, and this is Adam's boyfriend, Jerome. Adam here is a Satanist, these other two we aren't so sure about." Ashley later said she was an atheist, Jerome an agnostic. The audience was completely pin-drop silent.

"You know about me, you've seen my YouTube videos?" Larson said, then flicked his mic toward Adam.

"Yup," Adam replied.

"You've read my blog?"

"Yup."

"What happens when you go to the shopping mall? Does everyone stare at you?"

"Oh, well . . . I don't go shopping that much."

"Why all the piercings? The bones?"

"It's like having a Christmas tree around all year, I guess."

"And this—here he has a patch," Larson said, pointing to Adam's knee and looking at the audience in shock, "that depicts Anton LaVey, the founder . . . of the Church of Satan . . . himself!"

▲ ▲ ▲

"Zeena, if this new Satanic century truly does come into being, if your numbers increase in the Church of Satan and, as you hope, the number of Christians decrease and suddenly you are the people of the new social order, describe to me what that social order would be like."

Challenging Satanists is old hat for Rev. Larson.

"Well, I think it would take on its own momentum. What we would see is nature taking its course, because that's all we stand for is to let nature dictate what our actions are, whether it's a moment-to-moment or gut-instinct level . . ."

"Can you be more specific?"

That was Larson in 1989, debating Satanists Zeena and Nikolas Schreck. Larson is wearing a similar suit, but his orange hair and beard is fuller, his face more youthful.

Zeena, dressed in black, with pulled-back blonde hair, ruby red lipstick, and high arched pencil eyebrows, at the time was known by her maiden name, LaVey, and was the daughter of Church of Satan founder Anton LaVey (d. 1997). At the time of the debate, Zeena LaVey was the Church of Satan's high priestess, and her husband, Nikolas Schreck, also dressed in black, with a widow's peak and missing an ear from an assault, was leader of a different group, the Werewolf Order. They were the "First Family of Satanism," as Larson dubbed them, selling a VHS of the debate under that name.

The year 1989 was in the thick of a period in the 1980s and '90s known as the Satanic Panic. This was when Satan and his minions, we were told by Larson and others, were everywhere and looking to capture children with their claws. They were in heavy metal music, role-playing games like Dungeons & Dragons, comic books, and Hollywood movies. Wild, unsubstantiated stories of a mass Satanic network kidnapping and sacrificing children during black masses spread and were treated as fact.

It was a Renaissance period for Larson, a former musician who played in a band called the Rebels before being reborn. Larson had already been promoting the dangers of the occult, starting with his 1967 book *Rock & Roll: The Devil's Diversion*, followed by 1969's *Hippies, Hindus and Rock & Roll*. In the 1980s Larson began challenging Satanists to meet him face-to-face to debate.

The debate caused a sensation—wow, real Satanists!—and Larson repeated the act by routinely having heated confrontations with Satanists on his call-in radio show, *Talk Back!*

Guests included the likes of Glen Benton, of the Satanic death metal band Deicide, and members of Mayhem, GWAR, Obituary, and Napalm Death. Soon it became a little too routine. But then Larson had another idea. Instead of interrogating this parade of black-clad, dreary Satanists, why not try challenging the demons themselves to debate?

▲ ▲ ▲

"So you don't do any of the rituals, you just look strange?" Larson asked Adam the Satanist. He was doing kind of a one-man good cop/bad cop routine on Adam and his friends.

"Don't you think he looks strange?" Larson challenged Adam's boyfriend, Jerome, who was wearing a suit and skinny tie and had a floppy black wave of hair.

"Exotic," Jerome responded.

Larson asked if he could say a prayer for the three. They agreed. Larson reached for a container of holy oil. "I anoint you in the name

of the Father and the Son and the Holy Ghost," he said, sticking a
thumbprint of holy oil on Ashley's forehead. He then repeated the
process on the other two.

"I'm not doing this for a theatrical reason," Larson said, turning to us. His voice had become really soft and tender. "I genuinely
care about these young people. And you know what? They're here.
And I'm grateful for that. So I want the devil to know something: I
claim these young people for Christ." He turned and looked deeply
at Ashley.

"Interesting enough, Ashley . . ." dramatic pause, "you have the
most demons."

Ashley smiled, a little taken aback.

"If there were demons, I would probably believe that," she said.

"People would think him," Larson said, casually looking at Adam
before returning his gaze to Ashley. "But you . . . they're looking at
me." Larson grabbed a large silver crucifix and tipped the cross end
onto Ashley's forehead. She looked a little frightened now; her joke
in attending this thing had gone too far.

"I bind you, Satan, for all the things you've done to hurt this
young woman!" Rev. Larson said, staring intensely at Ashley's face.
"For all the pain you've caused her. In the name of Christ . . ." he
removed the cross and stared at them silently for a second.

"Thank you all for coming," he said, softly again. "I want to say
one more thing. I bless you. I bless you. I bless you." He turned to the
audience. "Does that surprise you? How many know that's Biblical?
Reach out your hands to these people." Everyone in the audience
reached their right arm forward and spread out their fingers. Some
people did it with both arms. I awkwardly followed suit and extended
my right arm with my fingers out.

"Repeat after me," Larson said into the mic, while Adam, Ashley,
and Jerome stood dumbfounded next to him. "We the people of
God (*we the people of God*) bless these young people (*bless these young
people*) with the favor of God (*with the favor of God*), and we pray (*and
we pray*) that God will shine his favor upon them (*that God will shine
his favor upon them*) in the name of Jesus (*in the name of Jesus*). Now I
want you to tell them that you love them. (*We love you.*)"

"OK! Are you ready to break your curses?"

"All right! Amen!" someone called out behind me.

▲▲▲

Larson offers a way for you to find out if you are at high risk for a demon possession. For a mere $9.95, you can take his Demon Test® and answer twenty-one questions that will calculate the odds for you from the comfort of your own computer. Determined to find out if I was possessed (and possibly showing a demonic journalistic bias), I paid up* and began answering the test questions as honestly as I could.

Number 2: "Have you ever experimented with two or more forms of the occult?"

Number 12: "Do voices tell you to commit illegal acts, blaspheme God, or indulge in illegal acts?"

And a follow-up: "Have you asked Satan to take your life in exchange for something?"

More questions dealt with abusive family members, failure at relationships, financial hardships, and substance abuse.

I clicked the Submit button and waited and wondered as the Demon Test® worked out the results. To my surprise I was informed, "Your test score is 19. You are at low risk for demonic oppression/possession."

If you are oppressed (which is demons just harassing you) or possessed (which is when demons are actually living inside of you), the site recommends you set up a one-on-one session with Rev. Larson. If that is a bit out of your range, Rev. Larson again embraces technology, offering an exorcism session via Skype. Plug in, log on, and get your demons out. One-hour online exorcism session: $295 suggested donation. Other things you are able to pick up from Larson's site for your demon battle include *Larson's Book of Spiritual Warfare* ($19.99) and a replica of the same silver cross that Larson and the Teenage Exorcists use, blessed and anointed by Larson himself ($100).

▲▲▲

---

* Probably the strangest thing I'll ever claim as a business expense.

"The Rev. Larson claims he is not profiting by doing these exorcisms, but Fox 6 takes a closer look. You'll want to stick around because at ten forty-five we reveal what we uncovered," news anchor Estha Trouw intoned in a 2006 report for Fox 6 San Diego.

"For several years, Larson has been dogged by finances and how they relate to his ministry," the station's investigative reporter, John Mattes, explained. He found Larson had gotten $142,242 in compensation for the year as well as $28,000 for his pension. When confronted with the financial report, Larson tried to say the money was used for travel, "but we found another part of the report that said *the ministry* paid for travel expenses," Mattes explained, as the screen highlighted part of the report for travel—$186,683. Cars were also paid for by the church, and the report found that over $24,000 a year was being paid for food expenses.

"Is this the homeless you're feeding, or you?" Mattes asked, pointing at Larson, with the report in his hand.

Larson smiled angrily. "I'll be happy to answer questions, but these are gotcha journalism questions."

"No, final question. Has the ministry treated you well? Financially?"

"Heh heh heh. You know, that's one of those questions like 'When did you stop beating your wife?'"

▲▲▲

Larson was about to start the main portion of his seminar, having his assistants hand out pens and paper to those who needed them. But first he strongly suggested people buy copies of his book *Curse Breaking*, and they might as well buy copies of his last book, *Demon Proofing Prayers*, too.

"We make it available for fifteen dollars; if you want both books you can have them for twenty-five dollars. Now that's a deal! Here's what we're going to do—now follow carefully. If you want just the *Curse Breaking* book, hold up one finger. If you want both books, hold up two fingers. If you want a slip to pay by credit card, make a letter C with your fingers." Fingers went up, and Larson directed his assistants to step up.

"Quickly, who's got the credit card slips? Mike, come to the front and work back, that'll be more efficient! Envelopes, where's the envelopes? Two books right here, quickly. Anyone need a credit card slip? This is not the offering, that's later. Books, right here. I need you guys to keep up. Run! You never would have kept up with me in the Ukraine! Anyone didn't get one? Get ready to hand the baskets. Anyone else need an envelope for credit card? This is not the offering, just to pay for the books." After a whirlwind of book orders, Larson settled down.

"Turn to page thirteen—that's where we're going to start."

Larson led us through a couple pages of *Curse Breaking* and explained how people get the curse of demons. He drew an illustration of a stick figure with a bird flying above it on a dry erase board.

"It's like a bird flying around that wants to land on your head," he explained, tapping out swirly dotted lines indicating the bird's flight pattern. "It's flying around waiting for you to give it permission to land on you. But guess who else can give it permission? Your ancestors. Your ancestor is promiscuous? You'll marry someone who fools around. Dad's a drunk? You'll struggle with it. Mom's an addict? You'll become one. It's a curse!"

Larson decided it was time to pitch enrolling in his International School of Exorcism, which, he explained, was having a limited time offer of a reduced enrollment fee of $200 per class level, all three levels for "just $600, now that's a deal." As testimonial, he called up an exorcism student, a giant, jolly-looking African American man with a bald head and a beard.

"I am so honored to have Pastor James Vivian here with us tonight. He pastors in Kansas City, one of my dearest friends. He has started Do What Jesus Did deliverance teams all over Michigan and Illinois and Missouri. He is just a mighty, mighty man of God. James, come up here and say hello to these people!" Applause. "If you're a demon, you don't want to mess with my friend James!" Larson added.

"Hello everybody! God bless y'all!" Pastor Vivian said cheerfully. "Oh Satanists, my heart goes out to y'all," he said, smiling and gesturing to Adam, Jerome, and Ashley. "I got twenty-one grandkids, five great-grandkids, ten children, and they don't all believe in it. I was in psychiatry, that was my field, and I didn't believe in it, but now, demons don't want to mess with me! So God bless y'all. We gonna be prayin' for you on my team . . . we gonna whup demon . . ." he stopped himself from saying "ass," covering his mouth and laughing.

"I love y'all," he told the three, "but we come to whup demons!"

"God bless you!" Larson said, throwing his head back and laughing heartily.

▲▲▲

"Get wild. Go with it. Go wild," Larson told us at the conclusion of his talk on curse breaking. This was the big finale of the seminar, when Larson went headfirst after the demons. The tension in the room was rising.

"Some of you can already feel yourself getting fidgety—that's good. As we break these curses, focus on the personal pain. Think about the worst things that have happened to you. The curse is attached to the pain in your life, not in the joy. They're embedded in the negative stuff! That's where the demons are. They live in it! They live in your misery! A lot of preachers will smile at you and tell you everything is all right. I'm here to kick demon butt! Are you ready?"

"Yes," the audience murmured.

"I want you two up here ready to give me a hand," Larson called to his assistants.

"I'm going to lead you in a prayer and tell the devil to leave you. Do you know in the Ukraine over half the audience manifests demons? It's not that they have more demons, they are just more transparent before God. Americans are just too cool. Whatever you feel, just feel it. Honestly, if you came here with demons, don't you want to get rid of them? Think about the pain. Focus on it." Larson lifted his crucifix up to chin level and began walking slowly down the aisle, pointing the cross at various people in the audience. He led a long prayer in a firm voice.

"In the name of Jesus," he started.

"In the name of Jesus," the audience repeated.

"I confess (*I confess*) Jesus Christ (*Jesus Christ*) rose from the dead (*rose from the dead*) defeated the devil (*defeated the devil*). I want the devil to be defeated . . ."

Larson's prayer did have an impact on the people around me. The young woman sitting to my left, whom I suspected might just be another fan of Bob Larson's Exorcism Channel, suddenly burst into tears and began weeping. Michelle, two rows behind me, began speaking in tongues or perhaps ancient Egyptian.

"Ho dun tay ch chh chh," she chanted. "Hooooooe!" she yelled out a few seconds later. A woman across the aisle began weeping, too. Then the woman directly behind me began wailing: "Oh please, God! Please, please help me! Oh help me, help me, please! Please, please, please! Help me, God, please! Please!"

"Move these chairs up here," Larson instructed his assistants.

"Oh please, please, help me, God, please!"

"Ha cho hay ha ch ch."

As this was happening, I realized I had been holding my breath, so I started breathing again. Larson walked up to my row and gestured to the weeping woman sitting next to me.

"Come here," he said. Then he selected the young woman weeping across the aisle. "Come here," he said. He led them to the chairs in front of the congregation.

"By the name of God I smite you for what you've done," he said angrily, staring down at the two women. "You're going to release these people and let them go! I release you in the name of the Father and the Son and the Holy Ghost. I put the torment of God in you!"

Larson told the young woman who had been sitting on my left to stand up.

"When I asked people a moment ago to focus on some hurt, what did you focus on?"

"My abortion."

"You had an abortion. OK. How old were you at the time?"

"Twenty-one or twenty-two."

"Well, people make mistakes. Are you Christian?"

"Yes."

"You've asked the Lord to forgive you?"

"Yes."

The woman went on to tell Larson she was raised in a "terrible home" that she was kicked out of by an abusive father.

"What were you feeling back there?" Larson asked, pointing to the empty seat next to me.

"Pain. And hurt. And misery."

Larson anointed her with holy oil. "Don't try to figure out anything I do here, just go with it. And if you feel something evil inside you, let it rip. Look at me."

Larson stared at the woman and began to angrily scold Satan for cursing her womb. He yelled at the demons Death and Murder. "Just let it overtake you, let it look at me—it's evil. Look at me. You're going to stop, Satan, you're going to *stop it now!*"

No demons manifested. The woman just stood there, looking like she might be hyperventilating, with tears streaming down her face.

"You've got demons. You're so terrified, you're getting in the way of them. I understand; I'm not making a criticism, just an observation. Your terror is getting in the way of me getting to the demons. You need to relax and in your mind say, *Lord, let me be in your presence so I can be healed.*"

Larson switched his message back to the demons: "You won't be able to hide forever, Satan! How long do you think you can hide? I know Death and Murder are there, I know my old nemesis Jezebel is there . . . who else? Well, if I don't get you now, I'll get you later. Do I just need to put you in torment? OK, you got that, Satan? Torment . . . *torment!*"

The woman just continued to stand there, weeping, frightened. With no demons manifesting, Rev. Larson explained that she should step to the side and he would return to her.

"OK, we're going to get to this. It's just right now you're just so emotional about all this, it's a bit of a challenge, but that's OK."

▲▲▲

"I want you to come up here. C'mon. What's your first name?"

"Kimberly," said the woman who'd been sitting across the aisle from me.

"Kimberly? How old are you, Kimberly?"

Kimberly said she was thirty-one, single, and had three children. Larson led her through a curse-breaking prayer to ensure they were "bastards no more."

"What were you so touched by out there?" Rev. Larson asked, pointing to her empty chair.

"Oh . . . I . . ." she said, beginning to sob heavily. "I . . ."

"Help me out here."

"Since I was a uh . . . a little uh . . ."

"Since you were a little girl what?"

"It came in my room . . . at night . . . and I couldn't move. And . . . it's embarrassing."

"What?" Rev. Larson said. Kimberly was so upset that Larson couldn't understand what she was saying.

"It's embarrassing."

"What?"

"Embarrassing."

"What? Nothing's embarrassing. You were asleep and couldn't move, and you felt like someone tried to have sex with you,* or touch you, or molest you?"

"Yes."

"Of course, it happens to lots of women; it's just no one wants to talk about it. Don't feel badly. It's not your fault! You're not some kind of pervert. It's just, there's a curse somewhere that's opened you up to this. It's happened to a lot of women in this room. They're just

---

* There is a name for this type of demon—an Incubus. The female equivalent is a Succubus. These demons allegedly appear in dreams in the form of humans to seduce their prey into sexual activity.

embarrassed to talk about it. Bring her a Kleenex. What other problems you got?" Larson asked, as she wiped her face with the tissue.

"I can't sleep at night. I lost everything . . . because of my boy . . . friend," she could hardly say the word.

"Who's your boyfriend? Is he a bad dude?"

"Yeah."

"How bad? Drug addict?"

"No, he's abusive."

"Abusive to you?"

Kimberly nodded, tears streaming down her face. "He got my house tear-gassed up."

"He had your house *tear-gassed?*"

"The police."

"The police came after him?"

"Yes."

Larson led her through another curse-breaking prayer. No demons manifested there either, so he had her go stand by the first woman, then called up the woman sitting behind me, who had been saying "Please, please, God, help me" over and over. With the three crying women at the front and Larson with his dyed hair, clashing suit, and microphone, he looked like the host of a strange '70s game show, *Let's Meet Your Demons!*

$$\blacktriangle \blacktriangle \blacktriangle$$

"My opinion of Larson's activity is that it is more akin to primal scream therapy than legitimate exorcism," Father Jack Ashcraft told me. Father Ashcraft is also an exorcist and a Byzantine Catholic priest from Kentucky. He has embraced new technology like Larson has, maintaining a blog titled *The Bare Fisted Cleric*, but has used that forum to criticize Larson as "the unreal exorcist."

"Suffice it to say that Larson is not considered a valid exorcist by any legitimate church, as he is not Catholic, Orthodox, or Anglo-Catholic, is not a priest, and has no formal training under a priest who has experience in this area of ministry," Father Ashcraft blogged.

I asked him to explain what he thought was going on in Rev. Larson's exorcism sessions.

"In all of the videos I've seen he appears to manipulate his audiences' emotional hurts and perhaps religious predisposition to acting out (most of these appear to be from the fringes of the evangelical movement) and, rather than acknowledging the mental and emotional scars as psychological issues in need of pastoral counseling and perhaps psychological assistance as well, these people act out the trauma by assigning it a name (such as lust, fear, witchcraft, death) and emote dramatically," Father Ashcraft wrote me. "This also may be a way for them to add some sort of affirmation to their faith by manufacturing a 'religious experience.' Do I believe he is actually performing exorcisms? No."

▲ ▲ ▲

"What's the issue, Carol?" Larson was making his last-ditch effort with the last one he called up, the one saying "Please, please, God, help me."

"Tormented by demons. It's always attached to me, follows me. Terrible smells."

"You stop following this woman, Satan! She doesn't want you anymore! You get out of her life! I take the sword of the spirit and I pierce you with it!" Larson pressed his Bible against her.

But this woman, Carol, just stood there crying, too.

"All these demons are hiding tonight! I can see them. Let your fear out, get it out. Get out of this woman's life!"

"Help me," Carol sobbed.

"OK, I'm trying to help you, but let me tell you, here's the problem. When you're in a sense of despair, I can't get to the demons. I mean, that's just the way it works. You have to be in a fighting mentality."

Larson, feeling he had exhausted his demon possibilities, decided to wrap it up and get to the offering. "It's not uncommon to meet roadblocks like this," Larson explained to us on the failed demon appearances.

"We're going to take an offering. No one's said anything about money all night. Not a word! Just teach, minister, help. Well, we got some bills to pay. I got a plane ticket to buy, and I need your help to do it. If a buck is all you got, that's wonderful. We got to finance this thing . . . we need some of you to give $5 if that's all you got, but I need some of you to give $500 or $1,000. And I don't apologize for that. And for everyone who gives a gift of $100 dollars or more, I'm going to give you a cross, and I'm going to pray over it and anoint it, and you're going to use it as an instrument to bash the devil!"

After offering more incentives—all the books and doodads on a list for $500 or more, Larson added, "I'm going to ask you to take out that checkbook, that credit card, and help us in a very, very generous way." Larson was about to lead us in another prayer, when he was distracted by an audience member with a question. I used the opportunity to exit the room faster than I've ever exited a room in my life.

It was extremely hot and stuffy, and I gasped to breathe the secular air as I walked down the hallway. All of the yelling and crying had left me emotionally drained, too. I felt angry, like maybe one of those alleged demons had come to roost on me, like in Larson's stick figure illustration.

As I walked back to the Blue Line, I thought of the name of Larson's ministry: Do What Jesus Did. I had a hard time imaging Jesus flying from airport hotel to airport hotel in a plaid suit, hawking two-for-one specials on his books and screaming through a microphone at alleged demons hiding inside of hysterical, sobbing women.

« 11 »

SOMETHIN' SKUNKY

IT WAS LATE WHEN WE PULLED INTO the Trail Lakes Campground. My friend
Sarah and I had driven from her home in Arcadia, Florida, to Naples,
where we picked up her friend Elette. From there we began cruising
into the Everglades on the Tamiami Trail, a passageway that starts
in Tampa and turns into a two-lane highway that connects Naples
on the west coast of Florida with Miami on the east. A chorus of
chirping insects filled the night sky as we cruised through the saw
grass lining the roads. Not a lot was out here—an occasional crab

shack or billboard for an airboat tour. Our destination was Ochopee, a small, unincorporated community close to Everglades City, a town of less than five hundred people.

Arriving at Ochopee, we followed a road down into the campground and found the "night office," a trailer where a heavyset, mustached man in a baseball cap was smoking a cigarette and leaning on the trailer's small wooden porch. He introduced himself as Kelly, "but folks call me Kell."

I explained to him that my friends were dropping me off and that I wanted a site to set up my tent so I could camp out for two nights. Kell jumped on a four-wheeler and led us deeper into the campground. There were giant piles of dirt and construction machinery everywhere—a bulldozer and a backhoe with a bumper sticker slapped on it, inviting the reader to ASK ME ABOUT THE SKUNK APE. It was a mix between a campground and a construction zone.

"This is a good one," he said, pointing to a site near a palm tree and a giant fern plant. "High ground, won't flood. The bathrooms are over there," he said, pointing into the complete darkness. "Make sure you shine your flashlight on the ground in front of you. There's potholes and piles of dirt and sometimes snakes."

"Snakes?" I said.

"Rattlesnakes, sometimes, yeah. Look out for them."

"Any other animals I should look out for?"

"Naw," Kell said, thinking a moment. "I haven't seen any gators here in a while."

I quickly set up my tent in the headlights of Sarah's car. Hundreds of bugs were descending, attracted by the light. I started a fire, and then Sarah and Elette wished me luck and took off. I sat down by the fire. Now I was alone in the swamp.

▲▲▲

The next morning I woke early, along with the hot sun, and stumbled toward the bathroom, keeping a bleary eye open for snakes.

"Mornin'!" I heard someone call, and saw a bald man wearing mirrored sunglasses, jeans, knee-high rubber fishing boots, and no shirt walking up the path behind me. I waved and kept walking.

As I approached the bathroom, it dawned on me who I had just encountered. Dave Shealy: Skunk Ape expert.

▲ ▲ ▲

People report Bigfoot-like creatures all over the United States and the world. They're also commonly known as Sasquatch, particularly in the Pacific Northwest. In the Himalaya Mountains, they're called Yetis. Australians call them Yowies. In China they are Yerens, and in South America, they're known as Mapinguaris.

Bigfoot is also spotted in the American South, where he is known by a variety of names. Some Southerners call him Wood Booger or the Stink Ape or the Swamp Ape. In the Everglades region and other parts of Florida, the creatures are most commonly called the Skunk Ape. As explained in *Cryptozoology A to Z*, the Skunk Ape gets his name from his "distinct and far-ranging aroma redolent of an unholy mixture of skunk, rotten eggs, and cow manure." The guide says spottings have occurred throughout Florida for a long time, dating back to the 1950s, with a wave of sighting and interest in the 1970s, followed by another wave in the late 1990s and early 2000s.

Loren Coleman, who has been to Florida several times to search for the Skunk Ape and interview witnesses, was also an investigator in a key piece of alleged Skunk Ape evidence: the Myakka Ape Photographs of 2000. The pictures depict a hairy, grimacing cryptid and were sent with an anonymous letter to the Sarasota County Sheriff's Office. The letter reported that the creature was frequenting the person's backyard, poaching apples from a basket on the porch.

Inevitably, speculation on what the photos depicted varied quite a bit. Some suggested the photos were a hoax, perhaps a cardboard cutout. Experts studied the photos, weighing in on the eyeshine, pupil contraction, and facial expression. Coleman suggested that the creature could be an escaped or feral *Pongo pygmaeus abelii*, a Sumatran orangutan.

Skunk Ape Research Center

Dave Shealy is a native of the Everglades. His grandfather and father grew up in Miami. In the 1930s and '40s, Shealy's father and his friends would spend their spare time hunting in the Everglades.

As the 1960s approached, Shealy's father grew tired of city living and wanted to establish some land out in the Everglades. In 1961 he bought the land that the Trail Lakes Campground currently stands on. Dave Shealy was born in 1963.

Shealy said his father "fell into" the campground business. People would stop by and pay or barter something to set up tents on the land to do some hunting. "It got kind of popular," Shealy said. In the late 1960s the land was officially licensed as a campground.

Shealy and his brother Jack took over the business after their father died at the age of fifty. They originally billed their business as the Florida Panther Gift Shop—a gigantic fiberglass panther still lurks by the side of the road near the campground—but in the late 1990s they switched the top billing from panthers to Skunk Apes.

The switch coincided with a string of Skunk Ape sightings in the Ochopee area that were the talk of the town. Among others, a busload of tourists spotted a "large, apelike creature" ambling through the swamp in 1997. Soon Shealy stepped in to declare himself a Skunk Ape expert. Shealy and Jack renamed their establishment the Skunk Ape Headquarters and Trail Lakes Campground.

Shealy claimed he actually first spotted the smelly creature at a young age. "The first time I saw the Skunk Ape, I was just ten years old and I was out hunting with my brother," Shealy said in an interview for a 2008 PBS documentary, *Escape to Dreamland: The Story of the Tamiami Trail.*

"We had a rule in the house that if we could kill a deer before the school bus came, we got to stay home and package the meat, so we were always eager to get out early in the morning and see if we couldn't bag a deer. That particular morning it was raining, just drizzling a little bit. We walked on back, and my brother saw something in the distance, but I couldn't see it because I couldn't see over the grass. So he had to pick me up, and when he picked me up, there it was, a hundred yards out, definitely a Skunk Ape. We had heard about them growing up, and we were like ten years old, but there it was right in front of us. It was amazing."

After he established his Skunk Ape Research Center, fortune again smiled on Shealy, he claimed. He said he spent an hour or two every evening in a tree stand he set up, just a short distance from my tent, every day for eight months. Finally, on September 8, 1998, he spotted a Skunk Ape strolling through the grasslands in the distance, and Shealy began shooting pictures. He took a roll of twenty-seven somewhat blurry pictures altogether. One of these photos is the center of a small display in the Skunk Ape Research Center.

"I dozed off for a little while, and when I woke up I saw it coming straight at me. At first I thought it was a man, but then I realized it was the Skunk Ape," Shealy said days after the sighting.

Shealy has tried to get support for his cause. In 1999 he attempted to get a $44,000 tourist-tax-dollar grant from the Collier County Commission. His breakdown was $20,000 to fund two expeditions to search for the elusive Skunk Apes, with the remainder financing Shealy's public appearances and a "Skunk Ape hotline" with operators who could answer Skunk Ape and general tourist questions in English, Spanish, and German.

Shealy's grant proposal was denied.

But Shealy began to get attention from far and wide with his Skunk Ape stories, and he started making media appearances. In some of those appearances, he was dressed rather like Crocodile Dundee, in a safari shirt and a hat adorned with a gator tooth. He was a mix of cryptozoologist, big-game hunter, and charismatic southern big fish storyteller.

He became the go-to guy when shows wanted to do a Skunk Ape story and get a quirky news bit. He continued to pop up regularly, particularly on the "strange travel" type of shows popular on cable. The night before I arrived in Ochopee, he had been featured on the Travel Channel's *Weird Travels* program.

▲▲▲

After waking up, seeing Shealy, and going to the bathroom, I headed up to the Skunk Ape Research Center to pay for my campsite and introduce myself. Shealy was sitting on a bench outside, the sun beating down on him, a pint glass of iced coffee in his hand.

"I'm just going to sit here and talk to people about Skunk Apes for a little while," Shealy called over to his brother Jack. Then he spotted me approaching and stood up to shake my hand.

"Good mornin'!" he said. "Got in late last night, huh? What brings you here?" he asked, smiling. I told him I was there to learn about Skunk Apes.

"Well, you came at a great time!" Shealy said, while Jack smiled in the background. "I got a show, a new show that they shot here, about to be on the Discovery Channel! October 8," he said. That date was about ten days away.

"Great!" I told him. "I'll be sure to check that out. Yeah, I'm actually working on a book where I'm traveling around meeting different monster hunters and writing about them . . ."

I immediately saw some sort of alarm bells going off with Shealy. He was now giving me a wary, suspicious look. He looked at his brother Jack, and the two passed communication to each other through facial expressions. I read Jack's face as saying, *Who is this guy? Be careful what you say.* Dave's cool expression in response was *Roger that, good buddy.*

I don't usually drop in unannounced on people, but in this case, it had seemed like the best option. I had tried to e-mail a couple times, with no reply. Maybe they don't have a lot of Internet time in the swamp, I surmised. Next, I tried calling. After the phone rang a dozen times, someone picked up.

"Yeah," a voice said.

"Uh . . . is this the Skunk Ape Research Center?"

"Yep."

"I'm traveling down there in late September, and I'd like to reserve a campsite."

"Don't need no reservation that time of year."

"Oh, OK. I'm working on a book about monsters—like the Skunk Ape—and people that study them. I'd like to talk to Dave Shealy about them . . ."

"Yep. He's the Skunk Ape guy. And he's here all the time, so he'll be here. OK, then?"

I decided it was best to just take a gamble and show up and see what happened. And now I was standing in front of Dave Shealy, Skunk Ape expert, trying to explain myself. I realized my Midwestern accent clearly pointing to the fact I was a Yankee wasn't helping my case, so I made a note to slow down my speech and try to filter that twang, try to drop the nasally "-ing" sound on my present participles.

"So," I continued, "I hope you don't mind me hangin' 'round here and listenin' to what you have to say about Skunk Apes."

"Yeah," Shealy said. I could see him calculating his next step with me.

"Yeah. OK. That's great. And we're glad to have you here . . ." He said that in a weird tone, like someone trying to back out of a hostage situation. He backed away from me and shot a glance to his brother, who was smiling politely and remaining quiet.

"And you . . . why don't you come with me? You can meet Rick! He's our reptile expert!"

We walked through the Skunk Ape Research Center, which was actually just a souvenir shop with a small shrine dedicated to the Skunk Ape in a corner. The display had a photo and a plaster cast of a Skunk Ape footprint. There was a giant, red-eyed statue of a gorilla in the middle of the shop, a popular photo op for the tourists. The shop offered a variety of stuffed alligator heads and merchandise—T-shirts, shot glasses, beer cozies—that featured a Skunk Ape on it. We walked through the shop into what looked like a remodeled airboat hanger–style garage. There were a couple dozen giant tanks and a large cage in the middle of the space.

"Rick? Rick!" Shealy called, looking around. A bald man in a tank top and shorts appeared in an open garage door leading to a small outdoor enclosure, where the squawking of parrots could be heard.

"Oh, there you are! This here . . . this—gentleman—is here . . . he's workin' on writin' a—book—and here, Rick'll show you around here and tell you all about our reptiles."

"OK," I said. "Thanks, Rick."

"OK, then," Shealy said, backing away from me. "I got a bunch of dirt here—you probably seen all the piles of it. I got a guy comin' in, gonna help me with movin' it around. I can talk to you maybe an hour, but it'll be ten minutes here, a few minutes there, whenever I get a few minutes. You just come and find me."

"OK," I said. "Sure. Whatever works for you."

And then Shealy retreated and I was alone with Rick.

Rick began leading me through his reptile zoo, starting by plopping a baby alligator in my arms. It felt like a cold leather bag. He called out the window of the hanger to the full-grown alligators in an enclosed pen with a small pond in it. He told me the gators' names were "Lumpy, Grumpy, and the Other One." Grumpy was getting some sun while the other two lurked in the pond. He showed me a snapping turtle and some rat snakes. Most impressive in the collection was the biggest snake I had ever seen—a huge, fat reticulated python named Goldie. Rick said it was about thirty-two feet long and 250 to 300 pounds. We walked outside to the enclosed area.

"Most of these animals are rescues. They've been given to me by people who either didn't want them or weren't in a position to take care of them," Rick told me, offering a pair of tortoises an apple. He placed a noisy cockatoo named Dodo on my shoulder while a macaw screeched nearby. After the tour, I stopped back in the Skunk Ape Research Center, where I picked out a T-shirt and Shealy's guidebook, *Everglades Skunk Ape Research Field Guide*, a seventeen-page photocopied booklet written by Shealy and illustrated by Kell, sold in the gift shop for $4.95. It featured a variety of tips for tracking the highly elusive Skunk Ape as well as facts on the lives of Skunk Apes that Shealy appeared to have collected through unknown methods. For example, he claimed in his guide that "7 to 9 Skunk Apes make the Everglades their home." He also said Skunk Apes probably got their foul odor from hiding out in alligator caves.

"Evidence suggests that Skunk Apes spend a great deal of time in these underground caverns. Many people believe that methane gas, emitted by decaying matter in these low-lying areas are what gives the Skunk Ape its unique skunky / rotten egg odor," the guide said.

Shealy's brother—heavy, red-faced, sweaty—rang up my purchase. "I don't know nothing about monsters," he said. "You'll have to ask Dave about that. He'll be glad to autograph your book, here, too. Just ask him."

I left the gift shop and headed back to camp to eat. Later in the morning I walked around and looked for Shealy. I didn't see him anywhere. Hours later, early in the afternoon, I spotted him with his hands resting on the top of a car. I walked toward him.

"He should be here in a couple hours, and then we're goin' to work," Shealy was telling the man in the driver's seat. "We're goin' to work until dark! Today's my birthday. I'm fifty. Yeah, fifty right now. We're getting old, Donald! October 8, yep," he said, and the car drove off.

"Well, happy birthday!" I told him. I found out later it was a significant milestone for him. Shealy's father had died at the age of fifty. His mom died around the same age, too.

"Thanks," he said.

"So what's going on here?" I asked, gesturing to a row of dirt piles.

"That's the state making up for some wrongdoing," he told me. "I just put a truck of asphalt on the parking lot. I'm making some sites, expanding my tenting area. I'm not putting cabins on all of them, but I'm just making them nice, landscaping. I got to have them all done in thirty days!" Shealy gestured toward his campground in general.

"My son is fixin' to take over the business soon, and I don't want to work so hard anymore, so I've been double-timin' it. I've only had one day off in a hundred days. One day! One hundred days. It's my birthday today and I'm workin'!" Now appraising me again, Shealy started to back up.

"Well, Jerome is not here—he's the guy running equipment. . . . But when he's here, that's when we can sit down and talk a minute," he said, turning and walking up the dirt road out of the campground.

It was early afternoon by now and despite being the end of September, it was intensely hot. It was too hot to be inside my tent, so I dragged a blanket out, put it in the shade, and took a fitful nap. I woke up sweating, and when I opened my eyes, I saw a couple of buzzards circling above me.

Well, that's an ominous sign, I thought.

I got up and walked around the campground. I didn't see Shealy anywhere. In fact, the whole place seemed deserted. I took a short walk through the swamp but didn't see—or smell—anything skunky.

My notes on the day after the reptile zoo tour had one entry: "No sign of Dave."

▲▲▲

As the sun set, I made a campfire. Then I reached into my cooler and grabbed a beer. I had brought the beer along as bait for Shealy to talk to me. Through various sources, I had gleaned that the man liked to drink, and there is nothing that will get someone to start telling his life story and deepest confessions like a steady supply of alcohol.

A few beers in and I was deeply reflecting on just what I was doing here in the middle of the Everglades when I saw headlights roll into the campground and then heard heated voices. One was Shealy, intoxicated and arguing with someone.

"You and your people—that's the reason these *damn trails got ruined! So get the fuck out!*" he screamed at someone, slamming a door.

"Whatever, Dave," I heard a disgusted voice respond, then a door slamming.

I stoked the fire and opened another beer. *Probably not a good time to approach Shealy,* I thought. I began to cook up some lima beans I had brought along. The lima beans were something of an inside joke. I chose lima beans for dinner because that was what Shealy recommended as bait for Skunk Apes.

From the *Everglades Skunk Ape Research Field Guide*: "Black eye peas, pinto, and kidney beans all work well, however large lima beans are the recommended bait and should be considered your first choice."

But the joke of the lima beans now fell a little flat with me. Before I even pulled into the campground, I was pretty much 100 percent certain that the Skunk Ape—well, Shealy's alleged Skunk Apes, at least—were fake.

Hoaxers

"What do you know about Dave and his claims?" Loren Coleman had asked me at the International Cryptozoology Museum. I had told him that the Skunk Ape Research Center was my next stop after I visited him.

"Well," I said, "I hear a lot of claims that he's a hoaxer."

"Oh, he's all but admitted it!" Coleman replied. "It was his brother in a suit."

Coleman continued, "The thing about David—it's like a lot of people you meet in this field—one-to-one, he's a wonderful guy. He's nice, he donated a statue that he sent up with a guy from Connecticut, he's always said good things about me, and I want to say good things about him. He was arrested for marijuana trafficking [and got] three years—I don't hold that against him.

"What's wrong with David is he is so interested in attention seeking that he'll hoax these films. My whole notion about the Skunk Ape of Florida is that they are chimpanzee-sized creatures that go down on all fours. David is the focal point for so many journalists going down to talk about Skunk Ape and his museum roadside attraction, and his descriptions of the Skunk Ape are that it is six or seven feet tall and always upright, because that's the suit he has.

"It's not so much about David but what he's done to the field down there; he's polluted it so much that it's now distracted in the wrong direction. Even though I've been investigating these things since the '60s, if I get on a program and say they are littler, they go down on all fours, people say, 'You don't know what you're talking about!' because they got the mythical Skunk Ape in their head now."

The Internet seems to be in agreement about Shealy being a hoaxer.

On the forum Above Top Secret, an author using the name "maxhile" posted an entry on November 2, 2010, that claimed his mother was an old friend of Shealy's and had told him (along with others) that Dave and Jack had hoaxed the Skunk Ape photos. Maxhile writes: "I eventually got the courage to ask Dave Shealy himself if it was just a hoax. Expecting a defensive rant he surprisingly started laughing hysterically and admitted to the scam. He said that he and his brother, along with some friends had conjured up the elaborate scheme while having a few tall ones around a fire on his campground, ultimately trying to get a rise out of the government and media."

This posting is from an administrator at the Mid-America Bigfoot Research forums: "After travelling to Ochopee many times, I had determined that anything happening in this area are hoaxes perpetrated by David, and probably his brother. Their agenda seemed obvious; getting tourists into their Gift Shop and Campsite."

I read several comments from people saying they were members of the Bigfoot community and the Ochopee community, and they all seemed to agree on one thing: Shealy and his brother Jack had concocted the Skunk Ape appearance at the Trail Lakes Campground as a publicity-grabbing hoax to boost business.

▲ ▲ ▲

I encountered another well-publicized hoax while writing this book. Rick Dyer, self-proclaimed "Best Bigfoot Tracker in the World," is a cowboy hat–wearing, soul patch–sporting used-car salesman who claimed he had lured a Bigfoot he dubbed Hank into his camp with a side of pork ribs, then shot him. After a lot of hoopla, Dyer announced he was taking Hank, stuffed and on display in a glass case, out on the road to give the public the chance to throw down some cash to take a look at him.

Bigfooters had already come to view Dyer as a four-letter word, a name that drew as much revulsion as Harry Potter's nemesis Voldemort. Dyer, along with his friend sheriff's deputy Matt Whitton, had already pulled a similar stunt in 2008, known as the Georgia Hoax. The duo came up with pictures of a Bigfoot body stored in a large refrigerator.

The case was reviewed at length by Matt Moneymaker on BFRO's website. Moneymaker said the two paired up with "infamous hoaxer" and Las Vegas showman Carmine "Tom" Biscardi. They then had the perfect trifecta for a con: Whitton's credibility as a deputy sheriff,

Biscardi's hoaxing experience, and Dyer's ability to talk out of both sides of his face at once. The goal: to make money.

On August 15, 2008, Biscardi, Dyer, and Whitton held a press conference in Palo Alto, California, that received a tremendous amount of coverage. Meanwhile, BFRO had already identified what was in the Bigfoot pictures. "The 'body' was a widely available Halloween costume stuffed into a large cooler and filled with rotting animal entrails," Moneymaker reported.

But the public has a short memory for such things, so when Dyer returned with claims of a new Bigfoot body and set off on his Time to Believe tour in 2014, a lot of media fell for the story hook, line, and sinker. "Fool us twice," they begged him.

I almost encountered Dyer and Hank. The tour had approached the International UFO Congress, asking to set up shop as part of the conference. As I power-walked around the convention floor with Maureen Elsberry, she told me that after Open Minds staffers discussed it, they decided to pass. "We talked about it for a minute," she told me, standing still for a second. "We thought about potential publicity and media for the conference but then determined we had a lot of good media already and didn't want to be associated with what is a pretty obvious hoax."

Despite rejection in Arizona, the tour went on to have success elsewhere, and one source puts Dyer's tour earnings at about $60,000. For reasons unknown, Dyer admitted the hoax on his Facebook page in April 2014, and it soon came out that this time, instead of relying on a commercially manufactured Bigfoot suit, he had paid a costume and prop maker to create the body out of latex and fake hair.

"Dyer is a bump in the road, one we have experienced too often," Loren Coleman wrote in a blog post. "But he is not cryptozoology. That is for certain and those that wish to dig deeper will soon discover that fact."

▲▲▲

Hoaxing is still a pastime for some, one greatly aided by the gullibility of the Internet. Fake or doctored videos and pictures spring up all the time and circulate through social media. A simple download of a phone app can help insert UFOs and ghosts into a photo with a flick of a fingertip.

I thought about all this as I stared at my fire in the campground. I had been hoping to get a chance to talk to Shealy and try to see what he had to say, but it looked like it was a bust.

A Voyage to the Circle K

I awoke with the sun again the next day and again made my first destination the bathroom. I was walking back toward my tent when I heard Shealy's voice say, "Hey, how long are you around for today?"

I looked around and saw Shealy standing in the screen door of his trailer. I had immediately figured that this was his house. A carved sign that read EAGLE'S NEST was posted above the door. Centrally located, Shealy's trailer was elevated and overlooked a small pond, giving him a grand view of his campground kingdom and the Everglades beyond.

"I'm gettin' picked up around eleven or twelve today," I said.

"Well, I got to make a run to the Circle K in Everglades City. You want to ride along?"

"Yeah, absolutely," I said. He told me he'd pick me up from my site in fifteen minutes.

When Shealy pulled up in his truck, I hopped in the passenger seat. He immediately began laying out the story of his land and the struggle he had had with it.

"The government stepped in and built five campgrounds around me twenty-five years ago," Shealy explained, growing bitter at the memory. "If you go in their visitor's center and ask them where to camp, they won't even tell you I exist! They told my son they are trying to stop 'socially transmitted behavior.' That means 'Don't grow up to be like your old man, or we're going to treat you like we treated him,'" Shealy said, staring at me as he wheeled his truck around. "That's fucked up!"

He continued, "If you look at my financial records over the last twenty-five years, I've lived in poverty. Less than $12,000 a year went into my pocket for food and stuff because I sacrificed everything. My whole life I've sacrificed to hold on to this place. And they"—Shealy always means the government in some form when he says "they"— "they've taken my airboat trails—illegally—and put them into their campgrounds, my swamp buggy trails. It's all been illegally taken!"

We pulled into a site where a couple of tents were set up next to some trucks. Shealy explained that some young people had come out to celebrate one of their twenty-first birthdays. I had heard them partying the night before.

"We're going to Circle K in Everglade. You need anythin'?" Shealy asked a shirtless young man who looked badly hungover. He shook his head no.

"OK. That drink knocked me on the ground. I don't know if it was the shots or the drink, but I went out like a light!" Shealy laughed, then pulled out.

"So last night I ran into this guy named Nate—he made my Skunk Ape video, and he works, but his work. . . . He's got this big house in Naples with a big yard and a barn, and his work is music, and he has a studio and friends over and parties and going to this tavern and this cigar bar and this hotel and having *fun!* Sometimes when he talks to me, when I tell him I've been living in poverty for twenty-five years, he just sees what's in front of him.

"'Oh, how can you say that? This isn't poverty,'" Shealy said, imitating a stupid, whiny voice. "I do without food. I do without food to pay the light bill! So I said, 'Fuck you, motherfucker!' We got in a fight. Not a fistfight—he just don't see." That explained the argument I had heard in the dark.

We stopped to check in with Kell on our way out of the campground.

"Those kids still out there?" Kell asked, puffing on a cigarette.

"Yeah. They give you any trouble last night?" Shealy asked.

"No, no problem. They went out and I was just wonderin' if they came back."

"Those are some sweet little girls," Shealy told him, grinning dev-ilishly. It soon became clear to me that Shealy's libido had been cook-ing out here in the hot sun. "He told me they would have brought me a sweet little girl out, but they were heading this way when I told them I was looking for one. I think on my fiftieth birthday a nineteen-year-old girl would probably kill me anyhow!" Shealy chortled.

Realizing a writer was sitting next to him in his truck, Shealy decided further clarification was in order. "His birthday is the same birthday as mine. Young people come in here to have parties, and I ain't never had any problems. And I never screwed any teenybopper, never even thought about it, believe it or not, even though I'm a horndog. . . . I know my age limits." Later in Everglades City, Shealy pointed out a club where he said a manager was "a lush. She's got big tits." And another spot where an employee "has big titties."

Next we stopped by the parking lot outside of the Skunk Ape Research Center.

"Hey, Jack!" Shealy called out. "I'm riding over to Circle K. You need anything? No? OK. Good morning."

"You got someone in there with you?" Jack asked suspiciously.

"Yeah, guy back from the tent area. I didn't get a chance to talk with him much yesterday, so we're just going to shoot the bull and go for a quick ride."

Now on the Tamiami Trail, I asked Shealy about the history of the land and his father's decision to buy undeveloped Everglades property.

"The government sold it to him knowing there was no way he could pay for the land, no way he could come up with that money. My dad . . ." Shealy paused. "He was a hard worker. He had a lot of friends, and he wasn't afraid to bend the law if he had to. So before he developed the land, he made a foot trail from 41 to the back of the property, and he built a giant moonshine still back there.

"He brought in this guy named Mousey, who wore these big Coke-bottle glasses. Loved Chihuahuas. Mousey produced thou-sands of gallons of jugs of moonshine, rum. They had a wagon with what looked like a fuel tank, but there was moonshine in it, and they shipped it up to Miami and Liberty City. They made *a lot* of money. So the land was paid for. My dad worked, too. While Mousey was making moonshine, my dad was doing equipment repair.

"They finally got my dad with the moonshine still, but that was quite a few years later, because I remember it. There was a bunch of cars that pulled in back where our trailer was, and they got out and knocked on our door. My dad said, 'I don't know nothing about it.' They destroyed the still but didn't arrest him."

Like father, like son they say. Shealy got in trouble for his own illegal dealings in the 1980s. "Rum running, feather plume hunting, alligator hunting, and then marijuana running was my generation. I went to prison for that. You knew that, right?" he asked, looking sideways at me before turning his attention back to the road.

"Yeah," I said. "I saw a video on YouTube where you talked a little about it."

"I spent three years in prison on an air force base. I was maybe going to get sixty-five years, but I got three years for it, 1987. I got caught moving four tons of weed—that's over eight thousand pounds. There were two hundred of us arrested. We were arrested by Bush Sr.'s presidential task force. They had all the roads sealed up here," Shealy said, gesturing to an intersection ahead of us. "I was arrested in what was called Operation Peacemaker, which was the final pickup of a three-part drug raid that lasted a couple years. There was a lot of people in jail and a lot of people that didn't want to go to jail. Well, things started to get violent. And what happened was, there was an investigation, and a key witness started to point fingers. He said, 'Yeah, Dave was there, I saw him.' A car exploded; he got killed with a car bomb. And so I became a suspect, because here was this guy that was going to testify against me, and all of a sudden his car blows up. Of course I didn't do it."

Though cleared of the car bombing, Shealy still faced his marijuana smuggling charges. "I got up and pleaded guilty. I said, 'I made a bad decision, I'm sorry. . .'" Shealy took a long pause, staring at the road, thinking of that day long ago in court. "I apologize. I'm guilty."

The judge was lenient and gave him three years.

▲ ▲ ▲

After buying a coffee and a few packs of cigarettes at the Circle K, Shealy decided to head over to the docks to say hi to some fishermen he knew.

"I got my television series gonna start October 8 on Discovery," he told them. "They're gonna do a one-hour special. I was on Travel Channel last night." After chatting with them, we stopped in a bait and tackle store for a chat with the employees.

"I told your brother to order me some Skunk Ape golf shirts," one of the shopkeepers told Shealy. "Collared ones. I'll buy half a dozen to send out to people."

"OK, I'll get you some. We're going to be getting that stuff in probably sixty days. I got my series starting on Discovery Channel— October 8." Shealy bought us both a can of Coke and a handful of Slim Jims. Then we cruised around Everglades City a little bit, and I asked him about his upcoming reality show.

"I would say in about ten days I'll get offered a million dollars. So it'll all come to an end. Thank God! I'll finally get my life back. But I'll probably have to do twenty more episodes. Each one takes a week, so twenty weeks. I'm cruisin' for a bruisin'! But I need the money."

But with fame comes certain headaches, and Shealy had already begun to feel the hardships of being the Skunk Ape expert. "It's . . . everyone wants to be the man, everyone wants to be the guy. When you walk in the bar, everyone is like, 'Hell yeah! Whoa! *Woo woo!*'" Shealy explained, whooping it up while he drove. He grabbed the wheel with one hand and ripped a Slim Jim package open with his teeth.

"You know, you get what you ask for, but it's hard being a public figure like that, because you always got to be on your game," he said. Shealy's fame had also made him a target of various other Bigfooters, who derided him as being a scam artist.

"There is a lot of jealousy in the Bigfoot community. It was really awful in the beginning when I decided I was going to go public with it," Shealy told me. "They saw me as a threat to them. Because Bigfoot was talked about, they would call me up, belittling me, giving me a hard time."

"Did that surprise you? Did it piss you off?" I asked him.

Shealy thought about it, then said, "It's something I'll never forget. Because I know who they are."

Shealy has also had troubles with relationships, due in no small part to his pursuit of the Skunk Apes and his Everglades lifestyle. A 2010 short student documentary titled *They Live in Trees* featured Shealy, and he explained to the documentarians the personal troubles he's faced: "There's a lot of things I should have done that I haven't done. It's been a roller coaster ride. Bad relationship after bad relationship. I was on television one time, and the girl left me over it. I was on *The Daily Show*, Comedy Central, *Talk Soup*. She said all her friends at the office said I looked like an idiot," Shealy told the camera, raising his eyebrows. "And she left me! After, like, seven years! Let me tell you somethin,' shit flows downhill, and I live at the bottom of the hill."

"The more ratings, the more likely they are to send me an immediate payment to get it to go to series," he told me, as the road led us back to his world-famous Skunk Ape Research Center. "I hope it happens. I need the money."

▲▲▲

On October 8, Discovery Channel did air the first two episodes of *Skunk Ape*, back-to-back. The promo for the program shows Shealy inspecting the ground in the swamp just behind his campground, dressed in a camouflage windbreaker.

"I smelled that, right now," Shealy says, looking over his shoulder at the camera. "There's been a Skunk Ape here! Recently. Do you smell it?"

The camera follows him into the swamp in pursuit of the cryptid. Or maybe just in pursuit of fame and the money to be had from it.

"Yeah! There's definitely been a big animal in here," he says, examining the ground.

Unfortunately for Shealy, his quarry would elude him. After the episodes aired, *Skunk Ape* was dropped and did not go to series.

« 12 »
THE ACCIDENTAL WEREWOLF CHRONICLER

ISCONSIN AUTHOR LINDA S. GODFREY didn't set out to become a leading expert in the Manwolf phenomenon. She just kind of fell into it during the cold winter of 1991.

"I call myself the accidental werewolf chronicler because it was nothing that I thought of in my previous life as a career I might

219

someday have," Godfrey told me. She lived in the "quiet, conservative community" of Elkhorn with her husband and children. In the early 1990s she got a staff job at the small Walworth County newspaper the *Week*. Her original aim was to be an editorial cartoonist. She got her foot in the door at the paper when the editors agreed to run her cartoons if she accepted the small fee they paid for syndicated cartoons.

"As much as I liked it, I was finding it hard to be outraged by everything, which you need to do to draw an editorial cartoon every day. You need a really strong point of view, and I can usually see both sides of an issue," Godfrey told me. She next tried to develop a concept for a daily comic strip but found a career in the comics biz can be almost as difficult as trying to find a cryptid, which is what Godfrey would be doing next.

Like the staff of many small publications, Godfrey began wearing many hats and was soon using the skills she learned in journalism class to report news. One day she received a strange tip. "Someone told me that people around Elkhorn were reporting seeing something that reminded them of a werewolf on Bray Road, which is a two-mile stretch of country road just outside of town. So, just for fun, I checked into it. I found out a lot of people were talking about it, and I discovered our county animal control officer had a file folder in his office that was marked WEREWOLF. That fact made it news."

Godfrey tracked down some of the people who had supposedly witnessed the creature and began to piece together a frightening mystery. "[The witnesses] didn't strike me as jokers or liars. They seemed very sincere and frightened over what they experienced," Godfrey recalled. One of them even reported that they had seen the werewolf squatting by the side of the road munching on some roadkill.

Godfrey's article ran in the *Week* on December 31, 1991. "We thought it would probably cause some chuckles and be gone, but in two weeks it became national news," she told me. The two-page spread was just the first of hundreds of pages she would end up writing on the topic.

The Beast of Bray Road, as it had come to be known, drew attention from across the country. News vans rolled through Elkhorn to get reaction quotes from citizens and to shoot footage of Bray Road. As I would soon see when I went to visit Godfrey in Elkhorn, the country lane isn't quite the creepy Transylvanian forest people hope for but a tame stretch of subdivisions and cornfields.

Elkhorn reveled in its newfound celebrity monster as werewolf fever hit the town. A local bakery peddled "werewolf cookies." A tavern offered "silver bullet specials." The *Week* produced a T-shirt featuring an illustration of the beast by Godfrey that quickly sold out. A mayoral candidate even staged a publicity photo, claiming he had been endorsed by the cryptid.

All of this had the makings of a local legend, a small-town Wisconsin answer to Point Pleasant's Mothman. Soon Godfrey had another surprise, though: she discovered that similar reports of the creature were heading her way, not just from the Elkhorn area but from around the world.

"From that point on I sort of became the person people started sending their reports to and that media came to. As soon as the story appeared, I started getting phone calls and letters from all over." Godfrey continues to get these reports via e-mails, phone calls, and letters. She found that a similar creature was already legendary in Michigan, where it is commonly called the Dogman. She began researching the Algonquin legends of the Wendigo, a half-human beast associated with cannibalism that purportedly stalks the woods of the Midwest and Atlantic coast. Terrified and confused people have sent her reports from as far away as Germany.

Digging through a stack of recent e-mail correspondence she had printed off, she told me of a report sent earlier in the year from a hunter in Jefferson Parish, Louisiana. Godfrey said he reported he was hunting for wild boar and deer when he and his dog stumbled on a seven-foot Wolfman. "[He said] it was covered in black fur with some grayish stripes here and there. He backed up slowly and felt like it was following him. He felt threatened and fired on it, and it stumbled off into the brush."

▲▲▲

Godfrey began compiling all of this incoming information and her research into book format. *The Beast of Bray Road: Tailing Wisconsin's Werewolf* was her first book on the topic and was published in 2003. She began to record reports of other mystery animals—Bigfoot, Thunderbirds, Lizard Men, Lake Monsters—and she profiled these in books like *Monsters of Wisconsin* and *Weird Michigan*. Godfrey's magnum opus on the Manwolf phenomenon is a collection of reports on sightings published in 2012 titled *Real Wolfmen: True Encounters in Modern America*. Despite the title, Godfrey preferred to call the creature a Manwolf, because unlike the Hollywood werewolves we are familiar with, reports don't involve a human turning into a wolf under a full moon.

One of the most hair-raising stories in her recent book is from a chapter titled "Manwolf Multiples," in which she tells the story of a terrified couple from Palmyra, Maine, who claim that they were trapped in their home by a pack of Manwolves in 2007.

"They were sitting on their front porch at night and found themselves being stalked in their own yard by a total of five upright, wolf-like creatures, who were walking on their hind legs and flanking them. They were about seven feet tall, which they based on comparison to a door they passed by. They held them hostage in their house all night. The man couldn't get to his guns because they were locked in an outer building. They called 9-1-1, who told them to call a game warden. They could see the creatures lurking and prowling around their house."

With no nearby neighbors and fearing for relatives' safety, the couple braved the night until the creatures vanished in the early morning. "It's one of the longest contacts, and two credible witnesses who saw the same thing," Godfrey noted.

Skinwalkers

According to the Navajo (or Diné people) creation story (*Diné Bahane'*), the first monster hunters were twin brothers named *Naayéé' neizghání* (the Monster Slayer) and *Tó bájísh chíní* (Child of Water). In the brothers' world at the beginning of time, the land was overrun with the *Naayéé*, a group of gruesome monsters that devoured the brothers' people.

After disobeying their mother, the brothers caught the attention of *Yé'iitsoh* (Big Giant) and thus sought out their father, *Jóhonaa'éí* (the Sun) who provided them with the proper weapons to slay the giant. Wanting to rid the land of the bloodthirsty *Naayéé*, the brothers systematically used their brains and brawn to ambush *Déélgééd* (the Horned Monster) and *Tsé dah hódziiłtáłii* (Monster Who Kicks People Off of Cliffs), among others. After slaying these monsters and leaving their decapitated heads and hides spread across the desert, the brothers made the world a safer place for its new occupants, the Earth Surface People.

"All of these things happened a long, long time ago, it is said," according to the *Diné Bahane'*.

But there are still some who say the strange and the sinister still lurk in the Navajo Nation.

▲▲▲

Crypto Four Corners is a group based in Teec Nos Pos, inside the Navajo Nation. This, according to one of the group's founders, JC Johnson, is apparently a Fortean vortex. Johnson told me that his group has tried to track down a variety of cryptids in the Four Corners region of Colorado, Utah, Arizona, and New Mexico. These include (but aren't limited to) Sasquatch, Thunderbirds, Small People (three-foot-high people in traditional Diné dress, similar to Leprechauns), and something they dub the "Night Stalker," a flying, clawed monster that a New Mexico family claimed was terrorizing them.

And just like Linda Godfrey, they've investigated several reports of the Manwolf, or as Johnson prefers to call it, the Dogman. In Navajo Nation, though, Johnson says reports of Dogman can be confused with the *yee naaldlooshii* or Skinwalkers, which, according to Navajo beliefs, are evil witches who have the ability to shape-shift into animals. They can turn into any animal, but a common form is as a coyote or wolf. It's said if you look at their eyes, you'll be placed under a powerful mind control.

Johnson, a burly outdoorsman, founded C4C along with cryptid investigator David Ortiz and Diné chief Leonard Dan. They've investigated Skinwalker encounters, including one in a cave-dotted gorge locals have nicknamed Skinwalker Canyon. C4C is composed of an eclectic lineup of investigators, "half Navajo Diné," Johnson says. With their camo fatigues, generous supply of firearms, and a few heavily tattooed members, C4C looks like a zombie apocalypse survival team straight out of *The Walking Dead*.

C4C's eldest member, "researcher/tracker" Chief Dan, says that he first heard of the Skinwalkers from his grandparents. He says they were at one point helpful to the Diné people, spying on Spanish conquistadors, but eventually chose to take an evil path.

Johnson said in an interview that in order to become a Skinwalker, you must "sacrifice a loved one, sibling, child, someone close to you." You then "bring in the body to the group, that they might practice necrophilia, and then feast on some of the body parts. Later they will take some of the organs and make powders and potions." Skinwalker apprenticeship then begins.

The main difference between a Skinwalker and a Dogman, Johnson told me, is that a Skinwalker appears to be a normal person most of the time. "They could be sitting next to you in Sunday school at 9 AM, and at 9 PM they take the form of a wolf," Johnson said. Dogman, on the other hand, is a cryptid stuck in humanoid wolf form permanently.

A Trip Down Bray Road

Months after my phone interview with Linda Godfrey, I took a trip out to Elkhorn on April 12, 2014, with my photographer friend Lacy Landre. We met up with Godfrey at Vasili's Cafe, a classic diner in downtown Elkhorn. The plan was to have breakfast, and then Lacy and I would bravely check out the legendary Bray Road for ourselves.

"This is my go-to place," Godfrey told us after we arrived. Settling into a booth near the window, Godfrey told us about her newest book—*American Monsters: A History of Monster Lore, Legends, and Sightings in America*—which details reports she's collected of various cryptids across the country. She has also recently taken a stab at fiction, authoring a fantasy novel titled *God Johnson: The Unforgiven Diary of the Disciple of a Lesser God.* Talk then turned back to Bray Road.

"It's not isolated. You're going to drive down it and be like, *Why would a monster be on this road?*" she told us.

Although the major hoopla at Bray Road happened in 1991–92, sightings of the cryptid in the Elkhorn area still filter in to Godfrey. She documented a case from October 2008, from a middle-aged couple who saw it run in front of their car on Bray Road and jump a guardrail.

"They said they could see the fur flowing as it ran past," Godfrey said.

And as the waitress delivered omelets and refilled our coffee mugs, Godfrey told us about a sighting just a couple months before Lacy's and my arrival to Elkhorn. "There was one in February. It wasn't on Bray Road, but it was in the vicinity," Godfrey told us cautiously.

"Can you tell us about it?" I asked.

"Um . . . I can't tell you a lot about it. The person is really antsy about remaining anonymous and is afraid his neighbors will figure it out. But the gist of it was he was working in his outbuildings, like at 3 AM in February, when it was really cold, and he heard some of his animals acting weird, making noises, so he looked out in his field and there was a bipedal running brown shaggy-furred thing with a muzzle and ears, hunched over but running on its hind feet, chasing a coyote. He chased it off into a field."

She added, "It's a pretty reliable source."

▲▲▲

"This way is a little simpler, actually. Turn left, then turn right, and you can take Court Street, which is the next street up—that'll take you to Highway 11, and that takes you all the way to Bray Road," Godfrey told us as we reviewed directions to get to the scene of the story. She added that most of the sightings had been at the far ends of the road, near the intersections of Bray Road and Hospital Road and County NN. We headed out.

It was a cold April, and Wisconsin was still in hibernation from a long winter. The sky was overcast and gray, a fresh rain reflecting off the narrow two-lane country road. The trees were bare as we cruised slowly down Bray Road, passing barns and cornfields shorn close to the frozen ground. Ravens hopped around, foraging for food. An occasional house, a small patch of trees. As Godfrey said, it hardly resembled a scene from a horror movie, just another stretch of country road, the same type of scenery that stretches across hundreds of miles of the Midwest.

"Not much to it," I said to Lacy, shrugging, and we headed home.

▲ ▲ ▲

What is this "upright canine creature" supposed to be? Godfrey has heard theories ranging from unknown or evolved animals to black magic to extraterrestrial visitors. She once got a phone call from Scotland from a man who explained his theory to her that they were werewolves from the fourth dimension. There's even some debate on it amongst cryptozoologists, especially when Bigfooters got wind of the story and determined the cryptid was invading their turf.

"[Some Bigfooters] are very possessive, very adamant about their own theories: 'I'm totally right and you're totally wrong.' They were calling it the Snouted Bigfoot, because everything had to be a Bigfoot," Godfrey told us, smirking. "If you went to Africa and were studying chimpanzees and then you saw a hyena, would you call that a snouted chimpanzee?

When I asked skeptic Ben Radford about the Beast of Bray Road, he told me he believes it not to be a Manwolf or a Snouted Bigfoot, but a hodgepodge of "mystery mongering."

"For a lot of these cryptozoology types, a good story is better than the truth, and they just throw all these theories out there, hoping that something sticks," he said, waving his hands at the webcamera during our interview. "And it could be ghosts, it could be aliens, it could be fucking Dracula, here's a dozen theories, some I pulled out of my ass! There's no serious investigation or journalism. It's mystery-mongering, and I find it distasteful.

"All these reports get force-fitted into this new story—that there's werewolves running around Bray Road, which is fine, except . . . " Radford leaned into the webcam, "there is no good evidence for werewolves!" He laughed.

Evidence is indeed limited to the anecdotal for this cryptid. Photos and video have all turned out to be faked. Godfrey recalls in one of her books that she met a woman who claimed she had a Manwolf scat sample. It was analyzed and determined to be from a raccoon.

Godfrey's stance on the Beast of Bray Road is similar to Mothman promoter Jeff Wamsley and other cryptozoologists like Lyle Blackburn and his examination of the Fouke Monster. She told me she thought people had certainly been seeing something, but she couldn't say what, and viewed herself more as a documentarian of the Manwolf mystery.

"I don't know whether the mystery can ever be solved," Godfrey admitted. "Just when I think I have it pinned down to one idea or another, I'll get a slew of reports that show something else. I just feel I have become the inadvertent keeper of the lore and reports, and I hope that by recording these things that people send me, we'll be able to get a database that people can refer to and they can make up their minds one way or the other."

« 13 »
NIGHT VISITS

Aᶠᵀᴱᴿ ᴬ ᶠᴱᵂ ᴹᴼᴺᵀᴴˢ of paranormal investigation, I began setting up one-on-one interviews with the five core members of Paranormal Investigators of Milwaukee (PIM)—Noah Leigh, Michael "Gravy" Graeve, Missy Bostrom, Jann Goldberg, and John Krahn.

I had slowly learned some details about Krahn during downtime on ghost investigations. Like me, he was a huge comic book fan; his favorite was Wolverine. He had a cat named Loki. Unlike me, he was an avid bagpipe player, able to blast out traditional Scottish pieces and hits like Johnny Cash's "Ring of Fire." I was curious what had happened to him and what had led him to walk with a cane at age forty-five.

The Hero Cop

"Old Hickory," John Krahn said during setup of one PIM investigation, holding up his cane. "I actually had a priest bless it so I can chop a demon's ass in half with it," he said jokingly, swinging it through the air with a *swoosh*.

Krahn had obviously been in some sort of accident, but I didn't feel comfortable asking him about it at that time. Several months later, when I sat down to interview him over coffee, I decided it was time to ask. And after he told me what had happened, I understood why the possibility of coming face-to-face with a demon probably didn't frighten him much anymore.

On the morning of Memorial Day 2009, Officer Krahn was out helping direct traffic in Elm Grove, a small village west of Milwaukee, for the Memorial Day parade. Krahn had been on the police force for twenty-one years, working as an undercover narcotics officer before accepting a job as a uniformed officer in Elm Grove.

Krahn was assigned to work traffic control at an intersection that had become congested. One minivan sat idling on the railroad tracks that crossed the road. Suddenly, the railroad warning gates dropped and the alarms began flashing, the bells clanging back and forth. The minvan, trapped by vehicles in front and behind, was unable to move.

As the railroad warning lights and bells activated, Krahn ran toward the tracks to be sure it was clear of pedestrians and cars. The frightened woman driving the minivan was still stuck on the tracks. Krahn saw the situation and ran toward the trapped vehicle. He was sprinting "as fast as I've ever seen anyone run," a bystander said later.

As Krahn was running, he was shouting "Get out of the car!" But the woman was frozen with fear, because now she saw the behemoth

Canadian Pacific freight train, ninety-four cars long, approaching her, its whistle blasting. Krahn tried to get her to move to a grassy area to the right of the tracks, but as she wheeled around, her tire got hooked into the track. Panicking, she floored the gas. The wheel spun and the minivan swung around, face-to-face with the oncoming train. Krahn yelled at the woman to get out of the vehicle, but she was frozen.

"She was like a deer in headlights," Krahn told me. She didn't respond to any of his instructions.

A new sound filled the air—the squealing of metal grinding on metal as the train conductor applied the emergency brake. Krahn tore open the door, unfastened the woman's seatbelt, pulled her from the seat, "and I threw her as hard as I could, because my back was to the train and I couldn't see how close it was."

Any relief he might have felt on the rescue quickly evaporated, because now the woman snapped out of it and screamed, "My baby! My baby boy is still in the backseat!"

Krahn hadn't noticed the child because he couldn't see through the van's tinted windows. Meanwhile, the woman's husband arrived. He had been in his own car, stuck in traffic. Krahn desperately tried to hit the van's unlock button while the boy's father tried to open the rear driver's-side door. Krahn said he stopped looking at the oncoming train through the windshield because he had made the decision he was not leaving until he had rescued the boy.

There was the blaring train whistle, the screeching brake, and a new noise—the train crashing through the front end of the van. The impact of the train threw Krahn and the woman's husband about sixty feet through the air, Krahn said. As he lay there, his leg badly twisted, onlookers rushed toward him.

"Don't worry about me," he told them. "Go check on that kid!"

The train had picked up the minivan and pushed it about two hundred feet down the tracks. Miraculously, the two-year-old boy was unharmed and still strapped into his car seat.

Krahn and the boy's father were both rushed to the hospital, where Krahn spent the next two and a half weeks. His recovery, including eight surgeries, was slow and difficult for him, his wife (whom he had just married seven months earlier), and his daughter, who was seven at the time of the accident.

"I had a compound fracture of my tibia, fibula, torn ACL, broken pelvis, four broken ribs, punctured lung, broken shoulder blade, and my left side was one big bruise. I almost lost my leg. It's called compartment syndrome, where the tissues fill up with fluid and the blood flow can't get to the rest of the limb. I ended up with permanent nerve damage in my left leg. Tried all kinds of stuff, but after a year and half, doctors said, 'There's no way you're going back to work.' So here I am," Krahn told me.

Slowly, he moved from a wheelchair to being able to walk on crutches to using a cane. He returned to do desk work for Elm Grove Police Department, but even that was too much, and soon he settled on full disability.

Krahn was praised in the media as a "hero cop," although he humbly said, "I was just trying to do the right thing, just doing my job." He was honored for his valor at a special luncheon in Washington, DC, in 2010 during National Police Week. He also was given a Carnegie Hero Fund Award.

▲ ▲ ▲

After Krahn told me this story I was visibly dumbfounded, which is a bit out of character for me. Months later, Krahn gave me a ride to my parents' house in Waukesha. We were driving toward some train tracks when the gate came down, bright red lights flashing, bells clanging. Krahn hit the brakes hard. He stared ahead and took a deep breath, then looked at me. "Sorry," he said. "Obviously I have a strong reaction to this type of thing."

The event completely changed Krahn's entire life, and in a 2011 interview, he admitted that he thought about the accident daily and often suffered from nightmares related to it.

"I don't . . ." I paused, then started again. "That was a very brave thing to do."

"I generally don't talk about it a lot," he said, nonchalantly.

While he recovered, Krahn had a lot of time on his hands. He told me he always had been fascinated with the paranormal, ghosts, ESP, cryptozoology, and mysteries, like the curse of the Hope Diamond. "I was surfing the Internet looking for places in Milwaukee that are supposed to be haunted and I stumbled across Paranormal Investigators of Milwaukee. I was like, *What the hell is this?* because I never got into *Ghost Hunters* or anything. I didn't even know there was amateur groups going around doing this."

Krahn checked out other local groups in the Midwest but came back to PIM's page.

"I liked the fact that Noah was a scientist. I had wanted to be a scientist before I became a cop. I just like the way he was organized and had his shit together, so I filled out the online application and he called me up and took me into the fold." Krahn joined the team in 2011. "I'm the type of person that wants to experience it firsthand."

▲▲▲

Krahn was not alone at our interview at the Colectivo coffee shop. He had brought along his friend Susan Benzine, knowing I was curious to talk to her, too. The two of them had been getting into some interesting experiences of late, joining up with a team of people supporting an exorcist.

"In September, Sue contacted Noah because she's been involved with this group called Christian Support Ministries and she was interested in doing some paranormal investigation with our group, so she told Noah she had been on some exorcisms," Krahn explained. Leigh told her he was interested in her group's methods but was busy at the time, so he sent Krahn to check it out.

Krahn met the members of Christian Support Ministries, led by the Reverend Michael Schroeder of Madison, Wisconsin. Rev. Schroeder, referred to by the group simply as "the Reverend," became an "ordained exorcist" through the American Association of Exorcists. (Like Rev. Bob Larson's school, this is an Internet correspondence course.) He established Christian Support Ministries to investigate reports of possession and to perform house blessings and exorcisms. In a 2013 interview, Rev. Schroeder said he was performing an exorcism per week or more.

Sue found out about the Reverend through her church and joined his demon-fighting team.

▲▲▲

Krahn's first foray with the group was an exorcism that was somewhat uneventful, he told me. But "the next one I experienced was totally crazy." It was with a woman I would later meet. I'll refer to her here as Mary.

"We went to her apartment, and she said, 'Oh, hi, I'm [Mary],'" Krahn said, imitating a meek, polite voice. "She seemed normal, but [the Reverend] started saying a prayer and all of a sudden her head drops and she's quiet.

"'[Mary]? [Mary]?'

"And all of a sudden she just starts laughing hysterically. And she goes, 'She is such a fucking bitch.' I'm like, 'What is going on here? Who is she talking about?' She gets up and starts screaming, runs outside. I go and bring her back in, she's in the kitchen and just goes bonkers, screaming and everything else, so I take her down to the ground to control her so she doesn't hurt us."

Mary continued to rampage in the apartment, slamming the bathroom door repeatedly, running amok until she was calmed down enough to attempt an exorcism.

"So then the Reverend starts doing his prayers, and she starts getting physically ill. She throws up a little bit. They're holding a bowl out for her," Krahn said, stretching his arm across the table of the café. "And she projectile vomits. It goes in an arc, right into the bowl," Krahn said, recreating the arc with his hand.

"I mean, that's what you saw, right?" he asked Sue.

"Yeah."

"It just went, every drop, into the bowl. And I was an EMT in our department, all our cops are EMTs. I've seen a lot of vomiting. It doesn't happen like that—it's like a shotgun blast coming out."

"She almost filled up a popcorn bowl of puke," Sue told me. I must have made a face at that, because she added, "I know, it's gross."

"She was going back and forth, laughing and crying, going in and out," Krahn said.

Krahn also captured an EVP at the exorcism, which he had a file of in his iPhone. He looked it up in the café, then got ready to hold it up to my ear.

"The Reverend is talking and saying 'You'll be judged,' and something about the world on fire, then he pauses, and about five seconds later you hear a long, drawn-out, gravelly sound. The speaker's right up there."

Sure enough, I heard the Reverend talking and then a ghostly voice saying, "Aaaaa . . ." something.

"Yeah, I heard it," I said, nodding, though I wasn't sure what I had heard.

"I wasn't sure what it was, and I sent it to Noah. He said, 'It sounds like someone saying "Allison."'" Allison? There was no one there named Allison, so why would it say that? Well, Sue looked it up: there actually is a demon named Allocen, A-L-L-O-C-E-N."

Later I decided to look that up in the *Encyclopedia of Demons in World Religions and Cultures* by Theresa Bane but found that the entry produced more questions than answers:

ALLOCEN

Variations: Alocas, Alocer, Allocer, Alloces, Alloien

According to Johann Wierus's *Pseudomonarchia Daemonum* (*False Monarchy of Demons*, 1583) Duke Allocen is a FALLEN ANGEL who commands thirty-six legions of demons (see DUKES OF HELL). He is described as looking like a soldier mounted upon a great horse. His face is very red and looks like a lion with flaming eyes. His voice is hoarse and he speaks very loudly. Allocen is summoned for his ability to give good FAMILIARS; he also teaches astronomy and liberal sciences. Some sources list Allocen as one of the seventy-two SPIRITS OF SOLOMON.

Another odd occurrence John and Sue told me about involved Sue's car keys. While the exorcism was happening, they heard a clanking sound. Later Sue was looking for her keys, which had been on the kitchen counter, and couldn't find them. She had a small ball attached to the key ring so she wouldn't lose them. Eventually she found that the keys had moved from the counter to a thin space between the counter and the refrigerator, suspended by the ball.

Two exorcisms were performed on Mary. Despite this, she claimed that three demons still inhabited her body and she was contemplating another exorcism.

Sue and John were not sure what the next step would be, but I asked them to keep me in the loop. A month or so later I joined them on the case. But first, they had a warning for me.

"I was waiting for my wife to come home from work. It was snowing lightly. I heard the screen door creak open and the doorknob rattling, like someone is pulling on the doorknob. I was like, *What the hell?* I was watching TV," Krahn told me at the café.

He thought the noise at the door was his wife. "Did she go back to the car and get lost or what? So I go and look, and there's no tire tracks, no footprints on the porch at all. And it wasn't one of those things like, *Did I hear that or not?* Apparently that type of stuff isn't uncommon; it's something trying to intimidate you and dissuade you."

Sue nodded her head in agreement. "They say when you have a case coming up you will know because stuff will happen to you," she said. "They call it the night visits. When Mary started getting close to me, stuff started happening to me. I've had unbelievable things happen."

Sue explained to me that thirty years ago she had a life-altering event,* "and I came to know the Lord as my Savior."

"I know this sounds nuts, and at the time I didn't want to tell anyone about it because I was afraid they would think I was nuts. In a six-month period I had three visions of angels and demons. I ran away from it because I was afraid of the devil; I had a healthy fear of it," Sue said. She attends a Lutheran church in her hometown of Oconomowoc.

And then, just a couple months before joining up with Christian Support Ministries, she had an encounter. She says it was a mani-

---

* I later contacted Sue and asked if she could tell me what this life-altering event was, and she responded with a two-part e-mail typed all in caps that didn't list any specifics. The gist of the e-mails, I guess, is that she did not admit she was a sinner to God and suffered because of this.

festation of the Dark Lord himself, and it matched her vision from thirty years prior.

"I was driving down the road at eleven fifty-nine that night; I worked third shift. This man comes walking out of a ditch—it was May 25, I'll never forget it. He came walking out of the ditch and I recognized him. It was Lucifer, from my first vision thirty years ago. He was dressed in a long trench coat, from like the 1880s, a very good-looking man, looked like Tom Cruise," she said, laughing.

"Or perhaps Tom Cruise is Lucifer; that could be, too," Krahn interjected.

"He had a great big book under his left arm," Sue continued, ignoring Krahn. "It didn't have a cross on it and it didn't say HOLY BIBLE, but to look at him, you'd think he was a minister from the 1800s. Well, he came walking out in front of my car, and I recognized him right away from my visions. I rebuked him, and he put his head down and walked away. There was part of me that wanted to stop, but I said no. I drove by and looked at him out of the corner of my eye, and he was chuckling."

Sue warned me that I was entering this sinister landscape myself when I joined up with them.

"If you get involved, things will happen to you personally. We call it the 'Oh shit' moment," she said, laughing. "Like, 'Oh shit, this stuff is real!'"

"OK," I told John and Sue, flipping my hands up in the air. "I'm ready for it."

They looked at me and laughed.

I kept my ears open for a night visit, but living in the city, I naturally tune out background noise. There is always a steady supply of traffic, loud music, snowblowers, and dogs, and if I hear a mysterious knocking, I'm likely to assume the upstairs neighbor has gotten drunk and lost his keys again.

The Demon Apartment

A couple of weeks later, March 22, 2014, I was cruising with John

Krahn from his home in Muskego to Sue's home on a farm in Oconomowoc. There, we switched Krahn's paranormal investigation gear
to Sue's car, and she drove to Beaver Dam, a town where Mary was
staying with a friend. She was too afraid to go back to her apartment
in the nearby small town of Juneau (about three thousand people),
located deep in the farmland of Wisconsin.

As we drove to Sue's house, a robotic British female voice ticked
off the GPS directions. Krahn talked to me about Ed (d. 2006) and
Lorraine Warren, the couple who popularized the term *demonolo-
gist*. Sue was a big fan of their work, he told me, but he described
them as "hacks" and "scam artists." The Warrens' association with
the paranormal goes back as far as 1952, when they founded the
New England Society for Psychic Research. Lorraine claims to be
clairvoyant herself. The Warrens' most famous case is known as the
Amityville Horror, in which the Lutz family moved into a house that
was the scene of a grisly murder, where a man had killed six family
members. The Lutz family said demonic entities sent them packing
twenty-eight days after moving in. The Warrens were among the
first to investigate. The case has been the basis for several books and
eleven movies to date.

The films *The Conjuring, Annabelle*, and *The Haunting in Connecticut*
are also based on their cases, which they claimed ran into the thousands. The Warrens began to amass a collection of creepy artifacts,
which they housed in a private Warrens Occult Museum in their
house.

One of the more famed pieces in the collection is a Raggedy Ann
doll named Annabelle that supposedly was possessed by an evil entity
that gave the doll mobility and left cryptic notes for a little girl and
her family. (The doll also appears in *The Conjuring*, and *Annabelle* is
based on this story.) Annabelle is now trapped (hopefully) in a glass
case in the Warrens' home with a sign on it that reads, WARNING,
POSITIVELY DO NOT OPEN.

"It was pretty much revealed to be a hoax," Krahn told me of the
Amityville case. He said the motivation for the Lutz family hoaxing
their experience was money, and he fingered the Warrens as being

guilty by association for promoting the case instead of investigating its flaws.

▲▲▲

After we switched cars, Sue drove and joined us in discussing the case.

"What if she was demonized and all that's left now is mental illness?" Krahn theorized. Sue told us that the demons had been terrorizing Mary and making her life hell. After a house blessing at her friend's house, "the demons were screaming at her and hitting her for two weeks."

Mary was unemployed. "Every time she gets a job, the demons scream and yell at her," Sue said.

Mary was struggling with other things besides demons—alcoholism (which she said she had recovered from), getting custody of her child, and run-ins with the law over her behavior.

I looked into court records for Mary and found a steady string of entries over the years—disorderly conduct, loud and unnecessary noise, resisting or obstructing an officer.

But Mary and Sue said it was witchcraft that led to possession. "Her ex put a spell on her using Satanic witchcraft," Sue said. She added that the apartment had a collection of books on Santeria and various forms of witchcraft.

"You get people that think they can fight bad stuff by using bad stuff," Krahn explained. "If you're relying on spells and witchcraft to protect you, that means you're not relying on God and Jesus to protect you."

Krahn told us one of his goals for our visit with Mary was to try to determine whether she was mentally ill, lying, or possessed by demons. He had a few tests he was going to try on her. In one, he was going to pour tap water into a bottle that used to contain holy water and see if she reacted to that. In another, he was going to hold an object behind his back and see if the demon could identify it for Mary.

"I'm trying to think of how to phrase it," he said as Sue drove.

"The Lord commands the demon to say what's in John's hand," Sue offered.

"No, we can ask the voice without acknowledging that it's a demon."

We cruised along County Road 5 through the farmland, bare trees, abandoned cornfields with the stalks shorn close to the frozen ground, and battered and faded red barns and silos. Beaver Dam had a foreboding entryway—a cemetery covered both sides of the street as we rolled past the town's population sign.

We arrived at Mary's friend's home, a normal-looking townhouse.

"The voices have been bad today," was one of the first things she told us after we arrived. Mary seemed to be a normal small-town Wisconsin girl with a plain look—blue jeans, a Green Bay Packers sweatshirt, slightly wavy blonde hair pulled back in a ponytail. She had a stocky, strong, farmer's daughter build.

We left Sue to stay with Mary so we could do an initial investigation at her apartment without her. We drove by the welcome sign that read, WELCOME TO JUNEAU, A CITY WITH A HEART.

Mary's apartment building was old, outdated. A streetlight flickered outside, and a simple playground in the backyard had a swing set and basketball hoop without a net. The hallway in the apartment smelled like cigarettes and sauerkraut, and I could hear pots and pans clanking down the hall.

At Mary's apartment I met some of the people who had been members of the former Christian Support Ministries team. After a disagreement about reporting a potential case of abuse they saw at an investigation, many members had left the group. They were not members of PIM, but Krahn had been joining up with them on occasion.

Later, Gravy snarkily told me this is the "B team." This is an ongoing PIM joke; when the team splits for investigations, much joking goes on about who is the A versus the B team.

Krahn had given the members (minus Sue) code names. The young guy wearing glasses was Biebs. This was from a mistaken EVP captured by a different team member who had thought they had recorded a ghost woman speaking. Krahn listened to the audio, recognized it as the earthly male investigator in front of me, and declared it sounded like pop singer Justin Bieber.

Canary, the dark-haired young woman sitting next to Biebs, got her nickname from a different investigation they went on. The team was afraid they were entering an unpleasant household in Iowa, and Krahn said she could go in first and act as the "canary in a coal mine." Another member, who is still a part of Christian Support Ministries, was dubbed Space Ghost because she wore her recorders on big wrist bracelets, which reminded Krahn of the cartoon superhero.

Krahn himself had picked up a nickname, House, tying his cane and his cantankerous attitude to the star of the TV show of the same name.

It was a small apartment. It was sparse and had several religious decorations—ceramic angels on the nightstand by the bed, a tile cross on the bedroom wall, a heavy-duty Bible on the desk, a calendar in the kitchen with a painting of Jesus Christ gazing upward toward the sky.

The Exorcism

While Krahn set up his cameras, I took the opportunity to ask Biebs and Canary about their experiences. The two had been friends for a long time and had joined up with the group because Canary's sister—we'll call her Lynn—had been one of the case studies. Canary told me that Lynn lived just outside of Oshkosh, Wisconsin. She had been possessed by demons.

"We thought it was just a haunting, but something latched on to her—there was a lot of stuff going on," Canary told me. "So [Biebs], being my friend, I brought him over for visits to sit with me and see if this stuff was really happening to me."

"Right, just these bizarre things," Biebs said. "When I came into it, we came to her house and her house was destroyed."

"Trashed, just trashed," Canary said. "No one had been there all day. I was with her, because she had been having these little things happen before that, lights turning on and off, doors opening and closing in the middle of the night, her dog freaking out like there were intruders."

As they walked into the house, they found a frightening mess spilling out of Lynn's living room closet. Lynn's Bible had several pages torn out of it that were scattered across the floor. A rosary had been ripped up. Lynn's confirmation photo was lying on the floor, her face on the photo scratched up.

As they were telling me this while sitting in Mary's living room, we suddenly heard a strange noise—an odd reverberating, echoing knock.

"What was that?" I asked.

"I don't know," Canary said.

"John, did you hear that?" I asked.

"Yeah, I heard it."

I got up to investigate, opening Mary's door. I looked down the hall, left then right. There was nothing.

I sat back down, and Canary kept telling me the story of Lynn's living room closet. After the incident, Canary visited her sister again, this time with her nine-month-old and three-year-old sons. Her three-year-old was playing on the stairs, but then Canary noticed he was missing.

"I said, 'Where's Jack? Why didn't he come back upstairs?'

"I looked downstairs and I hear him mumbling and babbling to this closet. He has the door open and he's just standing, looking up, talking into the closet.

"I was like, 'Jack, you need to come back upstairs.' He does this three separate times, going downstairs and talking to the closet, and I keep telling him to come back upstairs."

Things got worse.

"We saw her get picked up and *launched*, like literally thrown against the wall," Biebs told me.

"She was just like a rag doll," Canary added.

"You saw that happen?" I asked. I was trying to get a read on the two. Were they credible?

"Yes. She got lifted like three inches off the ground and thrown about my distance to the wall," Canary said, pointing to the living room wall a few feet away.

"It was so quick my eyes could hardly follow how fast she got whipped. It was insane," Biebs said.

"Not possible. The way she moved so fast and got lifted up and over," Canary added. "She had bruises on her legs from crashing into an end table."

In another strange incident, which happened when Canary and Biebs were visiting, they heard cries for help coming from Lynn's bedroom. Lynn was being pulled off the bed by an unseen force. Her fiancé screamed for help. Biebs ran to assist, but the bedroom door slammed shut and he couldn't open it. It was like an unseen force was holding it shut for several moments, he said.

Canary said her sister's temperament also became strange and unpredictable.

"One minute she'd call and ask for help—crying, scared—and the next she'd try to fight with me. It was like pulling teeth to get her to leave the house," Canary explained. "All these crazy things were happening, but she wanted to stay there, so that would baffle me. I was with my kids during the day, and every night I would go to her house and babysit her, basically. Her fiancé works on a farm, so he was gone a lot of hours."

A dark cloud had settled on the house, Canary said. "Walking into the house, I don't consider myself sensitive in any way, but Lynn's house had this overwhelming depressing feeling to it. You could just feel it in the air . . . tension—you could cut it with a knife. It was through her entire house that way. Just being there was unsettling. A lot of stuff happened to her when she was in her room, her bathroom, her laundry room. When she was in the shower, she'd get scratches, she'd get pushed, she'd get locked in the bathroom, she'd have lightbulbs busting out of the sockets. It was to the point that when I was there, I didn't want to go into any of the rooms. I didn't even want to go pee," Canary said, laughing. "I was afraid of getting locked in or having something thrown at me. It was terrifying being there, but I couldn't show that to her. I was the only person there for her, really."

The last major thing that happened to Lynn was the day before her first exorcism, Canary recalled. "I got a call in the afternoon from her fiancé telling me stuff was happening and I needed to help her. I tried calling over and over, and it would go straight to voice mail or I would just hear her crying for a moment and then lose the call. I finally got through, and she said, 'It pulled me down the stairs three times. It keeps hanging up my phone.'

"She was bawling and I was hysterical. I went and got my kids in the car and drove over there as fast as I could. She was covered from her shoulders down to her feet, front and back, with these welted, three-line marks all over her body. She said a demon had been pulling her down the stairs and scratching her. It wasn't like they were there a minute and then faded; they were there two or three days. They were deep scratches."

They decided it was time for an exorcism.

▲▲▲

Christian Support Ministries was called in to do the exorcism. John Krahn joined them. It was eventful.

"During the exorcism she was doing things—my sister is a hundred pounds wet, and she was overpowering seven people at a time, she had her eyes rolled back for hours; it wasn't like she'd break and look at you, they were rolled back and her lids open," Canary described to me, getting a little bit shaken up at the memory. "She went into a trance state, started talking crazy. She didn't sound like herself, she had this witchlike giggle. Her eyes were rolled back, she was overpowering people. She was kicking John's ass. Right, John?"

Krahn stopped working on his night-vision camera setup for a minute and sat down on the couch next to me. "OK, lean forward," he instructed me. I did. He swung his legs around and trapped me in a scissors lock. "This is nothing intimate," he said, locking my torso and pushing my shoulder with his hand. "Try to move forward." I pushed forward but was unable to move far.

"Three other people held her other arm and legs. And she was able to pull forward from us. The sweat was dripping off my face. What was pissing me off is she was laughing while she was doing it."

▲▲▲

The exorcism wasn't a success. So a second one was scheduled.

"The second one she was really lashing out at her fiancé," Canary said. "It was saying things like . . . John, what was it saying the second time?"

"'I'm better for you than he is,'" Krahn recalled. "'I can treat her better, and you're a coward. I've had her a long time. You'll never have her.' All these really crazy things."

"Every time they fought, the fireworks in the house would just blow up," Canary said. "Like it was happy they were fighting and wanted to be in their feud, too. The Reverend said, 'You will burn tenfold for not answering to me.' And it said, 'I'm already burning, and I don't answer to you.'"

▲▲▲

After the second exorcism, Lynn began to mellow out.

The events had been difficult for Canary and Biebs, and they decided they wanted to use the experience to find answers and hopefully help out other people in a similar situation.

"A lot of people don't know where to turn to," Canary said. "[Lynn] was afraid people would think she's crazy. I know I did at first. But she's had no mental health issues, she's not medicated, she doesn't abuse substances. I just wanted to help people, just seeing how confused and lost she was, because there are probably a lot of people like that, that need the appropriate help."

Biebs agreed. "Some of my family has said that: 'Why do you want to mess with that? Leave it to the priests.' But even the priests need help. They can't be everywhere."

"It's irritating because I feel like I don't have enough answers," Canary added. "My main question is—why did it pick her? She seems like she was doing everything right—she goes to college, she goes to church, she has a fiancé, she was working, she seemed like she had everything together. What part of her life opened up a door for something? Why did it feed on her for so long?"

▲▲▲

With Krahn's equipment set up, we started the paranormal investigation portion of the evening.

"I told Sue, we got to consider the possibility that she has mental issues in addition to she was maybe demonized before, she's no longer demonized, and now she's got leftover residual mental health issues. She could be schizophrenic and that's why she's experiencing the things she is.

"Sue said she got checked out. How does she know? 'Because she said she got checked out.' Well, 'I can walk across water.' Doesn't mean I can actually do it."

Krahn started an EVP session in the living room.

"Hello, my name is John; I'm here with my friends. And [Canary]," Krahn announced, giving a joking slight to Canary.

She let out a condescending laugh at Krahn's dig.

"We're here to find out why you've been doing what you've been doing to [Mary]. Can you tell us what your name is?" The rest of us sat in silence as Krahn made observations and asked random questions. . . .

"You can hear the wind blowing pretty good out there, too."

"Why are you here?"

"Car in the distance."

"Are you still here from the problems she was having last time?"

Silence.

▲▲▲

With an uneventful EVP session, Krahn decided to do some "religious provoking."

"OK, we can try some scripture," he said, and read a Bible verse from a packet of sheets titled "Group Prayers for Provoking Demonic Entities."

"Finally be strong in the Lord and the strength of his might," Krahn read, from Ephesians 6:10–20. "Put on the whole armor of God that you may be able to stand against the wiles of the Devil . . ."

Then, passing the packet to Canary, Krahn said, "OK, Canary, let's see what you can drum up." She read a verse, then passed it to Biebs, then me. I read John 3:14–21 (in part, "For God so loved the world that he gave his only son") and James 4:4–12 ("Resist the devil and he will flee from you, draw near to God and he will draw near to you").

Krahn grabbed a *Book of Psalms* and a bottle of holy water to do one more prayer. "I'm going to try to find this passage and spray some holy water around," he said, flipping through the book.

"Let God arise, let his enemies be scattered, let those who hate him leave before him," he read (Psalms 68:1–4), pausing to splash holy water on the living room wall, then moved into the bedroom to repeat the process. "The smoke is driven away, so drive them away as wax melteth before the fire, so let the wicked perish at the presence of God."

Nothing happened. Krahn decided it was time to call Mary and Sue over to the apartment.

▲▲▲

"How are the voices?" Krahn asked Mary when she arrived. Sue sat next to me on the couch, and Mary sat on the floor. "Are they loud now or not?"

"Not right now, no," Mary replied. She laughed nervously. "Sorry stuff isn't flying around, but it happens when it happens." Typically in the apartment, she explained, she'd experience kitchen cabinets opening and closing, ghost footsteps, disembodied laughter.

"I hear three different voices. I've heard them for three years now. There's a female voice I hear rarely and two male voices. I visually saw them three different times. That was really scary, but that was over a year and a half ago. I don't know why I haven't seen them again."

We sat in the dark in Mary's apartment, and I asked her how this had all started and asked her to explain her first encounter with the demons.

"I was at my sister's house. I started hearing numbers coming up through the vents. I was terrified. It was someone counting, 'One thousand six, one thousand seven, one thousand eight,' and then it whispered my name.

"I went outside because I seen someone baling hay, but it was at a super slow speed. I thought it was my brother-in-law because he has a farm, so I went outside because I was like, 'What is he doing? It's like four o'clock in the morning.'

"I went outside and got this overwhelming feeling of fear. I went inside and slammed the door and felt someone slam it at the same time as me.

"When I looked out, I looked around, and he was still baling hay and went like this to me," Mary said, slowly waving a hand. "Waving but like in slow motion."

"What type of things were the voices saying tonight?" Krahn asked.

"Um, everything: 'We're not going to help you.' I don't know what that meant. The same old stuff. I didn't hear 'Kill yourself.' That's a normal one. I heard them say 'Sleepy, sleepy' again. It's like they're just joking with me. That's what it whispers, 'Sleepy, sleepy,' right next to my ear. 'Bitch, bitch, bitch,' I hear that quite a bit."

Krahn decided to try out his tests.

"If you could ask, 'What is John holding in his hand right now?' Why don't you see what happens," Krahn said, holding a clipboard in front of one of his hands to hide the object.

"I can try. Sometimes I get an answer, and sometimes I get an 'F you,'" Mary said, sitting cross-legged on the floor. "He's holding his pen. I don't know, I'm just telling—"

"So you can just think a question and get a response?" Krahn asked.

"Sometimes."

Krahn was holding a flashlight behind the clipboard. "OK. How about, how many fingers am I holding up?"

"I'm not psychic, I don't know. First they said, 'He's holding three fingers, he's holding six fingers, he's holding three fingers, six.'"

"OK. I'm just trying to see what responses I get," Krahn said. He was holding four fingers.

Last, he offered Mary the bottle of holy water that was actually filled with tap water. "Do you mind sprinkling this on your hand?" She agreed and showed no reaction.

"All right, that's a wrap, folks," Krahn said. We began to pack up.

▲ ▲ ▲

"As far as I know, she's doing better now," Canary told me in a follow-up e-mail when I asked about her sister. But for Mary, not so much. She underwent a third exorcism, which didn't help her, she told me.

"With now three exorcisms and no relief, things are just as bad now as when they started," Mary told me in a follow-up e-mail. "So I'm worn out and tired because I don't know what to do. I know Sue, Reverend, and everyone has tried to help for years but sometimes I think it makes them more mad and it makes things worse!"

Sue was there for the third exorcism. She said the demon was hiding from her, but after she commanded it to come forward, "all hell broke loose. It cursed at me, used a different language, and screamed at me in a weird tone." Sue said a week after the exorcism, Mary had a vision of Christ and got on a better path but soon slipped into alcoholism and the demons returned.

"She knows she's brought it back on. However, she also knows the demons can't have her soul," Sue e-mailed me.

« 14 »

THE CASE OF THE HAUNTED HONKY-TONK

BOBBY MACKEY'S MUSIC WORLD is a honky-tonk bar and live music venue in Wilder, Kentucky. In 1991, the Reverend Glen Cole conducted an exorcism on Carl Lawson, the club's caretaker:

Lawson (growling): "You don't scare me."

Rev. Cole: "Well, you don't scare me, either."
Lawson (unintelligible yelling)
Rev. Cole: "No, you're going to leave."
Lawson (growling): "No, I'm not."
Rev. Cole: "Yes, you are!"
Lawson: *"I ain't goin' nowhere!"*
Rev. Cole: "Yes, you are!"
Lawson: *"I ain't never gonna leave!"*

▲ ▲ ▲

"Just because we went there and something happened, doesn't mean something will happen when we're there this time. That's a distinct possibility," Noah Leigh told me over the phone. He wanted to have some frank talk with me about an upcoming investigation I was joining PIM on, at a place he noted "is not your average haunted place."

He was talking about the notorious and frightening Bobby Mackey's Music World.

"The other possibility is that a lot of stuff could happen," Leigh explained. "And we're being told that if someone gets upset like they did last time, they have to leave. So if there's a situation where something happens to you, if you feel you need to leave, it's going to end up in all of us having to leave. And if you're not willing to go back into the location, you're basically going to end up sitting in the car."

The Expedition

I had heard of Bobby Mackey's when PIM initially investigated the haunted honky-tonk a few months earlier, in July. It was during part of an epic haunt tour, which I heard about at a PIM meeting in Leigh's rec room basement about a month after the trip on August 11.

Leigh had greeted me at his door, eager to get started, with a notebook in his hand, listing the meeting's agenda. The majority of the items on the list concerned discussing and reviewing evidence from PIM's out-of-state expedition in July. While some people use their vacation time to plan trips to Honolulu or Orlando, the members of PIM plot time off to travel to some of the most notoriously haunted hot spots in America.

Stops on their recent ghost road trip, which PIM termed the Expedition, included the Mansfield Reformatory (a historic prison in Ohio), Sedamsville Rectory (a 120-year-old rectory that was once part of Our Lady of Perpetual Help, located in the "armpit of Ohio," according to Jann) and the Waverly Hills Sanatorium (a Kentucky hospital built to accommodate a tuberculosis epidemic). All of these locations are well known to ghost hunters as being "active," but the one place everyone was itching to talk about at the meeting was Bobby Mackey's Music World.

▲▲▲

Northern Kentucky Music Legends Hall of Fame member Bobby Mackey wanted to be known for one thing when he opened his honky-tonk in 1978: music. And his venue, Bobby Mackey's Music World, was well known in the Wilder, Kentucky, area for offering the best of both types of music: country and western. On Friday and Saturday nights, Bobby Mackey's gravel parking lot fills up, and revelers file into the bar, order beer, and head out to the dance floor. On a busy weekend, upward of a thousand people might come through the doors. Up onstage you'll often find Bobby Mackey himself, backed by the Big Mac Band.

Over the years, Bobby Mackey's has become known for something else—it overshadows his country music legacy at times, and it goes bump in the night. Although Mackey isn't a believer himself, he quickly began hearing ghost stories after opening his doors. First his wife, Janet, who happened to be five months pregnant, reported a malicious spirit pushing her down a flight of stairs. After that, Janet was none too thrilled by the venue but couldn't convince her husband of the ghostly presence lurking in the dark corners of the club.

Then there was the strange case of Carl Lawson, who was hired as caretaker of Bobby Mackey's before the doors even opened. He soon moved into an upstairs apartment in the building. Lawson, familiar with local lore on the place, reported having lots of experiences with ghosts and then claimed he himself was possessed by demons. An exorcism, performed on him inside of Bobby Mackey's in 1991, was recorded on video. With "PM 9:24:42" floating in white letters in a corner of the video, exorcist Glen Cole points at Lawson, lying on the floor:

Rev. Cole: "Yer not gonna do anything, because I'm gonna find you, tonight!"

Lawson: "How you gonna fucking find me!"

Rev. Cole: "Because I got something inside me that tells me I can. You understand me?"

Lawson: "What the fuck you got? He's on the way. He's coming and a thousand strong! And I tell you what! There ain't a goddamn *fucker* ever can come in this place again and ever try to run any of us off!"

Rev. Cole: "Oh yes—"

Lawson: "There's thousands of us here!"

Rev. Cole: "I don't care."

Lawson: "We've been here six thousand years!"

Rev. Cole: "I'm telling ya, ya got to leave tonight!"

Janet Mackey passed away in 2009 at age sixty. Carl Lawson passed away in 2012 at fifty-three.

▲ ▲ ▲

Bobby Mackey was none too happy about these ghost stories coming from his wife and caretaker . . . and soon his employees, patrons, and bandmates. He thought if the stories circulated it would damage his business. Who would be crazy enough to hang out in a haunted bar? But the ghost was out of the bag. People continued to talk about Bobby Mackey's and his ghosts, and they began to weave together a mix of historical fact, speculation, and campfire ghost story.

There are a lot of stories about the land and building that houses Bobby Mackey's, many of them unsubstantiated. The honky-tonk is built on the grounds of a former slaughterhouse, which was in operation in the 1800s and is said to be the scene of a gruesome murder in the 1890s. Two men—Scott Jackson and Alonzo Walling—murdered a pregnant woman (five months, the same as Mackey's wife), Pearl Bryan, and cut off her head. Legend says that they threw it into the slaughterhouse's well as some sort of Satanic rite. The well, although filled in, is still in the basement and is now commonly referred to as a "portal to hell."

Lawson is the one who discovered the well after ripping up the basement's floorboards. He claimed spirits told him where to find it.

Although the story of the murder is true, it is unknown where Pearl Bryant's head was disposed of. Jackson and Walling were arrested and hung for the crime on March 20, 1897, in the gallows behind the Newport Campbell County Courthouse in Newport, Kentucky. Bryan's headless body was buried in Forest Lawn Cemetery in her hometown of Greencastle, Indiana. It is now popular lore that the ghost of Bryan and the malicious spirits of Jackson and Walling inhabit Bobby Mackey's.

The gruesome history continues into the Prohibition era, when the property became a speakeasy. It's said barrels of moonshine were smuggled up the Licking River and through the former slaughterhouse well. Shady dealings are said to have happened in the club over the years, and it's rumored the basement rooms were where cheats and mob stool pigeons were tortured and murdered.

In the 1930s E. A. "Buck" Brady took over the nightclub and casino and named it the Primrose. He soon found himself in trouble with the Cincinnati Mafia. Brady refused to sell the club to the mob, and violence escalated against him for years. Brady got out of the business in the '40s and committed suicide in 1965.

After Brady's tenure, the club was renamed the Latin Quarter and became a popular nightclub. One of the casino's popular dancing girls was an attractive young woman named Johanna. The story goes that her stern father, who owned the club, forbade her from seeing a club musician, a singer named Robert Randall. (Bobby Mackey's birth name happens to be Robert Randall Mackey. Coincidence?)

She ignored him, and her father had the young man murdered. Johanna got revenge by poisoning her father and herself. She died in one of the club's dressing rooms in the basement. Since her death,

Johanna's rose-scented perfume has still been smelled lingering in the air.

Bobby Mackey says his young daughter, who was scared of the place, said that it smelled "like roses on a grave."

The bar was converted into a Hard Rock Cafe in the 1970s and was reportedly shut down after a fatal shooting on the premises in the winter of 1978.

And then, one day in the spring of 1978, Bobby Mackey and his wife, Janet, pulled into the gravel lot of the building. After looking the building over, Bobby saw his name in neon lights, but his wife just had a creepy feeling.

Paranormal Fans

All of this lore has brought Bobby Mackey's a new breed of fans— ones not interested in tapping their toes to some country hits but wanting to investigate his premises for proof of ghostly activity. Mackey isn't a fan of the ghost stories (although he did write a song about one of the alleged ghosts, titled "Johanna"). We can speculate that once Mackey realized these groups were willing to pay a hefty fee to spend the night wandering around his basement, he saw the silver lining in the cloud.

Paranormal investigators began traveling to Wilder, Kentucky, from all over the country, and an investigation at Mackey's was added to many a ghost hunter's bucket list. Dozens of groups have conducted investigations in the building, everyone from the Central Ohio Ghost Squad to the Ghost Research Society to the Paranormal Investigations of Wichita.

Adding to the intrigue, the spot has become immortalized on shows like *Ghost Adventures* and *Ghost Hunters*, among other paranormal and spooky travel-themed shows.

Ghost Adventures used an investigation of Bobby Mackey's as its lead episode of season 1 in 2008. The show's mixture of cockiness, befuddlement, and shock tactics shown in this early episode made it an instant hit and a competitor of *Ghost Hunters*. The show stars a trio of investigators: Zak Bagans, Nick Groff, and cameraman and equipment tech Aaron Goodwin.

Inside Bobby Mackey's, Zak did an interview with Carl Lawson, explaining to the bewildered former caretaker that "I want to provoke the hell out of them. I just want to stand up to them. Who are they? Who are these spirits to be bullies and possess you? I want to taunt the hell out of them. I want to provoke them and give them a taste of their own medicine, see what happens when we do that."

After employing their gimmick of getting padlocked into the building, the creepy experiences started. First Nick went to use Bobby Mackey's men's room, when a ghost punched a nearby wall.

"Oh my God, that scared the living [*beep*] out of me!" Nick exclaimed to the camera.

"That scared me, too, bro. I'm shaking right now," Zak agreed. After another noise startled him, Nick began to run out, but Zak grabbed him.

"Stop! Stop running! Do not [*beep*] run! Do not run! Stop running! Do not run from this!" And then to the spirits in general: "We're not running from you!"

"Do it!" Nick challenged. "Do it again!"

The night became infamous for the group, and they returned twice to investigate it on the show, but they say they paid the price for the footage. On their first investigation, Bagans suffered a long scratch on his back, executed by a demon, he claimed. Afterward, the evil followed them home, they said, damaging their personal lives. Aaron Goodwin went so far as to say the bad energy was a major contributing factor to his marriage being ruined.

Zak ended the inaugural episode by intoning, "If there is a place that houses pure evil, Bobby Mackey's Music World contains it. We felt it, we saw it, and we heard it."

In one of the *Ghost Adventures* follow-ups, they brought along an archbishop to perform a cleansing rite on the building. I thought that before my own visit, it might be good to ask exorcist Father Jack Ashcraft for his opinion on the matter. He didn't have encouraging words, to say the least.

"First, it is an extremely dangerous practice to go 'hunting ghosts,'" Father Ashcraft explained to me. "From the viewpoint of the Church, this is necromancy and spiritism, both very grave sins. Additionally, demonic entities will pose as the spirits of the dead, so even if one were to validly make contact (which is extremely rare), one cannot honestly say it is not demonic. There are many dangers to contacting or showing an unnatural interest in such entities, including oppression and obsession.

"My advice would simply be, don't do it. If many 'ghost hunters' put as much effort into seeking God and His Son, I dare say the face of reality television would be quite different."

▲▲▲

PIM's first investigation of Mackey's in July 2013 was a memorable one. In fact Leigh said it was "the most stuff that's happened on any investigation I've been on."

PIM was getting a tour of the basement by Bobby Mackey's representative Wanda Kay when Leigh noticed PIM member Missy Bostrom fall to the ground. Leigh thought she had tripped, but after seeing the look on Missy's face, he knew something else had occurred.

"It felt like somebody grabbed onto my arms like this," Missy described at a team meeting, clenching the air, "then it pushed me backwards." PIM had not yet set the video equipment up, but you could hear Missy's reaction in an audio clip, which Leigh played at the meeting.

Missy: "What the hell!"

Leigh: "Are you OK?"

Missy: "What the hell?"

Wanda Kay: "Let's step outside a minute."

Missy: "Oh my God!"

In addition to Leigh, Missy, Tony Belland, and Jann Goldberg, PIM members Randy Soukup, Michael "Gravy" Graeve, John Krahn, and Chris Paul were gathered in Leigh's rec room.

Missy had a second encounter about an hour later in an area of the basement known as the Wall of Faces. Although this was caught on video, someone was standing between Missy and the camera. You can see part of a leg flailing and a shuffle and hear a scream.

"That's me screaming, 'cause yeah, she was pinned on the fucking wall, hanging there," Jann said.

"It looked like someone had her by the armpits by the way her arms were positioned," Leigh recalled.

"That time it felt like it pushed me in the chest, up against the wall, and that's all I remember, getting a really hard push," Missy said, still seeming a bit shaken up by the events.

Jann also had a life-altering event that night at Bobby Mackey's. She was walking around the building doing baseline readings. "I remember thinking how badass I was, walking around the most haunted nightclub in America." The feeling was short-lived.

"I walked into a wall. Not a real wall, but that's what it felt like," Jann told me at a later interview. At this moment, she said, she instantly turned from skeptic to believer. She had spoken to PIM's member who identified as "sensitive" but didn't have an understanding of the concept until now. "I can't describe the feeling. It's kind of like falling in love: you can't describe it to someone who hasn't felt it. It was like instant vertigo. I kept thinking I was going to puke. My stomach was turning like this," Jann said, clenching the air and twisting. "I almost burst into tears. I called Missy over and she said, 'Oh, I feel dizzy.' She got hit with it, but not as hard as I did.

"I've never been shaken like that before, never thought it would happen to me," Jann said. "My motivation [for investigating] was just to go grubbing around in dirty old buildings for something to do on the weekends. I never believed—it wasn't in my paradigm."

She said that her new sensitive ability brought her a couple of visitors at Bobby Mackey's. "I felt like I was talking for two people. One was a girl who, in my mind's eye, was right here," she said, gesturing by her right shoulder. "She had golden natural blonde hair, like Elizabeth Montgomery, kind of young Meg Ryan before she ruined her face with plastic surgery. Just kind of . . . 'Mmm, I smell like daisies and angel tears' type, and it seemed to me she hung out there because she liked the music."

Jann's face darkened as she remembered the other entity. "Then there's the guy I referred to as Tony Soprano, because that's what he felt like. That's what *I* felt like. I felt like I had a big beach ball gut, short, bowling ball head. Whenever Gravy would talk, it felt like someone was stabbing a screwdriver into my spinal cord. I just wanted to kill him, and Noah, too. It was a boiling feeling in my gut; it was like hatred, but without the passion, if that makes sense. It was a disgusting feeling because this guy didn't want to just kill them, he wanted to medieval torture them to death. Not so much blow their brains out as disembowel them. 'I want you to hurt to death.' It was like no feeling I ever felt."

There were times, Jann said, that she felt nagged, compelled to blurt her anger out. "Gravy was standing over by [Bobby Mackey's] mechanical bull, and I'm telling you, every time he opened his mouth I was just like, *Oh . . .* I just wanted to choke the shit out of him because I just thought he was an annoying little pissant! He said something—'Should I go ride the bull?'—and I was like, 'How about I take that bull and stick it up your ass?'" Jann laughed. "I had enough control where I told people to stay away from me because I wasn't sure I could prevent myself from punching someone. I remember going up to Noah, Missy, and Gravy and saying, 'I hate you, and I hate you, and I hate you!' Right in their face," Jann told me, shifting an angry pointer finger through the air.

"It was an interesting investigation,"* Leigh said. "Unfortunately we don't have good documentation of what happened. We have audio, but the video we have is blocked by someone standing in the way. So we have reactions and clips of body parts moving, but we don't have an end result."

PIM immediately began planning a return trip, and when I saw September 22 marked on its online calendar as a "Return to Bobby Mackey's," I told them I wanted to go along.

▲▲▲

---

* You can read PIM's report on this investigation (as well as all their other ones) in its entirety at www.paranormalmilwaukee.com. It's in the "Cases" section and is case #130724.

On September 12 I returned to Leigh's house, a nice house on a quiet residential street in the Milwaukee suburb of West Allis. Leigh lives here with his wife, Daphne, a high school math teacher, and their two young children. Leigh and his family had gotten their Halloween decorations out early—cloth ghosts hung from a giant evergreen in the front yard, smiling plastic jack-o'-lanterns and humongous purple tarantulas lined the porch, and a Bela Lugosi–style vampire lurked by a tree. Leigh greeted me at the door wearing a T-shirt with the message I CAN EXPLAIN IT TO YOU, BUT I CAN'T UNDERSTAND IT FOR YOU.

Slowly, the team members returning to Bobby Mackey's—Gravy, Jann, John, and most bravely, Missy, pulled onto Leigh's street. They were there to have a "dry run" to see how all of their combined equipment and bodies would fit into Missy's Chevy Tahoe.

Meanwhile, before everyone was present, there was a lot of joking around at each other's expense. Jann got a vicious razzing for her penchant for stealing people's pens and pencils, which the team called "pulling a Jann" or "Janning," and her missing an upcoming investigation of the First Ward School, an allegedly haunted schoolhouse in Wisconsin Rapids, Wisconsin, because she would be celebrating Yom Kippur.

"What is that, anyway?" Gravy asked.

"Jesus Christ. Haven't you seen *Fiddler on the* fucking *Roof*?" she retorted.

"Anti-Semitic, misogynist assholes," Jann huffed, turning to me. "Be sure to write that down and quote me on it in the book."

After Missy and her Chevy Tahoe arrived, a long line of equipment was gathered, and Leigh jumped in the backseat. "Now the Tetris game begins," he said. There were about nine big plastic cases of equipment, a half dozen duffel bags, backpacks, and tripod bags, and a dozen yellow industrial battery packs.

"We can put this here and this here," he said as Gravy handed him case after case. After finding a satisfactory stacking method, the group moved down to Leigh's rec room in his basement, where his kids' building blocks were spread across the floor. The team grabbed seats on his couch or the giant beanbag chairs on the floor.

There was a lot of talk, sometimes heated, between Leigh and Gravy, about what time to leave and what route to take. With a timeline mapped out, there was a discussion of what trigger objects needed to be purchased.

The motley trigger object list for Bobby Mackey's included makeup, pills, a single flower (for Johanna), as well as brass knuckles, handcuffs, a copy of *Playboy*, booze, a bullet, playing cards (for the malicious mob ghosts), and a baseball, marbles, and other toys (for the kid ghosts).

With all the details hammered out, the team called the meeting and started to head out. Everything that could be planned for had been, but what might happen was still unknown.

Return to Bobby Mackey's

"Investigating Bobby Mackey's this early in your paranormal career is like losing your virginity to Jenna Jameson," Jann told me shortly before I headed toward Wilder, Kentucky.

On September 22 I met up with PIM outside of Wanda Kay's Ghost Shop, just down the road from Bobby Mackey's on Licking Pike. PIM rolled up in a perfectly packed Chevy Tahoe a few minutes after me. They had driven a solid six or seven hours from Wisconsin to Kentucky. Wanda arrived shortly afterward and unlocked the ghost shop.

Wanda, a musician herself, had worked for Bobby Mackey's for a decade. She started as a DJ and had also hosted karaoke and country line dancing lessons. "He didn't know I was into anything paranormal and I didn't tell him. But after a while, he said, 'Why don't you do a gift shop?' and three days later he said, 'Why don't you start doing ghost tours?' And then we started doing investigations."

She would continue to handle paranormal tours and investigations for Mr. Mackey until 2014, when she and his management had a falling-out, and she has written a book on the bar's haunted history, *Wicked They Walk: The Tour Guide's Book.* Her shop offers her books and CDs, ghost detecting equipment, protective crystals, paranormal seminars, and classes and psychic readings.

After paying the investigation balance and signing waivers absolving Bobby Mackey's in the case of accident (or ghost attack), we drove to the bar. Bobby Mackey has reason to make sure his ghost-tracking guests sign the waiver. Ghost issues came to a head in 1994, when Bobby Mackey's went to court over a claim of assault . . . by a ghost.

Plaintiff J. R. Costigan said he entered Mackey's men's room when he was punched and kicked by a cowboy hat–sporting spirit in 1994. He tried to sue for $1,000 in damages and demanded a warning sign be put up. The judge opined that Mackey had "no control over ghosts" and dismissed the case. In a different incident, another witness, Ritch Lawson, said he saw a ghost with a handlebar mustache throw a garbage can against the men's room wall. The room became intensely hot, and the ghost cryptically told Lawson, "Die game."

At the urging of Mackey's attorney, for a long time, this handwritten warning sign was placed by the door of Bobby Mackey's: WARNING TO OUR PATRONS: THIS ESTABLISHMENT IS PURPORTED TO BE HAUNTED. MANAGEMENT IS NOT RESPONSIBLE AND CANNOT BE HELD LIABLE FOR ANY ACTIONS OF ANY GHOSTS / SPIRITS ON THIS PREMISES.

▲▲▲

"Eight oh six and eleven seconds, Bobby Mackey's, September 22, 2013," Leigh time-stamped as we walked from the gravel parking lot up to Bobby Mackey's front door. I took a deep breath and walked in.

Jann and Gravy began walking around the perimeter of the dark bar to take EMF and temperature readings, while I strolled around slowly, taking in the layout and details.

I walked past Bobby Mackey's collection of framed 45 rpm records lining the length of the bar. I stuck my head in the gift shop, which had T-shirts and Mackey's CDs. Wanda used to operate out of that space, but she had expanded enough to move, which was OK with Mackey. Although he'd enlisted to Wanda to host paranormal groups, he still felt reluctant about promoting ghosts and tried to maintain a separation of his music and the paranormal.

"It's like pulling teeth," Wanda said. "That's why I have the shop up the street; he doesn't want paranormal here. He wants to be known for his music."

I took in the stage area; a spotlight illuminated a drum set and guitar amp. A banner draped across the back of the stage proclaimed Bobby Mackey's as the COUNTRIEST NIGHT SPOT AROUND.

"They're really good," Kay said of the Big Mac Band. "Bobby's had the same pickers for thirty-five years. That's unheard of. You can imagine how tight they are when they play. He just eats, sleeps, and breathes music."

Continuing to look around, I crossed over the empty dance floor to an area that had a somewhat creepy-looking mechanical bull and pool tables set up. There used to be a jukebox set up in there too, one that liked to mysteriously play "The Anniversary Waltz" by itself. Sometimes, it was alleged, even when unplugged.

We settled down for the first EVP session of the evening. I grabbed a table near the bar with Jann, while Gravy and John moved chairs and sat on the dance floor. Missy, Wanda, and Leigh sat near the mechanical bull.

"Did someone move a chair over there?" Leigh asked in the dark.

"That was me!" I replied, sheepishly.

"Tea, make sure to tag yourself loudly!" Leigh reminded. Then he heard some noises coming from an unplugged change machine. Everyone was quiet.

"Do you need some money?" he asked the phantom spare-changer. "I have some money here in my hand."

The incident is time-stamped 8:27:23. Leigh started the EVP session.

"Hello, my name is Noah. I was here, oh, a couple months ago now. We're not here to hurt you. We just want to find out more about you. If there is someone here who would like to communicate with us, could you please come forward and tell us your name?"

A few minutes later Jann and I heard a faucet running for a few seconds and we went to look in the nearby bathrooms. When Jann turned the faucet on, it sounded like what we had heard. I later found out that the ladies' room faucets turning on and off has been reported activity in addition to ghostly appearances in the men's room.

The EVP session continued. "Who is your favorite country music star?" I asked, and I was surprised to see a moving shadow along the bar, before I realized it was a bit of outdoor light from a car coming through a window.

"Can you show yourself to us?" Missy asked. "We want to see what you look like."

At 8:43:30, we moved up to George's Apartment, the former residence of the caretakers. Named after a caretaker from the 1920s and '30s, Wanda said, this was also where former caretaker Carl Lawson lived when he claimed he was possessed by demons. After an EVP session, we moved outside so the team could do a more elaborate setup in the club's basement.

The team got to work unloading the SUV full of equipment. For the next hour, Leigh and Gravy set up equipment in every corner of the basement and did some EVP sessions with just the two of them while John, Missy, Jann, and I hung around outside. We went for a short walk around the exterior of the bar. We went crunching along the gravel near the railroad tracks, crickets chirping, then we sat down by the van to wait.

▲▲▲

"Well, I made it out; Gravy wasn't so lucky," Leigh said, exiting the basement about an hour later.

"You capture anything?" Jann asked.

"A gnat," Leigh said. "All right, these are the people I was telling you about," Leigh said as we walked through the basement door.

"Hello, hello, I'm back," Jann said.

We immediately headed to a backroom of the basement known as the Wall of Faces, to start an EVP session time-stamped 11:31:44 PM. The room was so named because of the weird blotchy patterns on the basement wall that appeared to be creepy human faces to an imaginative eye. A chicken-wired wall contained some storage on one side of the room. A coffee table and chairs formed a circle in the room, set up for paranormal investigators. This was where Missy had her experience of being thrown into a wall.

"Is there any negative history associated with this particular area?" Krahn asked Kay.

"Yeah, the whole building," Wanda said a bit wearily. "Every inch of it. The outside, too. You're sitting on top of the slaughterhouse and the armory and battery where everyone was massacred. The grounds are layer upon layer upon layer of negative shit, to put it bluntly."

After settling in to the Wall of Faces room to do an EVP session, Missy had her second terrifying experience in the room—and one of the strangest things I'd witnessed. We were sitting there in the total darkness, throwing out questions, hoping to get a response, when we heard Missy struggling with her breathing. Here's a transcription of what happened next:

Leigh: "Hey, you're breathing weird. What's wrong?"

Missy (through short breaths): "I can't see anything in front of me."

Krahn: "That's because you're in the dark, Missy. What's wrong?"

Missy (sounding more upset): "I can't see anything!"

Leigh (turning on flashlight and shining it in her face): "Is this better?"

Missy (looking blankly ahead): "No!"

Leigh: "Look up. Her eyes are constricting fine."

Missy: "Yeah, I can't see anything. It's like, completely dark in front of me."

Gravy: "You don't see the light in your eyes?"

Missy (frightened): "Yes, I'm serious."

Wanda: "Close your eyes. Close your eyes, foc—"

Missy: "My hands feel weird, like they're shaking. Like inside, vibrating."

Leigh: "I don't feel them shaking, but your hands are cold."

Wanda: "Try to focus on a number, like twenty, and count backwards to one, and concentrate only on that."

Missy (breathing heavily): "My hands feel like—oh my God—my hands feel like awful."

Krahn: "What do you mean?"

Leigh: "Can you see now?"

Missy: "I can see now, but my hands feel really awful. Like they're numb. Like they're sleeping."

Leigh got Missy to move her arms around.

Missy: "I can see now."

Krahn: "Gravy, you got your EMF detector?"

Gravy: "No."

Leigh: "I got my EMF detector right here. 3.69 . . . 4.04."

Gravy: "Just keep breathing deep."

Leigh: "3.72"

Missy: "I can still see."

Gravy: "That's good. Are your hands feeling better?"

Missy: "No."

Leigh: "Take off your gloves."

Missy (after rubbing her hands together): "OK, it's gone. I feel fine again. That was weird."

The Farmer's Daughter

Missy was raised on a farm near Lebanon, Wisconsin, with ten brothers and four sisters. When I sat down to interview her, she told me that her paranormal investigation hobby had made her the black sheep of her family.

"The consensus in my family is, no, they don't agree with what I do. My side of the family, they think I'm playing with the devil. They just don't get it. They are very religious. One sister is supportive, one is tolerant. The rest of my family would prefer I didn't talk about it. My mom will say something once in a while, and it's always negative. We're stubborn Germans. Mom and Dad's family are both German farmers."

I asked her if her family's lack of support bothered her.

"I don't care. I've learned with my family to just be yourself and don't try to live up to their expectations, because you're not going to," she said, laughing it off.

Missy moved to Milwaukee to attend beauty school and met her husband, Jim, an engineer, on a blind date on Halloween. They married in 2001, and she says he's supportive of her hobby. "He's a very free-spirited kind of guy. He had just rode his mountain bike from Wisconsin to Oregon when I met him. That's just the type of guy he is. If he decides to do something, he just does it."

Things started getting supernatural when Missy, pregnant with her first son, and Jim moved into an old farmhouse in Dousman, Wisconsin. "We had some kind of goofy experiences there," she told me. Missy, diagnosed with high blood pressure and toxemia, had been given a doctor's order of bed rest. Missy's hands were swollen, so she took off her wedding ring.

"I went to see my doctor, and when I came home, I noticed my ring was gone. I'm freaking out, calling the hospital to see if they found it, couldn't find it anywhere. A couple days later, I'm just so distraught, and Jim says, 'Missy, I found your ring.'" He had seen a glint in the sunlight by the base of a big tree in their backyard.

"I don't know how the heck it got out there, because it's not on the path to my car, and that's all I walked."

Shortly after that, another incident happened after Missy wrote out a stack of invites to her son's baptism. "I left them on the night-stand and went to sleep, and in the morning they weren't there. Well, sure enough, they were found in that same golldarned spot where my ring was found. There's a couple other small things we found out there, too. And Jim would always get a sense of someone extremely tall standing behind him. His good friend Chad is really tall, so there's a couple times he'd think Chad was there. He'd turn around and say, 'Hey, Chad, what are you up to?' And there would be nobody there."

Missy added that after they moved from the house, she ran into an old neighbor at the grocery store. He wanted to know if anything strange had happened at the house, because the new tenants were having odd experiences.

▲▲▲

Missy, also inspired by *Ghost Hunters*, got a tip from one of her sisters living in Stevens Point, Wisconsin, that a coworker was a member of a new team there named Stevens Point Paranormal Club (SPCC), led by Valerie Kedrowski. Missy initially joined the team until she found out about PIM, in closer proximity. During her tenure with SPCC, she took a trip to Bobby Mackey's and Waverly Hills Sanatorium to investigate, but she said both were uneventful.

"Not much happened. Val got scratched on her back; it disappeared almost immediately. But nothing like the times I went with PIM."

▲▲▲

Missy: "Did someone do something scary to you like put something over your face where you couldn't see? I'm not going to lie, that was a scary thing. Did that happen to you?"

And . . . silence again.

▲▲▲

"It's quarter after twelve. We should move to the well room," Leigh said.

In the well room, I grabbed a chair right next to one of Bobby Mackey's most famous attractions: the portal to hell. I kept one eye on the rest of the team, or where I thought they were in the dark, and one eye out to watch for any demons springing from the well. Gravy sat across the room, also next to the well. Missy sat in a small chamber attached to the room, which Wanda said is a former jail cell, left over from when the building was used as an armory.

"I'm going to sit right here with my back to this opening, which I don't like, because it creeps me out. But I don't have any choice. Fight through my fears. Fight through the fears," Gravy said, smiling. We started the EVP session, and soon the fear grabbed Jann.

"Missy, can you come out of there?" Jann asked, her voice nervous.

"Why?" Missy asked.

"I just really would like it if you would. OK?"

"Why do you want Missy out of there?" John asked. Jann sniffed abruptly, her voice shaking.

"Because I'm afraid she's going to get hurt in there. *Please*, Missy, come out of there, please."

PIM's cameras positioned near the "portal to hell" in Bobby Mackey's basement.
TEA KRULOS

"Jann!" Gravy said. "Jann, sit and relax. Take a couple deep breaths."

"Missy's fine," John said.

"It's OK, I'll be all right," Missy said.

"She's not going to get hurt," Leigh said. "Gravy was in here before. Nothing happened to him."

"Gravy is exactly the one I would attack," John said.

"Thanks, John."

My ear hurts really bad," Missy said.

"You guys leave Missy alone!" Jann said. "They're the ones who threw her last time. Leave her alone!"

"No, these are different ones; they don't come out of there—they're stuck in there," said Wanda.

Krahn switched with Missy for a few minutes, but then Missy wanted to go back in.

"My ear feels fine now," Missy said.

"We brought your gal pal back," Leigh said.

"Why dontcha just tell them you're coming to show 'em a good time? See if they treat you different," Wanda said to Missy.

While the rest of us remained silent, Missy began an eerie entice-ment session with the male ghosts stuck in the cell. "Yeah, I'm here to show you a good time," she said. "You haven't had a woman here in a while, I bet. Any requests?"

Silence.

"Maybe you could start out by telling me what your name is."

Nothing.

"Do you know what my name is? My name is Missy."

Nothing.

"Why don't you whisper something in my ear, instead of making it hurt?"

No response.

"Can you touch me? I don't care where you touch me, but you got to do it so I feel it."

Nothing.

"Or maybe you can pull on my hair."

No response.

"Do you like me being in here? . . . I feel cold . . . colder."

Silence.

▲▲▲

The EVP sessions moved from room to room in the basement. We did one near what was said to be Johanna's dressing room, another one in the entrance of a tunnel—since filled in—that was said to be a former transport channel for moonshine, another in a room that was formerly a kitchen.

We returned to do sessions in the Wall of Faces room and the well room, but no further noteworthy incident occurred.

▲▲▲

"Thank you very much for communicating with us if you did. We have to go now," Leigh said. He time-stamped the end of the inves-tigation at "two thirty and twenty-five seconds."

"Lights coming on, watch your eyes," Wanda said. The team broke down equipment while I chatted with Wanda, and around 3 AM, we walked out into the crisp air and the chirping crickets.

▲▲▲

PIM always tries to view the encounters they have from a scientific perspective, so although Leigh wasn't quite sure what happened to Missy, he said one explanation could be some kind of panic attack.

"I think it is possible she had a psychological event that resulted in what she reported," Leigh said, also noting that the same room was where she had her terrifying previous encounter of being pushed. So was this experience psychological or paranormal? "In the end," he continued, "we will never definitively know what caused it."

▲▲▲

The incidents at Bobby Mackey's had affected Jann on a much deeper level than I had suspected at the time. It was the starting point for an ugly falling-out she had with PIM in January 2014. Around the time of PIM's holiday party, I noticed testy exchanges between her, Noah, and Gravy, and shortly after, she loudly quit the team. This came as a surprise to me, because in my first interview, she had specifically told me how she considered the team to be almost as tight as family.

After PIM's first Bobby Mackey's investigation, their next stop was Waverly Hills Sanatorium near Louisville, Kentucky. Jann said she was exhausted and looking forward to a more typical PIM investigation. The group brought along a baby doll as a potential trigger object for a ghost of a woman who, legend had it, killed her own baby in the sanatorium.

"I thought this being able to sense things was going to be a strictly Bobby Mackey's phenomenon," Jann told me. She said that soon she had tuned in to one of Waverly Hills' ghosts.

"I felt this *va-voom!* You get these pins and needles, not just on your skin, but through your guts. You ever take a Percocet? It's a feeling like that, like *aaaaah.* Then I started feeling these emotions—sorrow beyond anything I've ever felt, unimaginable, heart-wrenching sadness. I had these nagging thoughts again: *Secret baby, secret baby, secret baby.*"

Jann said she began to get impressions. The ghost was "smart and funny, like Diane Keaton," she said, and she was able to tell that the woman had been forced to undergo an abortion by a sanatorium doctor who had impregnated her—the "secret baby."

"It's not so much she was mad as she was like, 'Oh, Christ, another group of fucking idiots with a baby doll.'" Jann said that PIM members later hid the doll without her knowledge to rile up the ghost. Jann said her senses led her to the doll and she confronted the team. Noah said Gravy didn't hide the doll adequately and Jann spotted it.

"One of the things that really set my Irish up was Noah having conversations two or three times where he was grilling me at this point and I'm trying to sort out my own head," Jann said. "I was like, 'Look, don't you get it? I didn't ask for this! I'm questioning my own sanity, I don't need your ass to do it, too.'"

Noah countered that questioning paranormal experiences with a skeptic's eye is fundamental to PIM.

"My understanding is that she's mad we didn't believe her. Well, I don't believe anyone—it's not a secret," Leigh told me. "It's not like I tell people, 'I believe you 100 percent' and then behind their back say they are full of crap. I question everything anyone tells me on an investigation."

The straw that broke the camel's back was a reality show appearance. PIM was invited to be on the *Ghost Adventures* spin-off show *Ghost Adventures: Aftershocks*, to talk about the group's experiences at Bobby Mackey's. The show producers told the team they would fly one, possibly two members to talk on camera in Las Vegas.

"Noah calls, and the first thing he says is 'You're not going,'" Jann told me. "He said, 'I think it's just going to be me and Missy.'" Jann, who talked to people behind the scenes, said she felt "screwed over" by her teammates. Eventually, just Missy was sent for the shoot. An angry storm of text messages followed between Jann and Noah about the show and other topics, and she quit. Another ugly debate appeared online when Jann and PIM fought over control of the group's Twitter page. Both Jann and Noah point fingers at each other and accuse the other of trashing a friendship over the *Ghost Adventures: Aftershocks* show.

"There are some members of the group who genuinely hate her for how she treated things and things she said. That is unfortunate," Noah told me over the phone. He sounded upset, admitting that she had been a useful member of the group. "Very unfortunate. It is the opinion of some of us that her virtual friends on Facebook were more important than the actual people she was associating with here in Milwaukee."

Not surprisingly, Jann's summation of PIM consisted of several four-letter words.

It's interesting that, despite the high level of drama the investigations of the haunted honky-tonk had caused, the allure of the place led both PIM and Jann (with an independently assembled team) to both plot return trips to Bobby Mackey's Music World in 2014.

EPILOGUE:
THE BOGEYMAN

"**A**LL RISE."

I stood up in the court of Judge Michael Bohren, who entered the courtroom wearing a red bow tie and with a neatly trimmed white mustache. He sat down solemnly.

Then-twelve-year-old Morgan Geyser was led through the court-room doors, handcuffs connecting her wrists and ankles, attached to a chain belt. She shuffled into the courtroom wearing the smallest prison jumpsuit possible. Two security guards twice her size led her to her defense lawyers. Her father, sitting a couple seats away from me, burst into tears and put his face in the palm of his hands.

Geyser was part of a terrifying incident that happened in Wauke-sha, Wisconsin—a midsize city outside of Milwaukee, where my parents currently live—while I was working on this book. This inci-dent took place just a couple miles down the road from their house. There, in an area of forest near a city park, two young girls' belief in a monster resulted in tragedy. Geyser and her friend Anissa Weier had come to believe that a mythical entity, Slender Man (sometimes written as Slenderman), was a real being and that if they gave him the blood sacrifice of one of their classmates, a twelve-year-old girl later identified as Payton Leutner, they would be granted access to Slen-der Man's kingdom in the Chequamegon-Nicolet National Forest, about two hundred miles away. There they would become Slender Man's "proxies" and live with the mythical entity, who is depicted as being tall and slim, having a gray head with no face, wearing a sharp black suit, and sometimes having tentacles protruding from his back. Slender Man was said to kidnap and kill children.

Geyser and Weier had had a sleepover party the night before, with their victim. They went roller-skating. The next morning, they went to play at David's Park. The girls originally planned to stab their friend in the park bathroom, letting her blood flow through a floor drain. They entered the bathroom. Geyser had a five-inch knife tucked in her waistband. But she had a "nervous breakdown," according to a report by the *Milwaukee Journal Sentinel*, and the girls abandoned the plan for the moment.

Next, the girls went to a thick forest bordering a quiet suburban backstreet on Rivera Drive, where Geyser and Weier created the ruse of playing hide-and-seek. Weier and Geyser jumped on their victim and stabbed her with a knife nineteen times. The victim cried out, "I hate you. I trusted you."

The *Milwaukee Journal Sentinel* reported:

Weier told the victim to lie down and be quiet—she would lose blood more slowly. Weier told police she gave the victim those instructions so she wouldn't draw attention to herself, and so she would die. Weier told the victim they were going to get her help; but they never actually planned on doing so. They hoped she would die, and they would see [Slender Man] and know he existed.

A couple days after the incident, I retraced the crime scene. Walking along Rivera Drive, I ran into three young girls, quietly carrying messages they had written on signboard. I approached them, and they told me they were classmates of the victim and were showing their support. You and Your Family Are in Our Hearts! Stay Strong, Bella! read one. The girls explained that Bella was the victim's nickname. Our Hearts Go Out to the Victim, read another sign, shaped like a Valentine heart. A pink teddy bear was placed next to it.

Geyser and Weier had left Bella behind to die and began to walk to Chequamegon-Nicolet National Forest, where they thought Slender Man would greet them. They packed granola bars, bottled water, and a change of clothes for the two-hundred-mile trek. Geyser packed a picture of her family.

Bella did not die. She managed to channel enough strength to crawl out of the forest to Big Bend Road, right by the spot where the girls I encountered were placing their signs. A horrified bicyclist found her, collapsed near the road. One of the girl's messages read, A Millimeter Away, and You're Still Here Today, referring to the doctor's discovery that one of the nineteen knife wounds had penetrated just millimeters from Bella's heart.

Police quickly picked up Geyser and Weier. Because of the severity of the crimes, the case was brought to adult court instead of juvenile court, and the two girls were held on $500,000 bail.

▲▲▲

The court appearance was a short one. Judge Bohren ordered Geyser be tested for "competency" to determine how the case would proceed. Weier's defense asked for more time to evaluate the case. Afterward, the lawyers were surrounded by a throng of media in the courtroom hallway.

Slender Man is not an old myth. He can be traced back to an online photo contest from 2009 that quickly became a viral hit. Soon people were featuring him in their own online fiction stories, short homemade movies, and video games.

But, then again, Slender Man is older than 2009. He is just a new version of an old, powerful archetype: the Bogeyman, that faceless, frightening creeper who has lived on in children's imaginations and nightmares for generations. With the gullibility and viral nature of the Internet, this Bogeyman soon took on a life of his own. The lines between fact and fiction, as they often do with paranormal subjects, began to blur. Some people began to believe Slender Man was real.

▲▲▲

In *The Mothman Prophecies*, John Keel talks of the theory that creatures such as Mothman or ghosts might be an actual manifestation of the human mind. He writes about an alleged haunted house in Greenwich Village. The home is the former residence of pulp writer Walter Gibson, and after he vacated the house, people began to report seeing an apparition "dressed in a long, black cape and a wide brimmed slouch hat, pulled down over its eyes as it slinks room to room," Keel reports. That description matches Gibson's most well-known creation, the mysterious pulp detective known as the Shadow.

"The Tibetans believed that advanced human minds can manipulate invisible energies into visible forms called Tulpas, or thought projections," Keel writes. "Did Walter Gibson's intense concentration on his Shadow novels inadvertently bring a Tulpa into existence?"

Aaron Sagers, of ParanormalPopCulture.com, speculates on this as well, specifically in relation to the Slender Man incidents. He says that in the paranormal community, there is an increasing amount of people who believe Slender Man is real in some form. Some think he has always been around and is just starting to get notice now, Sagers outlines in an article for the *Huffington Post*: "The other theory is that we created Slender Man by thinking about him. Not entirely unlike Tibetan Tulpas, Slender Man may be a so-called 'thoughtform.' Through people directing energy to him, crafting stories, fleshing out characteristics, and talking about him at length, the theory is we may have collectively given life to the monster and allowed him to enter our realm."

Sagers goes on to point to a case in the 1970s where members of a group called the Toronto Society for Psychical Research claimed to have materialized a spirit they created entirely with their minds—a seventeenth-century nobleman named Philip Aylesford. The group of eight created a fake bio on the ghost and communicated with him, they claimed, during a séance in which he communicated by knocking on the table.

▲▲▲

After a court-ordered evaluation, psychologists determined that Morgan Geyser was incompetent to stand trial. They determined, "[Geyser] exhibited disturbing behavior and beliefs during their interview with her," the *Milwaukee Journal Sentinel* reported, "squatting on her chair, laughing hysterically, constantly looking in corners. She had conversations with Voldemort, a Teenage Mutant Ninja Turtle, and repeated her belief in Slender Man, unicorns, and her own 'Vulcan mind control.'"

Evaluation of Geyser's and Weier's condition continued, and they returned to court in December 2014, with Judge Bohren hearing assessments from mental health experts. Geyser was diagnosed with schizophrenia, but despite this, the judge determined that both girls were competent to stand trial.

▲▲▲

"The Slender Man kids who wish to be allowed into the castle in the woods metaphorically equals the Christians going on the Crusades because someone imagines they will be able to enter the gates of heaven if they kill certain people," Loren Coleman told me when I asked him about the Slender Man case.

He said, "The existence of a fringe element in Fortean and unexplained studies, as well as vulnerable people 'believing' in the reality of some items that are not proven or outright creations and fiction is not common. But historically it does occur."

In June 2014 the International Cryptozoology Museum received 501(c)(3) status, and Coleman's visions for the museum continue to grow. That same month, the museum unveiled a new exhibit of artifacts donated by Tom Page, who bankrolled Bigfoot expeditions in California in the late 1960s and early '70s. On display are footprint casts and documents relating to the expeditions. The centerpiece of the display is Page's tranquilizer dart gun, which he hoped would take down Bigfoot.

When I asked Coleman what keeps him involved in the field, despite drama and struggles keeping his museum doors open, he had a simple answer: "The field of cryptozoology fills my life with passion, mysteries, and animals—three of my favorite things. Also, I absolutely learn something new every day, and feel more alive because of it."

▲ ▲ ▲

After I returned from my trip to Isabella, Jim Sherman had the recordings of the sounds we heard by our camp analyzed. The odd laugh-like chattering, he said, is still an unknown. But he determined that the terrifying howls we had heard so close to camp were most likely from an unusually aggressive coyote. That is what had trapped a Bigfoot tracker and an investigative reporter in a Jeep overnight: a coyote.

As for the UFO, I had a unique and somewhat humbling experience after seeing it—I got to experience the flip side. I had been scrutinizing with a skeptical eye, and now it was turned on me, to my surprise, by friends and family. They gave me that special look that implied I was lying or that I had been out in the field too long and had gone crazy. Jim's short video footage, not doing justice to the actual sight, did little to help. People told me what they thought

I had seen: airplane lights trapped in fog, a star shining at a funny angle, or a drone out for a late-night cruise. I do not maintain that what I saw was an extraterrestrial craft, but none of those other explanations satisfy me.

"Welcome to the club, haha," Jason McClellan of Open Minds Productions responded when I contacted him about the incident.

▲ ▲ ▲

Dave Shealy's next move with the Skunk Apes was to announce an expedition limited to five people with a price tag of $500 a head. The "exciting 2 day adventure," scheduled for late 2014, was to include "his home cook meal of frog legs, fish, etc." and a chance for "possible Skunk Ape sightings."

Rev. Bob Larson continues to tour around the country, from airport hotel to airport hotel. He had more than twenty stops planned for the first half of 2015, including eight days in the Ukraine.

▲ ▲ ▲

"Hello, my name is Noah, and these are my friends," Leigh's voice echoed across the stage of the Modjeska Theater, a historic venue on Milwaukee's south side that had been abandoned for seven years and was starting to decay. A development group had recently purchased the theater and was beginning the huge task of removing moldy carpet and flaking paint to restore the Modjeska to its glory days. PIM had been invited in to investigate the claims the Modjeska had accumulated over the years—an apparition of a man wearing a top hat who appeared before concertgoers in one of the balconies, items levitating, unexplained noises.

After setting up equipment in the main theater at the Modjeska, as well as audio and video recorders spread throughout a smaller side theater on the second floor, the hallway, and the theater's massive basement, PIM began its investigation. Nothing definitive was captured in that investigation or a second one the team conducted a month later. After my night with the team at the Modjeska, I parted ways with PIM.

"My reason for staying in this field that is filled with drama and way more questions than answers is twofold," Leigh told me about his motivation to keep investigating. "Are all these claims made-up, hallucinated, misperceived, etc., or is there legitimacy to a small percent of them? As a scientist that searches for that truth of whether or not the paranormal exists, it is too strong for me to resist, at least right now." PIM continues to book investigations around Milwaukee and beyond and made plans for a 2014 return road trip to investigate Sedamsville Rectory and Bobby Mackey's Music World.

"I also want to help people who think they are experiencing the paranormal. There are very few groups that take the stance PIM does, and being a strong voice of reason in a sea of disinformation is something I take great pride in," Leigh said.

▲ ▲ ▲

Meanwhile, Jann had continued her interest in paranormal investigation without the team. She described herself as an "orphan," tagging along with other investigators she had befriended. She joined TnT Paranormal Investigators, an Illinois team led by married couple Melissa and Tracey Tanner for an investigation at a business. For her birthday, she assembled a group of friends to investigate the Bird Cage Theatre, a haunted hot spot in Tombstone, Arizona.

She even returned to the site of her most intense investigating moment, Bobby Mackey's Music World, in June 2014. She teamed up with NightShade Paranormal, a group based out of Ohio, to bring in paranormal expert David Rountree, author of *Paranormal Technology: Understanding the Science of Ghost Hunting*. Rountree gave a seminar at Wanda Kay's Ghost Shop before joining the group for an investigation of the honky-tonk. This time, Jann told me, things were quiet.

"It was fun this time. That weird thing only happened with my stomach once," she told me. But why would she return again and again to a place where she had such frightening experiences? That was an easy question to answer, she told me.

"To find some fucking answers."

ACKNOWLEDGMENTS

Another book, another long list of people who have blessed me with their help. Again, I must first and foremost thank my friend and editor Jan Christensen, who looked over an early draft to help me clean it up and offer insight. A big thanks to my friends Erin Petersen and Chris Roth, both talented writers, who gave valuable feedback.

Other talented friends who helped with the book include David Beyer Jr., Jennifer Janviere, and Lacy Landre. Thanks to those who joined in the adventure in some way, my sisters Margot and Rita, Sarah Gonzalez-Myers, Tanner Stevens, and all my family and friends who have been supportive. Special thanks to Wendy Jean.

I'm grateful to everyone who offered time to me to be interviewed, but I especially want to thank Paranormal Investigators of Milwaukee, Loren Coleman, Jann Goldberg, Jim Sherman (and our friends at Isabella), Believe It Tour, and Maureen Elsberry for their extended hospitality.

Thanks much to Jerome Pohlen and everyone at Chicago Review Press for their hard work.

NOTES

Introduction: Invisible Monsters

Noah Leigh, interview with the author, McDonald's in West Allis, Wisconsin, January 18, 2014.

1. The Monster Hunter and His Museum

Loren Coleman, interview with the author and tour, International Cryptozoology Museum, Portland, Maine, September 25, 2013.

Course materials for Cryptozoology 101 class, Universal Class, last accessed July 24, 2013, www.universalclass.com/i/crn/7550037.htm.

Loren Coleman, "Top Cryptozoology Stories of 2013," *CryptoZooNews* (blog), December 18, 2013, www.cryptozoonews.com/top-cz-2013/.

NPR, "The Kraken is Real: Scientist Films First Footage of a Giant Squid," *All Things Considered*, January 13, 2013, www.npr.org/2013/01/13 /169274472/the-kraken-is-real-scientist-films-first-footage-of-a-giant -squid.

Loren Coleman, *Tom Slick: True Life Encounters in Cryptozoology* (Fresno, CA: Craven Street Books, 2002).

"The Yeti," episode of *Unsolved Mysteries*, NBC, aired February 12, 1992.

Loren Coleman, *Bigfoot! The True Story of Apes in America* (New York: Paraview Pocket Books, 2003).

Loren Coleman, "About Me," *Twilight Language* (blog), last accessed November 17, 2014, http://copycateffect.blogspot.com/.

Loren Coleman, "A Near Death Experience," *Cryptomundo* (blog), September 25, 2007, http://cryptomundo.com/cryptozoo-news/near -death/.

2. Time Stamp

PIM investigation of Riverside Theater, Milwaukee, Wisconsin, June 6, 2013.

PIM case report #110909 (Riverside Theater, September 9, 2011), www.paranormalmilwaukee.com/cases/riverside/riverside.html.

PIM case report #111203 (Riverside Theater, December 3, 2011), www.paranormalmilwaukee.com/cases/riverside2/riverside2.html.

PIM case report #120218 (Riverside Theater, February 18, 2012), www.paranormalmilwaukee.com/cases/riverside3/riverside3.html.

PIM case report #120323 (Riverside Theater, March 23, 2012), www.paranormalmilwaukee.com/cases/riversideclass/riversideclass .html.

Jann Goldberg, interview with the author, Colectivo coffee shop in Bay View, Milwaukee, Wisconsin, October 23, 2013.

PIM case report #130525 (Willow Creek Farm, May 24–26, 2013), www.paranormalmilwaukee.com/cases/willowcreek5/willowcreek5 .html.

PIM case report #090306 (Willow Creek Farm, March 6–7, 2009), www.paranormalmilwaukee.com/cases/011_willow_creek/.

Noah Leigh, presentation at Milwaukee Public Museum, October 10, 2013.

Noah Leigh, interview with the author, McDonald's in West Allis, Wisconsin, January 18, 2014.

Noah Leigh, follow-up interview with the author, Leigh's home, West Allis, Wisconsin, June 19, 2014.

PIM investigation of Brumder Mansion, Milwaukee, Wisconsin, November 9, 2013.

Sherry Strub, *Milwaukee Ghosts* (Atglen, PA: Schiffer Publishing, 2008).

3. The Slaying of the Chupacabras

Sharon Hill, interview with the author via Skype, January 9, 2014.

Sharon Hill, "Being Scientific: Popularity, Purpose and Promotion of Amateur Research and Investigation Groups in the U.S.," thesis paper e-mailed to the author.

Center for Inquiry Portland newsletter, December 2013.

J. Jason Groschopf, interview with the author via Facebook, June 9, 2014.

Loren Coleman and Jerome Clark, *Cryptozoology A to Z: The Encyclopedia of Loch Monsters, Sasquatch, Chupacabras, and Other Authentic Mysteries of Nature* (New York: Fireside, 1999).

Benjamin Radford, *Tracking the Chupacabra: The Vampire Beast in Fact, Fiction, and Folklore* (Albuquerque: University of New Mexico Press, 2011).

Benjamin Radford, *Scientific Paranormal Investigation: How to Solve Unexplained Mysteries* (Corrales, NM: Rhombus Publishing Company, 2010).

Benjamin Radford, interview with the author via Skype, June 16, 2014.

"Texas Chupacabra Captured, Family Says," Fox 8 News, April 3, 2014, http://myfox8.com/2014/04/03/texas-couple-claims-they-have-captured-a-chupacabra/.

Nicole Hensley, "Texas Captors Euthanize Alleged Chupacabra Dubbed 'Chupie,'" *New York Daily News*, April 4, 2014, www.nydailynews.com/news/national/texas-captors-euthanize-alleged-chupacabra-article-1.1745980.

Loren Coleman, follow-up interview with the author via e-mail, July 3, 2014.

Sharon Hill and Barbara Drescher, "I Doubt That— the Media Guide to Skepticism," speech to the James Randi Educational Foundation, video posted to YouTube by JamesRandiFoundation, January 6, 2014, www.youtube.com/watch?v=ybKMv_nvBjo.

4. Lake Monster Fever

Champ Camp, Button Bay State Park, Vermont, July 25–28, 2013.

Robert E. Bartholomew, *The Untold Story of Champ: A Social History of America's Loch Ness Monster* (Albany, NY: Excelsior/State University of New York Press, 2012).

Believe It Tour, "Tour of the Crystal Skull 2012," official website, last accessed November 17, 2014, www.believeittour.com/crystal-skull/.

Believe It Tour, "Old Haunts Transylvania," official website, last accessed November 17, 2014, www.believeittour.com/old-haunts-transylvania/.

Loren Coleman, "How Many Champ Sightings for 2013?" *CryptoZooNews* (blog), July 23, 2013, www.cryptozoonews.com/champ2013/.

Joseph W. Zarzynski, *Champ: Beyond the Legend* (Port Henry, NY, Bannister Publications, 1984).

Benjamin Radford and Joe Nickell, *Lake Monster Mysteries: Investigating the World's Most Elusive Creatures* (Lexington, KY: The University Press of Kentucky, 2006).

"America's Loch Ness Monster," episode of *MonsterQuest*, History Channel, aired October 31, 2007.

5. What Was That?

PIM walk-through of the "Smiths'" apartment, Milwaukee, Wisconsin, June 26, 2013.

Noah Leigh, interview with the author, McDonald's in West Allis, Wisconsin, January 18, 2014.

John Krahn, interview with the author during investigation at Bobby Mackey's Music World, Wilder, Kentucky, September 22, 2013.

PIM walk-through of "José and Maria's" townhouse, Milwaukee, Wisconsin, January 8, 2014.

Michael "Gravy" Graeve, interview with the author, Einstein Bros. Bagels East Side location, Milwaukee, Wisconsin, March 23, 2014.

PIM holiday party at the Jock Stop, West Allis, Wisconsin, January 11, 2014.

PIM investigation of Sarah's residence, Milwaukee, Wisconsin, February 1, 2014.

PIM case report #140201 (private residence, February 1, 2014), www.paranormalmilwaukee.com/cases/milwaukeeresidential /milwaukeeresidential.html.

PIM, "Paranormal 101: Types of Hauntings," official website, last accessed November 17, 2014, www.paranormalmilwaukee.com/paranormal101 .html.

PIM investigation of "poltergeist" at private residence, Wauwatosa, Wisconsin, April 11, 2014.

PIM case report #140411 (private residence, April 11, 2014), www.paranormalmilwaukee.com/cases/wauwatosaresidence /wauwatosaresidence.html.

PIM meeting, recorded April 27, 2014.

6. International UFO Congress

"Obama's New Advisor Is a UFO Enthusiast," episode 65 of *Spacing Out!*, Open Minds, released December 20, 2013, www.openminds.tv/obamas -new-advisor-ufo-enthusiast-spacing-episode-65/25495.

Jason McClellan, interview with the author via e-mail, June 17, 2014.

Maureen Elsberry, interview with the author via e-mail, August 7, 2014.

Twenty-Third Annual International UFO Congress, Fountain Hills, Arizona, February 12–16, 2014.

Jason P. Woodbury, "Phoenix's UFO Congress Probes What Believers Insist Comes from 'Above,'" *Phoenix New Times*, February 27, 2014, www .phoenixnewtimes.com/2014-02-27/news/phoenix-s-international-ufo -congress/full/.

The Roswell Project (documentary short), directed by Dennis Freyermuth, 2014.

"Secure Medical CEO John Rao Joins Histogen Board of Directors," Newswire Today, May 9, 2008, www.newswiretoday.com/news/33940/.

John B. Alexander, *UFOs: Myths, Conspiracies, and Realities* (New York: St. Martin's Griffin, 2012).

Emily Swanson, "Alien Poll Finds Half of Americans Think Extraterrestrial Life Exists," *Huffington Post*, June 21, 2013, www.huffingtonpost .com/2013/06/21/alien-poll_n_3473852.html.

7. The Terror and Subsequent Pride of Point Pleasant

Mothman Festival, Point Pleasant, West Virginia, September 21, 2013.

John A. Keel, *The Mothman Prophecies* (New York: Tor, 2002).

Jeff Wamsley and Donnie Sergent Jr., *Mothman: The Facts Behind the Legend* (Point Pleasant, WV: Mothman Press, 2002).

Jeff Wamsley, *Mothman: Behind the Red Eyes* (Point Pleasant, WV: Mothman Press, 2005).

Jeff Wamsley, interview with the author by phone, March 25, 2014.

Roger Ebert, review of "The Mothman Prophecies," *Chicago Sun-Times*, January 25, 2002, www.rogerebert.com/reviews/the-mothman -prophecies-2002.

John C. Sherwood, "Gray Barker's Book of Bunk Mothman, Saucers, and MIB," *Skeptical Inquirer* 26, no. 3 (May/June 2002): www.csicop.org /si/show/gray_barkers_book_of_bunk_mothman_saucers_and_mib/.

Loren Coleman, *Mothman and Other Curious Encounters* (New York: Paraview Press, 2002).

Lyle Blackburn, *The Beast of Boggy Creek: The True Story of the Fouke Monster* (San Antonio: Anomalist Books, 2012).

Loren Coleman, interview with the author, International Cryptozoology Museum, Portland, Maine, September 25, 2013.

"Mothman of Mason County," episode of *Mountain Monsters*, Destination America, aired July 20, 2013.

8. Drama with the Dead, Problems with the Living

RIP Midwest excursion to Bachelors Grove Cemetery, Bremen Township, Illinois, July 19, 2014.

Peter Crapia, "Bachelors Grove & Paranormal Activity," bachelorsgrove. net, October 14, 2011, www.bachelorsgrove.net/bachelors-grove -paranormal-activity.html.

Cindi Muntz, interview with the author by phone, January 5, 2014.

RIP Midwest, "Services," official website, last accessed November 17, 2014, www.ripmidwest.com/services.php.

Episode of *The Malliard Report* (Internet radio show), aired June 11, 2013.

Noah Leigh, interview with the author, McDonald's in West Allis, Wisconsin, January 18, 2014.

Noah Leigh, course material for Paranormal Investigation 102 class, taught through the West Allis Recreation Department, West Allis, Wisconsin.

John Krahn, Facebook message to the author, August 5, 2014.

William Kalush and Larry Sloman, *The Secret Life of Houdini: The Making of America's First Superhero* (New York: Atria Books, 2006).

"Mrs. X," interview with the author, Colectivo coffee shop in Bay View, Milwaukee, Wisconsin, June 17, 2014.

9. Squishes

Loren Coleman, *Bigfoot! The True Story of Apes in America* (New York: Paraview Pocket Books, 2003).

Loren Coleman, interview with the author, International Cryptozoology Museum, Portland, Maine, September 25, 2013.

Robert Sullivan, "The Men Who Dream of Bigfoot," *Outside*, February 12, 2014, www.outsideonline.com/outdoor-adventure/science/In-Search -of-Bigfoot-Hunters.html.

BFRO, "About the Bigfoot Field Researchers Organization (BFRO)," official website, last accessed November 17, 2014, www.bfro.net/ref/aboutbfr .asp.

Matt Moneymaker, e-mail to the author, June 11, 2013.

BFRO investigation at Isabella farm, Isabella County, Michigan, July 8–11, 2014.

"Bigfoot and Wolverines," episode of *Finding Bigfoot*, Animal Planet, aired
December 16, 2012.

"Super Yooper Sasquatch," episode of *Finding Bigfoot*, Animal Planet, aired
January 19, 2014.

Sharon Hill, interview with the author via Skype, January 9, 2014.

Jim Harding, interview with the author via e-mail, February 27, 2014.

Benjamin Radford, interview with the author via Skype, June 16, 2014.

10. We Come to Whup Demons

Rev. Bob Larson, Curse Breaking Seminar at the Rosemont Hilton,
Rosemont, Illinois, May 9, 2014.

Pricing and other details are from Larson's official website, www.boblarson
.org.

"About Us: Brynne Larson," Teenage Exorcists, last accessed November 17,
2014, www.teenageexorcists.com/brynne-larson/.

The Demon of Hate Didn't Have a Chance with Exorcist Bob Larson!, video
posted to Bob Larson's official YouTube channel, April 13, 2013, www
.youtube.com/watch?v=FT1b0o47JoQ.

Bob Larson Faces Jezebel and Lucifer Head On!, video posted to Bob Larson's
official YouTube channel, March 16, 2014, www.youtube.com
/watch?v=0WI9KcLl1Nk.

Kristen Bialik, "The Church of Satan Interviewed by Televangelist Bob
Larson: Not the Conversation You Think It Is," *Huffington Post*, May 25,
2012, www.huffingtonpost.com/network-awesome/church-of-satan
-interviewed-by-televangelist-bob-larson_b_1543751.html.

Local news report on Bob Larson, Fox 6 San Diego, video posted to
YouTube by Mark Bunker as "Bob Larson Exposed," December 30,
2006, www.youtube.com/watch?v=75TsvDIzIZc.

Father Jack Ashcraft, interview with the author via e-mail, September 4,
2013.

Father Jack Ashcraft, "Bob Larson: The Unreal Exorcist," *Bare Fisted Cleric*
(blog), January 6, 2012, www.trueexorcist.com/2012/01/bob-larson
-unreal-exorcist.html.

11. Somethin' Skunky

Campout at the Skunk Ape Research Headquarters & Trail Lakes
Campground, Ochopee, Florida, September 27–29, 2013.

Loren Coleman and Jerome Clark, *Cryptozoology A to Z: The Encyclopedia of Loch Monsters, Sasquatch, Chupacabras, and Other Authentic Mysteries of Nature* (New York: Fireside, 1999).

Loren Coleman, *Bigfoot! The True Story of Apes in America* (New York: Paraview Pocket Books, 2003).

Escape to Dreamland: The Story of the Tamiami Trail, directed by Timothy Long, PBS, 2008.

Michael McCormack, "Skunk Ape: Shealy Claims to Have New Photos of Elusive Legend," *Naples Daily News*, September 12, 1998.

Ralph Kircher, "Dave Shealy: On the Trails of a Skunk Ape," *Naples Daily News*, September 5, 1999.

Dave Shealy, *Everglades Skunk Ape Research Field Guide* (no publication info listed).

Loren Coleman, interview with the author, International Cryptozoology Museum, Portland, Maine, September 25, 2013.

Forum poster "maxhile," "Skunkape Is a Fraud, and I'm a Witness!" thread posted at Above Top Secret, November 2, 2010, www.abovetopsecret .com/forum/thread626008/pg1.

Forum poster "Stocking Hominid Research, Inc.," forum thread "Dave Shealy Hoaxes" posted at Mid-America Bigfoot Research Center official website, December 25, 2010, http://mid-americabigfoot.com/forums /viewtopic.php?f=26&t=2677&start=0 (site no longer available).

Matthew Moneymaker, "The 2008 Dead Bigfoot Hoax from Georgia," BFRO official website, last accessed November 17, 2014, www.bfro.net /hoax.asp.

Lee Spiegel, "Bigfoot Hunter Rick Dyer Confesses Again to Duping the Public," *Huffington Post*, April 4, 2014, www.huffingtonpost.com /2014/04/04/bigfoot-hoax-rick-dyer-confesses_n_5079861.html.

Guy Edwards, "$60,000 Later Rick Dyer Admits to Hoax," *Bigfoot Lunch Club* (blog), May 27, 2014, www.bigfootlunchclub.com/2014/05/60000 -later-rick-dyer-admits-to-hoax.html.

Loren Coleman, "Hank Hoax Dies: Bizarre Details Revealed in HuffPost Investigation," *CryptoZooNews* (blog), April 5, 2014, www.cryptozoonews.com/hank-dies/.

They Live in Trees (student documentary short), directed by Jimmy Avery, 2010.

The Skunk Ape Hunter, promotional video, Discovery Channel official website, last accessed November 17, 2014, www.discovery.com/tv -shows/skunk-ape/video/the-skunk-ape-hunter.htm.

12. The Accidental Werewolf Chronicler

Linda Godfrey, interview with the author by phone, October 23, 2013.

Linda Godfrey, interview with the author at Vasili's Café and visit to Bray Road, Elkhorn, Wisconsin, April 12, 2014.

Linda S. Godfrey, *The Beast of Bray Road: Tailing Wisconsin's Werewolf* (Boulder, CO: Prarie Oak Press, 2003).

Linda S. Godfrey, *Real Wolfmen: True Encounters in Modern America* (New York: Tarcher, 2012).

Paul G. Zolbrod, *Diné Bahane': The Navajo Creation Story*, (Albuquerque: University of New Mexico Press, 1987).

Navajo Skin-Walkers & Legends (documentary), directed by JC Johnson, 2010.

Chief Dan Talks About Skin Walkers & the Furry Ones, video posted to YouTube by JC Johnson, December 10, 2010, www.youtube.com /watch?v=kWOQuf02J3w.

Jeffery Pritchett, "'Navajo Skinwalkers and Legends' Interview with JC Johnson of Crypto Four Corners," Examiner.com, May 4, 2012, www.examiner.com/article/navajo-skinwalkers-and-legends-interview -w-jc-johnson-of-crypto-four-corners.

JC Johnson, interview with the author by phone, August 30, 2014.

Benjamin Radford, interview with the author via Skype, June 16, 2014.

13. Night Visits

John Krahn and Susan Benzine, interview with the author, Colectivo coffee shop in Bay View, Milwaukee, Wisconsin, March 2, 2014.

Linda Spice and Meg Jones, "Heroic Rescue; 2 Hurt," *Milwaukee Journal Sentinel*, March 25, 2009, www.jsonline.com/news/wisconsin/45982632 .html.

National Law Enforcement Officers Memorial Fund, "Officer John Krahn," official website, December 2009, www.nleomf.org/officers/month /otm-archive/december-2009-officer-of-the.html.

Peter Bukowski, "Hero Officer Steps Down Two Years After Train Collision," *Elm Grove Now*, June 15, 2011, www.elmgrovenow.com /news/123912484.html.

Emily Eveland, "Q&A with the Demon Doctor, Reverend Michael Schroeder," *Minnesota Daily*, October 31, 2013, www.mndaily.com /ae/weekend/2013/10/30/qa-demon-doctor-reverend-michael -schroeder.

Theresa Bane, *Encyclopedia of Demons in World Religions and Cultures* (Jefferson, NC: McFarland, 2012).

New England Society for Psychic Research, "Warrens Biography," official website, last accessed November 17, 2014, www.warrens.net/Warrens -Bio.html.

New England Society for Psychic Research, "Annabelle Story," official website, last accessed November 17, 2014, www.warrens.net/Annabelle.html.

Court records came from a search of "Mary's" name on the Wisconsin Circuit Court Access website, www.wcca.wicourts.gov.

Investigation of Mary's apartment, Juneau, Wisconsin, March 22, 2014.

Canary, follow up e-mails with the author, August 4, 2014.

Susan Benzine, follow up e-mails with the author, August 5, 2014.

"Mary," follow up e-mails with the author, June 28, 2014.

14. The Case of the Haunted Honky-Tonk

Footage of the Carl Lawson exorcism, video posted to YouTube by Doug Hensley, August 31, 2010, www.youtube.com/watch?v=iuQzZwCT1eo.

Douglas Hensley, *Hell's Gate: Terror at Bobby Mackey's Music World* (Outskirts Press, 2005).

PIM team meeting, Noah Leigh's home, West Allis, Wisconsin, August 11, 2013.

"Bobby Mackey's Music World," episode of *Ghost Adventures*, Travel Channel, aired October 17, 2008.

"Return to Bobby Mackey's," episode of *Ghost Adventures*, Travel Channel, aired October 1, 2010.

Father Jack Ashcraft, interview with the author via e-mail, September 4, 2013.

PIM case report #130724 (Bobby Mackey's Music World, July 24, 2013), www.paranormalmilwaukee.com/cases/bobbymackeys /bobbymackeys.html.

Jann Goldberg, follow-up interview with the author at Fuel Café, Milwaukee, Wisconsin, July 22, 2014.

PIM team meeting, Noah Leigh's home, West Allis, Wisconsin, September 12, 2013.

PIM investigation of Bobby Mackey's Music World, Wilder, Kentucky, September 22–23, 2013.

Wanda Kay Stephenson, *Wicked They Walk: The Tour Guide's Book* (self-published, 2013).

Noah Leigh, follow-up interview with the author by phone, March 24, 2014.

Epilogue: The Bogeyman

Court date for Morgan Geyser and Anissa Weier was at the Waukesha County Courthouse on July 2, 2014.

Ellen Gabler, "Charges Detail Waukesha Pre-teens' Attempt to Kill Classmate," *Milwaukee Journal Sentinel*, June 2, 2014, www.jsonline.com /news/crime/waukesha-police-2-12-year-old-girls-plotted-for-months -to-kill-friend-b99282655z1-261534171.html.

Bruce Vielmetti and Ashley Lutheran, "Judge Rules 12-Year-Old Incompetent, for Now, in Slender Man Trial," *Milwaukee Journal Sentinel*, August 1, 2014, www.jsonline.com/news/crime/lawyer-for-girl-in -slenderman-case-wants-mental-reports-on-co-defendant -b99319419z1-269441661.html.

Lauren Effron and Kelley Robinson, "Slender Man Stabbing Survivor's Parents: 'She's Meant to Do Something Special,'" ABC News, September 26, 2014, www.abcnews.go.com/US/slender-man-stabbing-survivors -parents-describe-horrific-ordeal/story?id=25787516.

John A. Keel, *The Mothman Prophecies* (New York: Tor, 2002).

Aaron Sagers, "Slender Man Is Real: From Cultural Conversation to Paranormal Topic," *Huffington Post*, June 10, 2014, www.huffingtonpost .com/aaron-sagers/slender-man-is-real-from-_b_5481349.html.

Michael Winter, "Judge: Girls Can Stand Trial in 'Slender Man' Stabbing," *USA Today*, December 18, 2014, www.usatoday.com/story/news /nation/2014/12/18/slender-man/20593281/.

Loren Coleman, "The Gun That Almost Brought Bigfoot Down," *CryptoZooNews* (blog), June 26, 2014, www.cryptozoonews.com/page -acq/.

Post on Skunk Ape Headquarters Facebook page, July 28, 2014, www .facebook.com/SkunkApeHeadquarters/photos/a.355155497856492 .80877.183155941723116/747219478650090.

"Events," Bob Larson official website, last accessed November 17, 2014, www.boblarson.org/religious-events.

PIM investigation of the Modjeska Theater, Milwaukee, Wisconsin, May 24, 2014.

Jann Goldberg, follow-up interview with the author at Fuel Café, Milwaukee, Wisconsin, July 22, 2014.

INDEX